"Never forecast what you can calculate."

Dr. Joseph Orlicky

"When it comes to Retail Supply Chain Management, people are beginning to understand that Demand Planning should start at store level. What we must now agree upon is that Demand Planning should also end at store level.
This book is dedicated to that objective."

André Martin, Mike Doherty and Jeff Harrop

Advance Praise for
Flowcasting the Retail Supply Chain

"Very often we read about Supply Chain principles such as Visibility, Collaboration, Flexibility, and Integration. We understand the concepts, agree with the principles, and look for ways to turn concept into reality. Flowcasting brings these principles to life. Its focus on simplifying Forecasting, combined with the tremendous versatility of time phased planning is both leading edge and executable today. Andre, Mike, and Jeff have done a great job of demonstrating the practical application ofFlowcasting concepts with everyday Retail challenges. Flowcasting is a great read, and worthy of serious consideration."

Geoff Frodsham
- Senior Vice President, Canadian Logistics
Loblaw Companies Limited

"André Martin has had a dream and vision to integrate end-to-end the "extended supply chain" all the way down to the store shelf. The future is now here and what was previously unmanageable in real life is now possible - driving the factory floor from the store shelf. Leveraging collaborative business processes along with the strength of the time series DRP orders forecasting methodology has positioned his dream into the industry's emerging best practice."

Robert Bruce - Former Vice President,
Supply Chain Strategies
Wal-Mart Stores, Inc.

"We live in an age of data. More plentiful and richer sources of data continue to emerge. The authors of Flowcasting The Retail Supply Chain have devised a means to make the supply chain visible by utilizing a stream of data to create a Flowcast, a forecast constructed from detailed demand data. What's remarkable about this concept is its utter simplicity. It's easy to understand and implement, and it can revolutionize the kinds of things we can do to improve supply chain operations. This book is an easy read, placing Flowcasting in the context of previous methods, and showing how it can be used to solve common supply chain problems. You will appreciate the potential of this method to cut through supply chain complexity."

Franz Dill - Manager
Procter & Gamble

"I had the distinct pleasure of working with Andre Martin on a concept called LogiCNet some 15 years ago. Andre, who conceived of and delivered on Distribution Resource Planning, believed that the principles of DRP could be applied at retail, using point of sale information as the engine that could drive the entire retail supply chain. It took a few years for DRP to be accepted and adapted by manufacturers and now DRP is broadly used through the manufacturing community.
Never one to give up on a dream, Andre and his colleagues Mike Doherty and Jeff Harrop have written "Flowcasting the Retail Supply Chain". The logic is sound, the challenges are significant, with the importance of a collaborative mind set ringing true throughout the book. CPFR® plays a major role in establishing the ground rules, expectations and initial planning that is paramount to successfully implementing Flowcasting.
We are hopeful that Andre, Mike and Jeff will see Flowcasting parallel the success that DRP has enjoyed."

Joseph Andraski - President & CEO
Voluntary Interindustry Commerce
Standards Association

FLOWCASTING
The Retail Supply Chain

Slash Inventories, Out-of-Stocks and Costs
with Far Less Forecasting

First Edition

André Martin
Mike Doherty
Jeff Harrop

Foreword by Thomas H. Friedman

Factory 2 Shelf Publishing
Winooski, Vermont

Flowcasting the Retail Supply Chain

ISBN-13: 978-0-9778963-0-1
ISBN-10: 0-9778963-0-7
Library of Congress Control Number: 2006924007
Printed and bound by RJ Communications, LLC
Book Design, Layout and Cover Design by Howie Green

Printed in the United States of America

10 9 8 7 6 5 4 3 2 1

A C K N O W L E D G E M E N T S

I first want to thank my co-authors Mike and Jeff. They convinced me to team up and do this. To me this book represents the last chapter of a journey that started sixteen years ago when I took what was supposed to have been a two year sabbatical to pursue my dream. Big thanks go to Steve Bennett who, for the third time since 1990, has taken the writings of a crazy French Canuck and made them readable. And finally, to my dear wife Régine, there are no words that are appropriate to describe the emotional and financial roller coaster I put her through these last sixteen years. If there ever was an example of a woman who stood by her mate come hell or high water she wins the gold medal hands down. Régine this is your book, Mike, Jeff and I were merely conduits.

André Martin

For a first time writer, there are many people I owe thanks to for their help in writing this book. My co-authors André and Jeff deserve thanks for sharing the passion and the workload. Darryl Landvater, author, consultant, and architect of one of the world's finest Flowcasting systems, spent many hours over the years with me discussing and debating how to solve supply chain problems using Flowcasting. Section 3 reflects these dialogues. Steve Bennett, a professional word-crafter if there ever was one, deserves special thanks for taking my often disjointed ideas and words and making them flow. My clients and colleagues deserve thanks as well. I continue to learn from them daily. Finally, my wife Kelly deserves the most thanks of all. Thank you for putting up with me and for giving me the space to write. This book is dedicated to you.

Mike Doherty

To André – Thank you for lending your knowledge, experience and immense credibility to this project. Without it, I don't think this book would have been possible.

To Mike – Thank you for challenging me every day. Virtually all of my thinking on supply chain management (and many other topics) has been shaped by you in one way or another.

To Steve Bennett – Thank you for your insight, skill and eternal patience! I would love to have your talent, but I wouldn't want your job.

To Kirsten – Taking care of 3 kids under 6 years old is a tough gig at the best of times. It was even tougher on you when I was working on the book and couldn't pull my weight. I dedicate this book to you, Jacob, Sydney and baby Mitchell, who was born while it was being written.

Jeff Harrop

F O R E W O R D

I like to call it the paradox of 'who knows best'.

It is the paradox that has plagued supply chain professionals forever. In the Extended Retail Industry, this has meant every member of the eco-system from retailer to manufacturer has created its own forecast with its own metrics for success. This has resulted in disjointed, incomplete and inaccurate planning, scheduling and execution across the Extended Retail Industry. It manifests in out-of-stocks particularly at store level, overstocking, higher expenses and disgruntled consumers.

For many years, André Martin, the Montreal-based consultant who wrote the seminal text Distribution Resource Planning, and two of his longtime colleagues – Mike Doherty and Jeff Harrop – believed they had a solution to this age-old paradox.

They have created a new supply chain movement called Flowcasting that seeks to improve product flow, forecasting and resource utilization.

In reading *Flowcasting the Retail Supply Chain*, I learned how a single product forecast in each store should replace all forecasts throughout the rest of the ecosystem. I saw how a hyper-focus on the original forecasts at the SKU level will engender trust among members of the ecosystem. I gained an understanding of how to improve inventory levels by cascading time-sensitive adjustments from systems in the stores to regional distribution centers to manufacturing plants. I discovered how Flowcasting improves promotional planning, product introductions, seasonal planning and operational/capacity planning. Last and certainly not least, I began to consider how this practice could reduce or eliminate cumbersome purchase order practices that constrain and often damage business relationships.

But these changes will not happen until the Extended Retail Industry reduces its dependencies on what Martin and his colleagues refer to as "a whole underworld of forecasts below the radar screen". Somewhat cynical in their view of today's forecasting practices, they claim there is an elaborate underworld of independent forecasts that overlooks consumer demand in favor of internal organizational metrics, goals and objectives.

Unlike some other forecasting initiatives, Martin and his colleagues are offering a forecasting concept that seeks to offer equally weighted benefits to manufacturers.

"Over time, as more retailers adopt Flowcasting, the manufacturer will gradually convert from a manufacture to stock (MTS) strategy to a manufacture-to-order (MTO) strategy for most of its business, and reap all the economic and productivity benefits that derive from MTO approach. Gone will be the uncertainty of demand, associated safety stocks, and associated warehousing and operating costs as well as last minute and very costly production schedule changes ..."

I strongly recommend reading this new book to improve your understanding of the paradox of current forecasting practices and eventually how Flowcasting will help you and your trading partners reap all the economic and productivity benefits in your extended supply chain.

Thomas H. Friedman
Founder and President
Retail Systems Alert Group
Newton, Massachusetts

SECTION 3: SOLVING BUSINESS PROBLEMS
WITH FLOWCASTING

Appendices

I N T R O D U C T I O N

Winning the Retail Supply Chain Race

Imagine that you're a race car driver, and you're minutes away from the most important event of your Formula 1 racing career. Your world class pit crew has prepped your car from front to end, and everything in between. All systems are go. Your team pushes your car into place at the starting line, and you climb in. The steering wheel is locked into place. The countdown begins, and the first starting light flashes. Then the second, followed by the third, fourth, and finally the fifth. The lights simultaneously flicker off indicating the start of the race. Your engine roars, and then you discover something terrible: the steering wheel isn't connected to anything, and you're out of the race.

This is an apt analogy for what happens in retail supply chains today. The retailer may have great wholesale and manufacturing partners, but if the retail store is disconnected from its trading partners, the retail supply chain will never win the race to cut costs while offering the best customer service. Instead, the retail supply chain will function like the race car with the disconnected steering wheel -- it will have tremendous brute force to push forward, but it will have little ability to steer a course, react to changing "road" conditions, or carry out a well-executed plan.

Because of this disconnect, the retail store is often considered the weakest link in the retail supply chain -- a notion supported by numerous surveys conducted over the past 10 to 15 years regarding out-of-stocks. Retail store out-of-stocks (usually in the 5 percent to 8 percent range) are indeed much worse than the percentage of out-of-stocks that occur elsewhere across retail supply chains. As you'll learn in this book, the nodes in a retail supply chain are highly inter-dependent. And when they're managed accordingly, the benefits that accrue to the trading partner are staggering in terms of reducing costs and improving customer service -- two keys in winning today's retail race.

Steering Linkage for the Retail Supply Chain

If you work within a manufacturing organization, you've probably heard of DRP (Distribution Resource Planning) and may deploy it in your company right now. DRP is a means of ensuring that goods produced at the manufacturing end of a supply chain reach the retail end in the most cost-effective way possible. The results from DRP, however, will be only as good as the ability to forecast what retail stores will actually need for routine and promotional sales activity. If you can't accurately forecast consumer demand, you'll need to rely on safety stock as a hedge against uncertainty. Whereas in the "good old days" inventory and capacity were cheap, today, no company can be competitive if a substantial portion of its inventory is held in limbo in case the forecast is incorrect. The only way to truly remove uncertainty about what you'll sell across a given retail supply chain is to forecast at the store level. Moreover, forecasting at the retail store level "drives" the entire retail supply chain; all plans for every trading partner can be derived from that single forecast.

Now wait a minute. According to conventional wisdom, you *can't* forecast at the store level! That's correct, as far as yesterday's conventional wisdom goes and before the advent of a revolutionary new concept called Flowcasting[1]. Today's DRP software packages, which do a superb job of planning for distribution and logistics management, are designed for manufacturing, not store-level, volumes.

---

[1] Flowcasting is a new concept and is derived from the DRP Process created and implemented by André Martin at Abbott Laboratories in the mid 1970's

Software packages for Flowcasting, in contrast, are specifically designed for forecasting, inventory management and replenishment, and driving the retail supply chain from the point of sale back, eliminating all other levels of uncertainty.

Flowcasting is a multi-echelon retail inventory management business process designed to 1) forecast products at the retail store level and 2) plan inventory, replenishment, people requirements, space, and equipment resources throughout the retail supply chain in a time-phased manner. Flowcasting continually monitors and controls the flow of inventory from beginning (the store) to end (the factory) -- the entire trading network. As inventory at store level increases or deceases above or below a set level, Flowcasting automatically recommends the adjustment of the flow and level of inventory across the Distribution Centers (DCs) and factories that service the store. The result is a balanced trading network, the elimination of shortages, increased sales, reductions in supply chain operating costs, and greatly increased inventory velocity (fewer inventories, greater turns).

The Flowcasting business process works as follows:
1. Flowcasting generates a baseline forecast that extends a year into the future for every item in every store.
2. Flowcasting allocates total planned promotion quantities to participating stores, thereby creating a total forecast of consumer demand.
3. Flowcasting takes the total forecast, deducts on hand inventories, considers on order quantities, applies the retailer's business rules, and creates a 52-week, time-phased model of how much product should flow into both retail stores and Retail Distribution Centers (RDCs), and when the product flow will occur.
4. Flowcasting calculates how much inventory will be necessary across all other nodes in the retail supply chain to support the total store and RDC's level forecasts every day for the next year.

5. Flowcasting enables the communication of replenishment schedules for both retail stores and distribution centers to wholesale and manufacturing trading partners over a 52-week planning horizon.
6. Flowcasting plans all required people, space, equipment, and capital resources necessary to acquire, transport, store, and deliver products from the final point of manufacture to the final point of sale.

The implications for retail supply chains are significant. Flowcasting not only eliminates the need for suppliers to forecast their retail trading partners' needs, but it ensures that the entire retail supply chain will be refreshed and automatically resynchronized on a daily basis, depending on whether sales at store level come in under or over forecast. In doing so, Flowcasting generates a detailed and realistic model of inventory based on the store-level forecasts of consumer demand. This model factors in all retailer specific constraints, schedules and rules, such as store shelf capacity, minimum shelf displays (including safety stock), minimum ship quantities to stores and DCs, transit lead-times between nodes, and shipping schedules.

The Flowcasting business process is made possible by several developments: advances in forecasting techniques that marry intrinsic and extrinsic forecasting at store level; the availability of new DRP-based, time-phased planning logic that can crunch and model retail store volumes on low-cost hardware; and advanced networking technology that enables trading partners to communicate on a level playing field. Of the many benefits that Flowcasting provides retailers, the following are particularly compelling:

1. Retailers and manufacturers can "flowcast," rather than forecast.
Flowcasting is a business process that gives retail supply chain trading partners the ability to model the stocks and flows of inventory, in a time-phased manner, from factories to final points of sale. Consequently, *sales forecasting and a myriad of other forecasting*

activities are completely eliminated at every node of a given supply chain except the only place where it matters: the final point of sale. The end result is the creation of a model of the business inside the computer and a totally synchronized retail supply chain aligned daily to pure end user demand. This process, upon reaching critical mass, enables manufacturers and their trading partners to transition from a make and ship-to-stock environment to a make and ship-to-order environment. Resulting benefits from this process are greatly reduced store out-of-stocks, inventories and cost reductions for all trading partners, ranging from 1 percent to 6 percent of sales depending on the company.

2. Better planning and execution of promotions.

Promotions may be the lifeblood of most retailers today, but they frequently become cost-intensive exercises in futility. Too often, manufacturing operations ramp up production in anticipation of a promotion -- in effect inventorying their capacity -- then deploy the inventory to their distribution networks where it sits until the retailers actually order. Since there's no visibility into the retail side of the supply chain (that is, into what and when trading partners will order), this strategy is akin to rolling the dice at Las Vegas or Monte Carlo. Maybe 50,000 cases of product wind up in the Chicago or Rome distribution center, but only 40,000 are actually needed. London and Milwaukee need another 10,000 cases, so the company ships the 10,000 cases from Chicago or Rome, incurring unnecessary added costs.

On the retail side, the situation is likely worse, because buyers, category managers, and planners are thinking about how many items they can sell in their 3,000 locations rather than about how many items they can sell *in a given promotion*. The result is that some stores wind up with excess inventory and the associated carrying and return costs, while others incur lost sales due to insufficient inventory.

In a Flowcasting environment, all of these problems vanish. Guessing and blind spots give way to a synchronization of the flow of inventory across the entire retail supply chain. This, in turn, makes it possible to plan and execute promotions that are profitable for all trading partners involved in the exercise.

3. A common language for all trading partners in the supply chain. Traditionally, entities involved in creating, distributing, and selling goods have been nations unto themselves, each speaking a different mother tongue. MRPII and DRP each eliminated a few floors of this "Tower of Babel," and ERP further promoted consistency throughout the manufacturing side of supply chains. But several key disconnects among trading partners still exist on the retail side. Disconnects occur between store inventory replenishment systems, RDC replenishment systems, merchandising systems, and trading partners replenishment systems.

Flowcasting resolves these major disconnects and introduces a means of consistent communication for all trading partners, one that enables them to easily share required people, space, equipment, and capital resources necessary to acquire, transport, store, and deliver products. Flowcasting makes anticipated people, space, and equipment constraints highly visible to all supply chain partners so they can deploy effective resolutions *before* the constraints become a problem. For example, take the after-the-fact-capacity considerations that often compromise the appointment systems of large retail chains. All too often, the retailer end of the supply chain orders a product and the manufacturer is ready to ship it immediately to an RDC. Unfortunately, the RDCs' receiving docks are all booked, and there won't be a delivery window for three days. The result is that stores may have stock outs which, in turn results in lost sales and reduced customer service levels. The manufacturers also pay a price, since they'll have to carry the inventory and replan logistics so that the order can eventually reach the RDC in a cost-effective way. With Flowcasting, receiving capacity considerations are taken into account before orders are released to suppliers resulting in the elimination of delivery delays.

Flowcasting creates a tight and natural linkage between consumer demand at the retail store shelf and output from manufacturing partners in the retail supply chain. Because Flowcasting models the flow of product in a time-phased manner, product will be pulled across the supply chain to distribution centers and retail stores only when it's needed. And because all trading partners are communicating in the same language, the flow will take place in an optimal way from a logistics standpoint.

4. Linking the supply chain to true consumer demand.

With Flowcasting, all trading partners win as forecasting moves from the individual nodes to the place where it counts: the point of pure consumer demand (the retail store). This is critical, because the biggest cost of doing business in a retail supply chain environment is the management of uncertainty on a daily basis. Flowcasting enables retailers to adopt a truly consumer-centric approach and focus on pure consumer demand. In this regard, Flowcasting might be called "Reality Planning and Modeling," since it synchronizes retail, wholesale and manufacturing plans to the reality of consumer purchases.

5. Instant business simulations, better reaction time.

Flowcasting enables retail supply chain trading partners to model the way they want to do business. The focus is on how product should flow from factories to store shelves. In seconds, trading partners can perform "what if" calculations that, at one time, would have required hours on costly hardware systems. By using Flowcasting, retailers can simulate their entire business and Flowcast their total supply chain on inexpensive computers and workstations. This enables them to react quickly to anticipated changes in demand and replenishment flows of products, and take appropriate actions.

So, rather than being caught by surprise with excess or insufficient inventories, retailers can respond to change in a way that enables them to minimize problems and seize new opportunities. The key is that trading partners are dealing with instant information, rather than information that is days old and out of synch with activity at the retail shelf level. Flowcasting enables buyers at all levels of the supply chain to truly make informed decisions, because the future has already been modeled and future flows of inventories forecasted on the basis of real-time consumer demand. What better way could there be to run a business?

6. Cutting costs at the core.

We recently analyzed 20 of the largest consumer goods (CG) manufacturers and 5 of the largest retailers in the world, comparing the cost of producing product to the cost that a consumer actually pays in a store. Our analysis showed that for those 20, depending on the product, consumers pay on average anywhere from 2 to 4 times the manufacturing cost. (Refer to Appendix G for complete details about the aforementioned calculations.)

While every retailer and manufacturer has its margin goals and pricing strategies, 45 percent (on average) of the cost a consumer pays represents the costs of manufacturing the product. Another 37 percent represents the way these companies market, sell, and distribute products. Flowcasting enables manufacturers and their retail trading partners to dramatically reduce their manufacturing, selling, distribution, and administrative costs. How much? We believe that the above mentioned 45 percent of the costs of manufacturers can be reduced as follows: materials 1 percent to 3 percent, labor 3 percent to 10 percent, and overhead 5 percent to 15 percent. We also believe that the cost of marketing, selling, distributing, and administration can be reduced in the range of 5 percent to 10 percent.

The bottom line is this: Trading Partners can reduce their cost of doing business in the range of 1 percent to 6 percent of their total sales volume. We calculated ranges because implementing the Flowcasting business process is a journey and is usually done one supplier or one retailer at a time, depending on who initiates the process. Therefore, the speed with which the process is implemented and the volume of business done by the participating trading partners will dictate the size of benefits achieved. Second, some companies are more efficient than others and, therefore, you have to allow for that.

According to the Economist, the Global Consumers Goods marketplace is a $10.36 trillion Industry. Reducing the costs of manufacturing, marketing, selling, and distributing products to consumers by 6 cents on the dollar (which represents the high end of the range) would generate savings of over $600 billion (USD) to be shared by trading partners and the consumer.

As you'll see throughout this book, Flowcasting opens remarkable opportunities for cutting costs while boosting profitability and customer service.

But...Does It Work

At this point you might be thinking, "Yes....but can you really eliminate forecasting everywhere but at the retail store level?" The answer is a resounding "yes." To test the Flowcasting concept, we conducted several simulations and pilots. Our latest simulation involved generating 378 different sales forecasts at the store/SKU level at a Fortune 100 Consumer Goods Manufacturer. To provide a context for the results of the simulation, we chose a study conducted by Georgia Tech's Marketing Analysis Laboratory. The study provides data, summarized in Figure 1, about the state-of-the-art in forecasting accuracy.

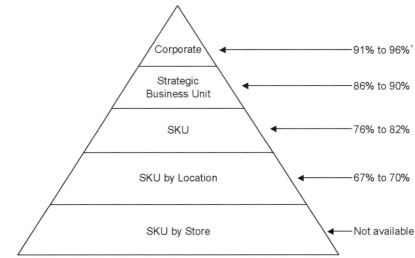

* Benchmark study of 40 Consumer Goods Companies by Georgia Tech's Marketing Analysis Laboratory

Figure 1: Benchmarking Sales Forecasting Performance by Kenneth B Khan, *Journal of Business Forecasting*, Winter 1998-'99.

As shown in Figure 1, our ability to forecast tends to improve at higher levels of aggregation. This makes good sense; it is far easier to forecast total corporate sales for the year than it is to forecast sales at the strategic business unit or specific product (SKU) level. Yet forecasting at the business unit, SKU, and SKU by location (retail, wholesale and manufacturing DCs) must be done. And the lower the level, the less accurate the forecast. Now what if, as a manufacturer, you had to forecast at the store/SKU level as well? Would your forecasting accuracy improve? Actually, it would most likely continue to deteriorate below the level reported in the study (67 percent to 70 percent), even though no statistics on forecast accuracy are available at the store/SKU level.

Can we improve on the current state-of-the-art? Let's return to our simulation for an answer. The objective for the manufacturer in our simulation was to use Flowcasting to forecast what one of its retail trading partners, also a Fortune 100 company (which we'll refer to as "Retailer X"), would sell during a given month for a sample of six products. The products included two high-volume SKUs, two medium-volume SKUs, and two low-volume SKUs sold across a group of 63 stores. The simulation would then subsequently forecast what Retailer X would purchase from the manufacturer for that month.

The simulation was performed on November 12, 2005. First, a sales forecast for December 2005 and the following eleven months was created for every product (SKU) in every store for a total of 378 separate forecasts. Then, the Flowcasting system netted store inventories (inventory on store shelves and back room) the morning of November 12, considered store/SKU safety stock requirements, and used each store's ordering rules (minimum ship quantities, lead times, and shipping schedules) to create a model of what each store would most likely order by day and week for the next twelve months.

The results were accumulated for the six products across all 63 stores and aggregated to show what Retailer X would specifically buy from the manufacturer during December. The information was kept for seven weeks. Then, in early January 2006, when the December 2005 orders from Retailer X had been received and shipped, a comparison was made between orders received in December and the forecast made seven weeks earlier for December.

Forecast Accuracy Summary – Retailer X

Product	December Actual Orders	December Orders Forecast	Forecast Accuracy
1	123,687	105,462	83%
2	13,500	11,940	87%
3	38,720	34,880	89%
4	67,200	75,600	89%
5	28,692	27,612	96%
6	79,464	77,352	97%

Figure 2: Simulation Results for Retailer X.

The level of forecast accuracy ranged from 83 percent to 97 percent for the 6 products as shown in Figure 2. In addition, Flowcasting gave hard evidence that Retailer X had ordered more inventory than it needed in anticipation of heavy sales during the holiday season. Had this not been the case forecasting accuracy at the store/SKU level would have been higher.

Hard evidence now exists to prove that sales forecasting accuracy at the store level can consistently be in the 80 percentage plus range. With the Flowcasting approach to retail supply chain management, forecasting uncertainty only exists at the store, so that the balance of the retail supply chain becomes a mere calculation. Therefore, with a Flowcasting business process in place, sales forecasting at all other levels in retail, wholesale, and manufacturing companies can be completely eliminated. The implications for retail supply chains are staggering, which brings us to the final point in this introduction: it's time to start thinking of Flowcasting as the gold standard for retail supply chain management.

The Flowcasting Imperative

If you look back at the introduction of new planning and execution business processes such as MRPII, DRP, and ERP, you'll see a similar pattern. Early adopters understand the vision and potential, leap in, and serve as guinea pigs while bugs and glitches are hammered out. And while they might be on the "bleeding edge," they're also the first to reap the benefits. Others soon follow, recognizing that the business processes will be essential to running a profitable business. Lastly, a group of companies adopt the business processes and supporting technologies because they've found themselves at a competitive disadvantage.

Where are we with Flowcasting today? A number of companies -- some at the Fortune 100 level -- are already implementing the Flowcasting business process and harnessing the immense power of planning based on a single forecast of consumer demand to gain a cost and competitive advantage. It's not a matter of if your competitors will adopt Flowcasting, it's a matter of when they'll begin using Flowcasting to improve planning, reduce costs, boost customer service, and reap all of the benefits of selling through finely-honed and well-synchronized supply chains.

And while Flowcasting represents a new paradigm for managing the supply chain, it's also an adaptation of existing systems that enables companies to easily transition to a new and highly efficient way of doing business. Unlike so many systems that require massive investments of time and money and the scrapping of existing systems, Flowcasting allows for the gradual adoption of new planning and modeling capabilities. Perhaps most appealing, Flowcasting simplifies the management of the entire retail supply chain.

Thirsting to know more? This book is designed to help you understand why it's critical to be on the earlier side of the adaptation curve and how you can use Flowcasting to gain a competitive advantage. It's divided into three sections that provide you with the essential information you need to know to adapt Flowcasting effectively in your organization.

Section 1 covers the current difficulties and challenges of forecasting and planning the retail supply chain, focusing on the difference between independent and dependent demand. It also reveals a little-recognized fact: most of the forecasting in the retail supply chain is unnecessary! Section 2 explains how to use Flowcasting to forecast demand at the store and integrate replenishment schedules among stores, DCs, and manufacturing plants. The third and final section discusses how problems that were previously tackled with disjointed forecasting can be solved more effectively using Flowcasting. It shows how Flowcasting, which creates a valid simulation of every future product movement, makes it easy to plan promotions, products' phase-ins and phase-outs, seasonal set-ups and take-downs, labor scheduling, capacity planning, load building, transportation, and financials.

Given the enormous benefits of Flowcasting, we hope you'll join in the new race for greater retail supply chain efficiencies, lower costs, higher customer services, and greater profitability. Don't wait -- some of your contenders are already rounding the first lap!

André Martin
Mike Doherty
Jeff Harrop
May 2006

Section 1:
Flowcasting Basics

C H A P T E R   1

The 21st Century
Retail Supply Chain
Doing Business with a Single Forecast

Back in 1958, Jay Forrester, then a professor at MIT, wrote a groundbreaking article stating that a volume increase of 10 percent at the retail store level actually cascades and translates into a 40 percent increase at the manufacturing level. His findings, which originally appeared in the *Harvard Business Review*, were later documented and published in a book entitled *Industrial Dynamics*. Forrester's work focused on the behavior of the flows of money, orders, materials, personnel, and capital equipment across what we refer to today as "retail supply chains." He found that these five flows were integrated by an information network. This information network gave retail supply chains their own dynamic characteristics.

Interestingly, Forrester calculated that the four-fold increase at the manufacturing level would take six months to manifest itself. This makes sense, given the fact that in those days, most business was done by snail mail.

Fast forward to the 21st century. Remarkably, the multiplier between retailer and manufacturer is still the same: four-fold. The only difference is that the ripple effect takes days or weeks, not months, to materialize thanks to the use of communication technologies that form the life blood of today's networked supply chains. The elapsed time may have shrunk, but the volume amplifier effect remains because we still manage the nodes in a supply chain independently, almost as if they're discrete islands or fiefs, blind to each other's needs. Because of this disconnect, pure consumer demand takes a back seat to business incentives, such as promotions, which create forward buys and diversions. Optimal shipping formats can also play a role in the multiplying demand. For example, the retailer may only require three cases of an item. But the manufacturer offers incentives to ship in pallet or truckload quantities. The retailer then winds up with more inventories than needed. Hence 10 percent at the retail store level becomes 40 percent at the manufacturing end of the supply chain.

This amplification of demand, coupled with the various disconnects across the supply chain, inevitably leads to uncertainty about the items, quantities, and delivery dates that various trading partners will need over the course of days, weeks, months, and beyond. That uncertainty, in turn, results in excess inventories and added costs. The good news, as you'll learn in this chapter, is that there are now solutions for gaining better visibility into the retail supply chain, so you can eliminate surprises without using inventory as a hedge. The first part of this chapter explores the problems with forecasting in retail supply chains today, while the second shows how forecasting at the retail store level is a far more accurate way to predict demand from the factory to the store shelf. If you believe that retail store level forecasting is impossible or just a dream for tomorrow, read on.

PART 1: FORECASTING IN A VACUUM

Every Node for Itself

The largest cost of doing business across a retail supply chain is dealing with the uncertainty of demand. This is directly related to not having visibility into what customers will actually buy, what quantities they'll purchase, and when they'll make their purchases. This lack of visibility and associated uncertainty results in major operating disruptions and significantly increased costs of doing business.

The lack of visibility is manifest in the fact that, in most supply chains, each node does its own forecasting. A retail store may have some sort of forecasting and replenishment system, but that system usually functions in a vacuum. The same holds true for the RDC, which looks at the needs of the stores it supports as an aggregate sum that's computed on the basis of history such as warehouse withdrawals. It is only a coincidence if the aggregate forecasts at the RDC level relate at all to what is actually happening on the retail shelves.

At the next downstream level in the supply chain, from the manufacturing DCs to the factory floor, you'll typically see tighter planning and data integration due to the use of MRPII and ERP. But even the most exquisite choreography among the manufacturing nodes won't improve supply chain management unless all the various nodes are connected with actual demand at the retail store level.

Nonetheless, few retailers today actually forecast at store level; instead, forecasting typically starts at the RDC, and is ultimately done throughout the supply chain. The farther from the consumer that the forecasting takes place, the less accurate the forecasts are likely to be. And depending on what's being forecasted, inaccuracies can have a significant impact on a business. Inaccurate sales forecasts across a given retail supply chain translate into increased operating costs and lower customer service levels for all trading partners. In addition, inaccurate sales forecasts lead directly to:

- Lost sales
- Dissatisfied customers
- Too much inventory
- Increased selling costs
- Increased distribution costs
- Increased manufacturing costs
- Increased purchasing costs
- Obsolescence

To appreciate the roots of forecasting inaccuracies, consider a typical retail supply chain (see Figure 1.1), which consists of two separate legal entities, a retailer and a manufacturer.

| Retail Store | Retail DC | Manufacturer DC | Manufacturer Plant |

Figure 1.1: A typical retail supply chain.

The retailer owns the first two nodes, which consist of the retail store and the RDC and the manufacturer owns the last two nodes, the manufacturing DC (MDC) and the plant. In an effort to generate the best forecast, both the retailer and manufacturer must forecast at multiple levels. Let's start with the forecasting on the retailer's side.

The Retail Nodes

Retailers typically begin forecasting at the total business level, based on a plan with a timeline that usually stretches out one year and beyond. This business plan normally includes a forecast of total sales expected for the business period, as well as assumptions about new store openings and closings, store renovations, new product introductions and deletions, and anticipated promotions. In addition, business volume forecasters will compare their forecasts to those of prior years, compare their data with key competitors' data by buying syndicated data, examine market share, and consider other critical economic and competitive factors as well. Figure 1.2 lists the various functional areas that create forecasts and the type of forecasting activities they typically perform in a typical retail operation; in aggregate, the number of different forecasts that are created is staggering!

Regardless of how many forecasts are created in a given retail company, they're done for high-level planning purposes. And the lit-

Who is Forecasting

	Top Management	Sales and Marketing	Stores	Distribution	Finance
What They're Forecasting	Revenues	Marketing plans	Sales	Transportation	Revenues
	Profits	Sales plans	Manpower	Warehousing	Profits
	Capital expenditures	Promotions	Inventories	Receiving	Cash flow
	Earnings per share	New products	Space plans	Shipping	
	New stores		Receiving	Customer service	
	Store closings		Shipping	Manpower	
			New products	Inventories	
				New equipment	

Figure 1.2: Retailer's functional forecasting activities.

mus test of a "good" plan is financial. Will the plan generate enough cash from operations to meet our targets? Will we have to borrow to support store expansions, and store renovations and closings?

In other words, the planning, by definition forecasting, is related more to the blessings or condemnation of Wall Street than to the planned flow of product from manufacturer to retailer to consumer. And therein lies the problem; these higher-level forecasts are not linked to the day-to-day business activities and lower level forecasts that drive replenishment into the stores, which in turn drives replenishments (purchases from suppliers) into the distribution centers. As a result, it would be a remarkable coincidence if the sum of the store and DC forecasts were to add up to the corporate sales forecast!

The Manufacturing Nodes

Like retailers', manufacturers' business plans must also include a forecast of total sales expected for the business period, which means forecasting at multiple levels. Typical forecasts must take into account the proposed marketing and sales targets, promotional plans, new lines of products, and product deletions. Given expected sales volumes, manufacturing must make adjustments to production capacities (adding or eliminating production shifts), and the addition, expansion, or closing of distribution centers. Figure 1.3 below depicts the major forecasting activities that functional areas of a manufacturing organization undertake as they plot the future.

Higher level plans in many manufacturing companies are disconnected from day-to-day business activities and the lower level forecasts that ultimately determine factory output and replenishment into manufacturing distribution centers (MDCs). What are the chances that the sum of the sales forecasts that drive both distribution replenishment and production will add up to the corporate sales forecast? Slim to none!

The Wrong Stuff

The problem with so many independent forecasts across the supply chain is two fold. First, the very fact that they're independent and dri-

Top Management	Sales and Marketing	Distribution	Production	Finance
Revenues	Marketing plans	Transportation	Production rates	Revenues
Profits	Sales plans	Warehousing	New equipment	Profits
Capital expenditures	Promotions	Receiving	Additional capacity	Cash flow
Earnings per share	New products	Shipping	Manpower	
		Customer service	Inventories	
		Manpower	Warehousing	
		Inventories	Receiving	
			Shipping	

Figure 1.3: Manufacturer's functional forecasting activities.

ven by internal metrics means that they do not mirror changes in actual demand at store level.

Second, the independent forecasts are expressed in mutually exclusive units of measure. People in sales will be forecasting in terms of the number of units that will be sold and the currency those units represent. People in distribution will be forecasting in terms of how many trucks will be coming and how many people will be needed to unload them, how much warehousing space will be needed, what kind of resources will be necessary for order picking, and so forth. And in manufacturing, people will be forecasting in terms of how many batches, pieces, or units the plants must produce, how many shifts will be needed, and so on.

The fact is, on both the retail and manufacturing side, there's a whole underworld of forecasts below the radar screen -- and none of them are connected.

PART 2: A BETTER WAY OF DOING BUSINESS

Doing—and Forecasting—Business Your Way

Given the patently clear shortcomings of the current "forecast everywhere but where it counts" approach, it's tempting to ask, "Why don't we just forecast the way we conduct business?" The question is so obvious that we rarely, if ever, bother to ask it. In part, doing business as usual is easier than questioning whether our planning tools map to our actual business. As we saw earlier, with marketing, sales and management people, sales forecasting is usually done at the corporate, regional, category, or product group level. On the operating side of the business (distribution, manufacturing, and purchasing), sales forecasting is typically done at the product and raw material level. Although these methods of forecasting have value, they bear no resemblance to the way we do business. Consumers do not buy products at the corporate, regional, category or product group level; consumers buy specific products in specific stores on specific days. Distribution people do not ship and receive products at the corporate, regional, category or product group level -- companies build distribution centers and ship products to support retail stores with the products they need. And factories produce and ship products to distribution centers. Until retailers, wholesalers and manufacturers step back and take a reality check on their planning practices, forecasting will continue to be out of synch with the actual flow of product throughout their supply chains.

Another reason that we forecast at the wrong place is our assumption that since we're dealing with supply chains, the answer to our problems lies in technological fixes and practices. So we keep developing new systems and practices that try to improve supply chain management. During the last several years, a number of initiatives such as Quick Response, Vendor Managed Inventory and Efficient Customer Response have improved overall supply chain performance. As good as some of these technologies and practices may be, none focus on the core issue: *you only need one unique sales forecast to drive a retail supply chain*. The retail store is both the beginning and the end of retail supply chains. It's the beginning of the information flow and the end of product delivery. So why not start there? As you'll see below, if you forecast at the retail store, the need to forecast anywhere else in the supply chain completely vanishes. The magic behind this lies in a concept called "dependent demand," which we'll turn to next.

Dependent Demand

Years ago in the auto industry, people realized that once you forecasted how many of a particular car model you would assemble and then sell, you could easily calculate the demand for tires, steering wheels, hubcaps and a variety of other parts. These item level forecasts were based on "dependent demand" -- that is, they depended entirely on another item's forecast (the assembly schedule).

Dependent demand is important in retail planning as well. Consider the supply chain shown in Figure 1.4. It consists of a distribution channel (or network) with four levels: a factory, a manufacturer's distribution center (MDC1), two retail distribution centers (RDCs 1 and 2) and four retail stores. At every node of this distribution channel, a customer/supplier relationship has been created. For example, the factory has one customer, MDC1. MDC1 plays a dual role -- it is the customer of the factory and the supplier to RDC1 and RDC2. RDCs 1 and 2 also play dual roles; each is a customer of MDC1, and each is a supplier to a specific number of stores (two each in this example).

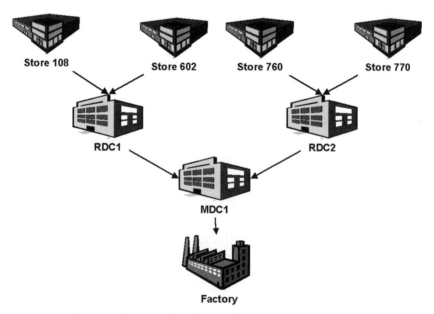

Figure 1.4: Dependent demand in a retail environment.

Suppose that when store 108 needs products, it orders from RDC1. When RDC1 needs products, it will order from MDC1. The product demand that RDC1 experiences will always be generated by stores 108 and 602. In other words, the demand on RDC1 is dependent on the needs of stores 108 and 602.

Another way to look at this distribution channel is to think of the way products will normally flow from factories to store shelves. Once you have forecasted what consumers will buy at the store level, you can calculate the demand flow through every node and trading partner within this distribution network. And this makes perfect sense. After all, we build distribution centers to serve the demands of other DCs and stores. So why not have forecasting and planning processes and systems follow in the same path that supports the way we actually do business?

One Retail Supply Chain, One Forecast

All retailers and their supply chain trading partners who sell and distribute products must answer the following "universal logistics questions":

1. "What am I going to sell?"
2. "Where will I sell it?"
3. "What do I have?"
4. "What do I have on order?"
5. "What do I have to get?"

As shown in Figure 1.5, the first question need only be answered at the final point of sale, the retail store. The calculated demand at each level, from retail stores through the supplier's factories, *is the one set of numbers that can be converted into meaningful units within each functional area of the supply chain.* (This is quite a contrast to the traditional approach in which each functional area has its own currency and is left to its own devices to develop a forecast that enables it to hit its bogey. The forecasts are done on the basis of history, application of "creative" formulas, and rules of thumb developed over the years through hard work and experience.)

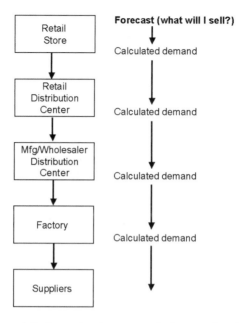

Figure 1.5: One sales forecast only at store level.

The answer to each of the subsequent questions lies in calculating and communicating demand to the next level of the supply chain where inventory is maintained. What sells at the retail shelf drives how much the retail store needs. What the retail store needs drives what the retail DC needs to provide, and so on until the entire retail supply chain is calculated and synchronized.

An important benefit of this approach is that the universal questions are answered not just for today, but for a planning horizon of 52 weeks into the future, in daily time increments. Imagine not only knowing your current inventory balance, but your projected inventory balance weeks and months into the future. Or what your expected purchases will be weekly for the next 52 weeks!

As desirable as this may sound, it's also tempting to ask, "Wouldn't it be more accurate to forecast at the retail distribution center level instead of the store level? Isn't this the law of large numbers?" The "law of large numbers" may be intuitive, but several pilots and simulations have shown that forecasting at the store-level only and Flowcasting back yields a more accurate RDC demand plan than forecasting at the RDC level explicitly, even though you're dealing with smaller numbers. This is because the law of large numbers still applies -- the only difference is that you're taking a sum of the store forecasts rather than a forecast of the sum.

Moreover, forecasting at the distribution center level actually introduces a significant source of error: store-level inventories. If the stores have too much inventory, any RDC level statistical forecast based either on aggregate sales history or warehouse withdrawals will yield forecasts that are larger than what is actually needed. The result is even more excess inventory. If the stores don't have enough inventory any RDC level statistical forecast based on the aggregate sales history or warehouse withdrawals will generate a forecast that is too low, resulting in out-of-stocks.

A multitude of factors make forecasting at the RDC level different from the sum of the POS forecasts at the RDC level supporting these stores. These include store on hand balance, shelf resets, delivery schedules, minimum shipping quantities, supplier ordering rule changes, product phase in/phase out, and so on. Figure 1.6, which is based on actual numbers from a simulation, shows the sum of the POS forecast for a product at a number of stores supported by a retail DC, as well as the projected demand (dependent demand calculation) on the distribution center from the same stores. It clearly shows the effect of one of these factors: inventory imbalances at store level.

The solid line is the sum of the POS forecasts for the more than 100 stores supported by this distribution center. The dotted line is the actual demand, or *dependent demand*, that the distribution center will experience once store level inventories are taken into account. Notice that in the first week, the dotted line demand is significant as the stores that are below the minimum display quantities are brought up to the minimum.

The differences between the dotted and solid lines indicate the degree of error that can exist between the POS forecasts and an accurate orders forecast (what a retailer will buy from suppliers). The typical orders forecast resembles the solid line, while the orders forecasts we are proposing would resemble the dotted line.

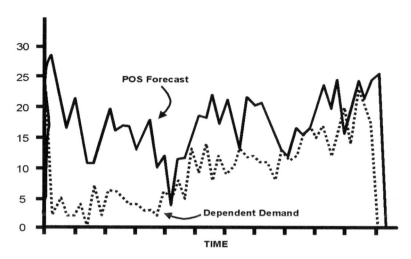

Figure 1.6: POS Forecast based on retail DC that supports more than 100 stores.

Figure 1.7 shows the effect of yet another factor that diminishes the value of RDC level forecasts: shelf resets at store-level.

The area of the graph on the left, beginning just before 9/28, represents the additional demand on the RDC as the number of facings for this product is increased at the stores. These changes are scheduled to occur on different dates at the different stores.

The area in the middle of the graph, beginning at 11/23, represents the depressed demand on the RDC that results from returning the number of facings to the original level at the end of the selling season. Again, these changes are scheduled to occur on different dates at the different stores.

Notice that there is a significant difference between the two curves, showing that the product forecasted has excess inventory at the stores that will take some time to sell off. This situation is represented by the lower dependent demand curve which, over the course of a year, finally catches up to the POS forecast curve. The point is that any calculation that does not take inventory at the stores into account on a store-by-store basis will provide the supplier with an incorrect picture of the future.

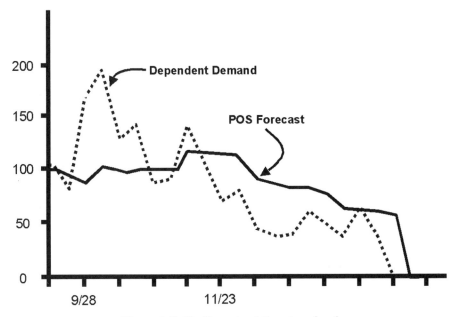

Figure 1.7: Shelf resets at the store level.

Summary

In this first chapter, we've looked at the traditional retail supply chain model in which hundreds of forecasts are generated by various functional trading partner groups. We've also commented on the problems associated with that model. Here are the key points to remember:

1. Traditional forecasting in retail, wholesale, and manufacturing companies is done to satisfy high-level business plans, which are based on aggregate numbers across a company's operations, rather than calculated on the basis of actual consumer demand.
2. Forecasting is done everywhere but where it counts: at the retail store level. The result is a collection of disconnected forecasts.
3. When forecasting is done in the traditional disconnected fashion, stock outs and excess inventories are inevitable and promotions become logistical and financial nightmares. As a

result, all trading partners experience higher operating costs.

4. Contrary to conventional wisdom, forecasting can, and should only, be done at the retail store level. Everything else throughout the supply chain can be calculated on the basis of the retail store-level forecast.

5. By forecasting at the retail store level, the need for hundreds of forecasts generated elsewhere in the supply chain vanishes. That provides visibility into the entire retail supply chain, which means that retailers, wholesaler and manufacturers can model the way they actually do business! The net result is that uncertainty is totally removed from the retail supply chain except the only place where it truly exists: the retail store.

6. By forecasting at the retail store level, all trading partners are poised to improve the way they do business.

The next chapter introduces a new concept, "Flowcasting," which provides unprecedented insight into consumer demand and every activity in a retail supply chain, from the moment product leaves the factory to the time it is purchased at the retail store.

CHAPTER 2

From Forecasting to Flowcasting
The New Art and Science of Managing a Retail Supply Chain

A Brief History of Supply Chain Technology

Since the advent of the industrial revolution, manufacturers built distribution facilities to match their unique needs. As they grew, manufacturing businesses found that it made sense to build distribution centers in geographic areas with heavy customer concentrations. Doing so enabled them to achieve economies of scale; they could manufacture products in a specific city, then ship full or nearly full truckloads to a given distribution center in another city, thereby reducing transportation, handling and warehousing costs. This approach not only saved money through newfound efficiencies, but it enabled manufacturers to improve customer service.

Wholesalers and retailers followed a similar course. Retailers, for example, found that it made sense to build distribution centers in geographic areas with a heavy concentration of retail stores. The motivation was the same as with manufacturers: achieving economies of scale in transportation, handling and warehousing costs, and improving service to retail stores and consumers. As markets further expanded, wholesalers and retailers began to look for additional opportunities to reduce their distribution costs. This led to the beginning of warehouse automation projects, many of which are still going on today.

During the 1950s and 1960s, companies also began to make investments in inventory management and replenishment systems designed to support the burgeoning distribution networks. The first inventory management systems were manual and included the visual two-bin system, followed shortly after by the visual reorder-up-to system. In the early 1950s, we saw the emergence of the manual Min-Max Kardex system, which was subsequently replaced by the manual, and then computerized, ReOrder Point system. For manufacturing, wholesale, and retail companies, the primary concern in inventory management was determining how much to order and when. Today, the emphasis is more on the "when" part of the equation. The attention has shifted to getting the right material at the right place and at the right time.

The mid-1970s saw the emergence of a new approach to inventory management and replenishment on the distribution side of a manufacturing business: Distribution Resource Planning (DRP), which revolves around the concept of dependent demand. DRP arose from the recognition that 1) within a manufacturing company, the capabilities of production facilities were out of synch with the needs of distribution facilities, and that 2) inventory management and replenishment practices had to accommodate inventory and production *dependencies* throughout the company's internal supply chain. Today, DRP is universally accepted in modern manufacturing and distribution operations in consumer goods manufacturing companies.

But what about managing inventory on the retail side of the supply chain? Back in the 1980s, it was recognized that DRP and dependent demand had applications in retail and that a complete retail supply chain was indeed interdependent. But the sheer volume of product/location combinations within large retail operations made the DRP approach to inventory management and replenishment impractical at the retail store level. (By contrast, the DRP system in a large consumer goods manufacturer may have to plan for, and manage, 250,000 product/location combinations. A large retailer may have upwards of *400 million* product/location combinations that need to be planned and managed.) As we stated earlier in the book, advances in technology and forecasting have made Flowcasting a reality.

In this chapter, we'll explore the benefits of forecasting at the store level through Flowcasting, and show how these accrue to retailers, wholesalers, and manufacturers alike.

The Power of One (Forecast)

Imagine how different the management of your company would be if you could operate and manage your total business on the basis of the single forecast described in Chapter 2. That one forecast would provide an unprecedented opportunity to reduce costs. Remember, the greatest cost of doing business today is managing uncertainty, and sales forecasting uncertainty *only exists at the final point of sale*. By forecasting only at the retail store (the underlying premise of Flowcasting), the entire retail supply chain benefits in two major ways: first, from simplicity (demand throughout the supply chain can be calculated from the store-level forecast), and second, from the ability to model several weeks into the future the flow of product from the store shelf to the factory.

This modeling capability is extremely powerful and places users in a proactive mode by establishing a "rack and pinion" customer/supplier relationship that starts at the retail store and connects every trading partner in the supply chain. By time-phasing recommendations for product over a period of several days, weeks, and months into the future, retailers can simulate the future in the way they actually do business. Such modeling greatly improves decision making and customer service while significantly reducing costs. In addition, it gives retail supply chain partners greater control of their business activities. The key is to think in terms of *"Flowcasting"* -- the ability to calculate, in a time-phased manner, the flow of products in and out of each node in a given supply chain from the factory to the store shelf.

The Flowcasting Concept

Flowcasting starts at the head of the retail supply chain (the store) by forecasting what consumers will buy each day over the forecast period -- typically one full year to capture the entire business cycle. It calculates dependent demand to predict how much inventory RDCs must ship to the stores, and when specified quantities of product must arrive in order to meet consumer demand from several days to weeks into the future. Flowcasting repeats this process for every supply chain node that a product will flow through on its way from the factory floor to the retail store shelf. Figure 2.1 shows the power of this approach within the first two nodes of a retail supply chain. The detailed logic and mechanics of flowcasting will be discussed in later chapters, beginning with Chapter 3.

The ability to Flowcast the inflow and outflow of products across each node in a given retail supply chain enables the translation of information into the various languages of the key functional areas within a retail company. For example, as shown in Figure 2.2, planned receipts (into a store or RDC) can be converted to receiving hours in order to plan receiving capacity. The capacity plan for receiving can also be expressed in terms of the number of trucks that need to be received in a given retail store or RDC, thereby transforming the typical appointment system into a forward looking system in which valid delivery dates can be stated on planned purchases before purchase orders (or supplier schedules, covered in Chapter

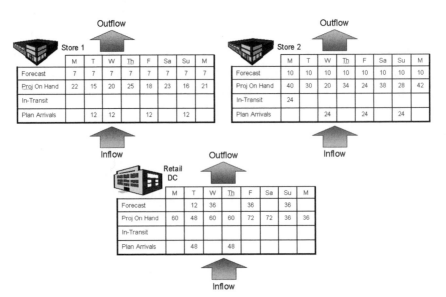

Figure 2.1: Flow of products in and out of retail stores and DCs.

Store 1

Outflow

	M	T	W	Th	F	Sa	Su	M
Forecast	7	7	7	7	7	7	7	7
Proj On Hand	22	15	20	25	18	23	16	21
In-Transit								
Plan Arrivals			12	12		12		12

Inflow

Store 2

Outflow

	M	T	W	Th	F	Sa	Su	M
Forecast	10	10	10	10	10	10	10	10
Proj On Hand	40	30	20	34	24	38	28	42
In-Transit	24							
Plan Arrivals			24		24		24	

Inflow

Retail DC

Outflow

	M	T	W	Th	F	Sa	Su	M
Forecast		12	36		36		36	
Proj On Hand	60	48	60	60	72	72	36	36
In-Transit								
Plan Arrivals		48		48				

Inflow

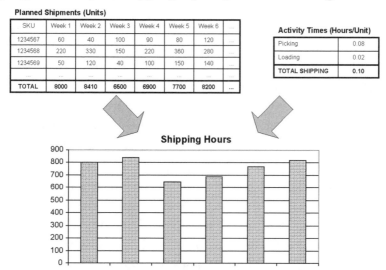

Planned Receipts (Units)

SKU	Week 1	Week 2	Week 3	Week 4	Week 5	Week 6	...
1234567	35	20	50	40	15	25	...
1234568	120	230	320	350	160	200	...
1234569	15	10	40	30	50	40	...
...	...	...	...	...	...	...	...
TOTAL	6000	6520	7790	8540	6480	6950	...

Activity Times (Hours/Unit)

Unloading	0.03
Verification	0.02
Put Away	0.05
TOTAL RECEIVING	0.10

Receiving Hours

Figure 2.2: Conversion of planned receipts into receiving hours.

5) are sent to suppliers. By using this approach, suppliers would no longer have to call in for appointments before making a delivery -- Flowcasting creates a receiving capacity plan for the planned inbound flow of traffic and can be used to match daily receiving capacity before sending out purchase orders.

Planned shipments to stores and RDCs can also be converted to shipping hours to plan shipping capacity as shown in Figure 2.3. This

Planned Shipments (Units)

SKU	Week 1	Week 2	Week 3	Week 4	Week 5	Week 6	...
1234567	60	40	100	90	80	120	...
1234568	220	330	150	220	360	280	...
1234569	50	120	40	100	150	140	...
...	...	...	...	...	...	...	...
TOTAL	8000	8410	6500	6900	7700	8200	...

Activity Times (Hours/Unit)

Picking	0.08
Loading	0.02
TOTAL SHIPPING	0.10

Shipping Hours

Figure 2.3: Conversion of planned shipments into shipping hours.

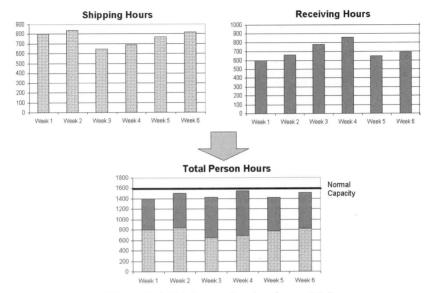

Figure 2.4: Total capacity plan for an RDC.

makes it possible, for example, to generate a capacity plan of total manpower for a given retail DC (see Figure 2.4).

Output from Flowcasting can also be used to make financial projections of planned product receipts from suppliers in dollars or euros (or any other currency) by week, by month, or one year into the future. These projections become excellent input for cash flow planning purposes. Companies can even take the projected product receipts from suppliers and offset them by their payment terms to predict the amount of accounts payable that product purchases will represent. Projected inventory levels can be converted to projected inventory *investment* in the currency of choice, as shown in Figure 2.5. The projected inventories can also be converted into cases and pallets in order to calculate how much warehousing space will be needed. Since information is generated by a single consumer sales forecast and is time-phased a year out, it drives every key function in a retail company. In other words, the consumer sales forecast becomes a "universal" set of numbers that can easily be trained to speak the various functional languages of the company.

In Chapter 11, we delve into significant detail on the benefits of using Flowcasting as a financial planning tool.

Projected On Hand (Units)

SKU	Week 1	Week 2	Week 3	Week 4	Week 5	Week 6	...
1234567	35	20	50	40	15	25	...
1234568	120	230	320	350	160	200	...
1234569	15	10	40	30	50	40	...
...	...	...	...	...	...	...	...

Product Data

SKU	Cost	Units per Pallet
1234567	$4.50	512
1234568	$9.35	144
1234569	$129.00	16
...	...	...

Projected Inventory (Dollars*)

Projected Inventory (Pallet Positions)

* or any other applicable currency

Figure 2.5: Projected inventory levels converted to inventory investment and space requirement.

Flowcasting for Lower Costs

By Flowcasting demand in a retail supply chain, companies can create numerous opportunities for reducing the cost of selling and distributing products. To appreciate the magnitude of these opportunities, consider the manner in which most companies order and deliver products today, as depicted in Figures 2.6 and 2.7.

Ordering Today

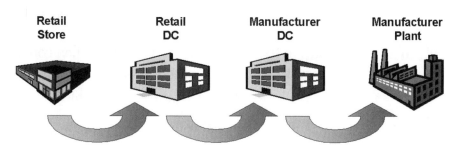

Figure 2.6: Ordering product in typical retail supply chains.

Delivery Today

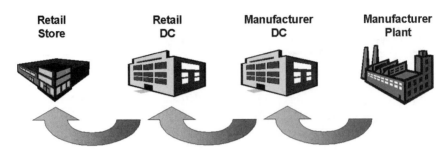

Figure 2.7: Delivering product in typical retail supply chains.

Normally, retail stores order from retail DCs, which in turn order from manufacturing DCs (MDCs) that place orders on the factories. Typical delivery cycles follow the same pattern, but in reverse: factory to MDC, MDC to RDC, and RDC to the store. (Note that we say "typical," because there are some variations. A retailer might, for example, cross-dock through a MDC or through an RDC. Or a retailer might bypass either the MDC or RDC.)

To Flowcast this supply chain, we would start with daily requirements at the head of the supply chain -- the store. Once those requirements are known, the entire retail supply chain can be synchronized to meet those needs. As a result, ordering and delivery requirements to retail stores will be completely visible to supply chain participants that manufacture and distribute those products. Trading partners will know the specific retail store needs today, tomorrow, next week and well into the future. The same visibility will apply to all other nodes in the supply chain. As a result, when conditions change (selling over or under forecasts), product flow requirements can be recalculated daily and communicated to supply chain participants.

Imagine how much supply chain partners could reduce selling costs if they had daily visibility into their customers' inventory levels, what and how much product their customers sell every day, and when their customers will order again. Now imagine this information being refreshed daily and shared among supply chain trading partners. The efficiencies and savings would be enormous!

Consider how the following trading partners would benefit if Flowcasting and the resulting Flowcasting process were implemented in their retail supply chains:

Retailers

• Retail distribution centers would become, over time, cross-docking and repackaging facilities. Products would arrive from supply sources and would then be repackaged when necessary in units of weekly store sales. Initially, most products would be cross-docked and inventory turn rates in RDCs would rise to 50 or more annually. Repackaging operation costs would be shared among supply chain trading partners. Over time, fewer retail DCs would be required.

• Retail stores would receive deliveries so that trucks would be unloaded in shelf placement sequence. Since repackaging would be done in RDCs (or in 3PL provider facilities), retail stores would be able to free up significant shelf space that management could use to fulfill other consumer needs. Backroom inventories would become a thing of the past. Retail store sales would increase 2 to 8 percent, while store inventory turns, over time, would rise to 50 or more annually depending on products' selling velocities.

• Retailers would no longer need separate forecasting and replenishment systems for their stores and RDCs. One common system would manage inventory in both stores and RDCs and interface with suppliers on a daily basis.

• The internal theft portion of product shrink would be reduced by at least 50 percent due to the hourly, and up to the minute, visibility of what is on the shelf, what is sold, and what is coming into the store.

• One common system would span cross-organizational boundaries. Store operations, merchandising, buying, category management, distribution, finance, and management would all be working from one set of numbers.

Wholesalers

• Flowcasting would enable wholesalers to become value-added partners for their manufacturing suppliers and retailing customers. Their businesses would transform as they become professional cross-dockers and repackagers for those retailers or manufacturers that cannot or do not want to take on those activities themselves.

• Wholesalers would only need to hold a few days of inventory, compared to the volumes they carry today.

• Wholesalers would require far less warehousing space. Many of their current activities in purchasing, distributing, marketing, and selling would be significantly reduced and, in some cases, eliminated.

Manufacturers

• A manufacturer's way of doing business would change completely. The timeframe for the change would depend on the size of their retail and wholesale customers, and how rapidly those customers adopt Flowcasting. For example, if the major global retailer of a CG manufacturer we've researched adopts Flowcasting, that manufacturer would no longer have to forecast 30 percent or more of its business. Over time, as more retailers adopt Flowcasting, the manufacturer would gradually convert from a manufacture-to-stock (MTS) strategy to a manufacture-to-order (MTO) strategy for most of their business, and reap all the economic and productivity benefits that derive from the MTO approach. Gone would be the uncertainty of demand, associated safety stocks, and warehousing and operating costs as well as last minute and very costly production schedule changes.

Finally, supply chain-wide inventory investment would drop significantly for those retail supply chain partners that adopt the Flowcasting way of doing business. We predict that once critical mass is achieved, finished goods inventories in the global consumer goods industry would drop by two-thirds. These inventories, which now range from 80 to 120 days on hand in the consumer goods industry, would drop to 30 to 45 days on hand, which would represent a substantial opportunity to reduce costs, product obsolescence, and returns.

Improving the Execution of Sales Promotions

As vital as promotions are to a retail business, they often result in lost sales and excess inventory. The root cause is almost always improper deployment. It's one thing to forecast how much you will sell in total for a given promotion -- retailers working with the supplier offering the promotion usually do a good job of this task. But problems begin when the retailer has to spread the promotion quantities over participating stores. Retailers usually ship the complete promotion quantity to a store just ahead of the promotion. Since most promotions last a week, there is little time to make adjustments. By the time the promotion is over, retailers inevitably end up with out-of-stocks in some stores and overstocks in others.

Promotions are also critical for manufacturers in the consumer goods sector. As much as 40 to 70 percent of a CG company's annual sales volume is derived from products that are promoted to retailers and wholesalers. In certain product categories, many wholesalers *only* buy from promotion to promotion. Unfortunately, manufacturers typically have significant problems with planning and executing the promotions. The major challenges center on production constraints. On average, most manufacturers promote their products three to four times per year for a period of three to four weeks per promotion. That translates into an enormous amount of inventory created in advance of promotions. By way of example, the U.S. grocery industry (as of 2005) manufactures and distributes roughly 50 percent of their annual volume to retail DCs over a 12-week promotional period as promotional inventory.

Regardless of the industry, promotions are scheduled well ahead of time. Since manufacturing people need advance information about the scheduling of promotions, they are normally able to plan production and accommodate capacity constraints accordingly. For example, let's assume that the maximum amount of product a manufacturer can produce is 1,000 units per day. Let's also assume that the manufacturer knows a promotion for the product will start in three months and that the promotion forecast predicts demand of 10,000 to 12,000 units per day (or 10 to 12 times the plant's daily production capacity). This means that the manufacturer has no choice but to start producing product and holding it as inventory several weeks before the promotion begins. In fact, many consumer goods manufacturers typically start making product *10 to 12 weeks* ahead of a promotion. In other words, they produce very large amounts of inventories ahead of the stores' needs and deploy it to their own DCs in anticipation of receiving retail/wholesale orders for a particular promotion.

Manufacturers must resort to this strategy because they have little flexibility to add or reduce production capacity without creating a major financial impact. That means for 40 to 70 percent of their annual production volume on promoted products, manufacturers have already produced *100 percent* of what will be sold during a promotion! That inventory is normally deployed into the manufacturer's own DCs six to eight weeks before that product will be sold in retail stores. So for promoted products, the problem is not with production -- *the real issue is one of executing proper product deployment from MDCs to wholesale or retail DCs and stores*. If there are constraints during promotional periods, they will be found outside the four walls of the factory, anywhere within the retail supply chain.

Impact of Flowcasting on Demand and Business Planning

The introduction of Flowcasting will bring with it the need for new approaches to planning. Like manufacturing systems thirty years ago, the planning systems in retail organizations as mentioned earlier are isolated today from one another. As a result, the top-level cat-

Figure 2.8: Disconnected retail systems.

egory plans are not directly connected to the systems that purchase and replenish products (see Figure 2.8).

Top-level plans are developed, but a reorder point system orders products when the inventory at a particular location drops to the trigger point. If the sum of these purchases adds up to the dollar amount on the category plans, it's just coincidental.

A Flowcasting system creates a direct connection between top-level plans and the execution systems that buy products. The same direct connection is also in place with respect to the systems that are used to make decisions about hiring full- or part-time associates, negotiate freight rates and/or increase the fleet size, and project profit and inventory levels into the future.

In a Flowcasting environment, the business planning process is similar to that used in manufacturing operations. Flowcasting, however, adds components to both demand management and resource planning that make it possible to link business plans with a single time-phased forecast that starts at the retail store end.

The left column of Figure 2.9a shows the overall business planning process. First the business plan, which is developed in the currency of choice, would be agreed upon. Next, product plans at a high level in the merchandise hierarchy or at the category level would be developed to support the business plan. These high-level plans would be translated into the demand side of the business; that is, what the consumers are expected to buy. At the "atomic" level (the store/SKU level), the plans are aggregated to confirm, or change and realign, higher level plans.

The right column of Figure 2.9a shows the four basic components of demand management that Flowcasting integrates. (These components, which will be described in detail in Chapters 3 through 5, enable effective demand management in a retail setting.)

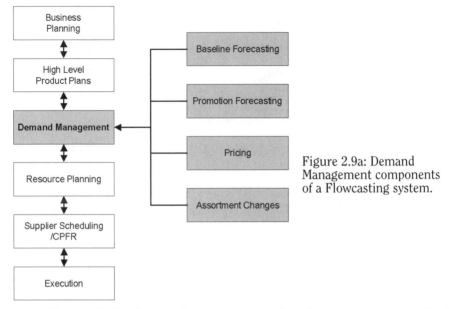

Figure 2.9a: Demand Management components of a Flowcasting system.

Figure 2.9b shows the resource planning components that Flowcasting injects into the planning process. These five components (see Chapters 6 through 10 for details) enable retail companies to effectively manage all their key resources -- inventory, people, space, and equipment.

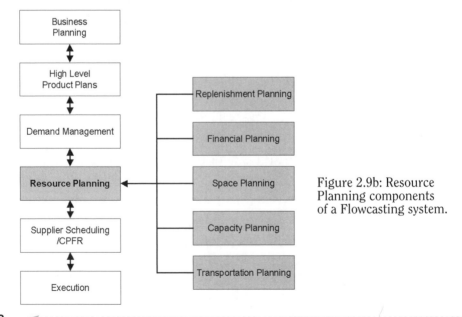

Figure 2.9b: Resource Planning components of a Flowcasting system.

The Demand Management and Resource Planning components of Flowcasting create a direct connection between the top-level plans of the business and the operating plans that actually order merchandise, schedule people's time, arrange for transportation, etc. For example, if a buyer decides to make a large purchase of an item, that quantity will immediately show up in the merchandise plans, along with:

- the amount of storage space needed (in the space plans)
- the weight and cube needed (in the transportation plans)
- the hours required to unload the shipment (in the capacity plans)
- the cost of this large purchase
- the inventory increase
- the change in gross margin (in the financial plans)

In short, everyone will be in the game using the same playbook. Best of all, there's still time to change the plans if business conditions change. From a planning perspective, this is vastly better than looking in a rear-view mirror and piecing together "what we should have done."

Flowcasting Will Spawn New Modes of Distribution

As a result of Flowcasting, distribution, and logistics professionals will finally be able to apply their expertise in their field and generate significant savings for their companies; distribution people have long known how to save money, but they've lacked the timely information necessary to do so. Flowcasting gives distribution professionals the visibility they need to take advantage of opportunities for bypassing nodes in retail supply chains when applicable. This will result in increased inventory velocity and reduced operating costs for trading partners.

As more companies adopt Flowcasting as a way of replenishing inventory across retail supply chains, new modes of distribution will emerge. Manufacturers, for example, will be able to collaborate and combine their efforts to reduce the cost of distribution and increase product velocity (see Figure 2.10).

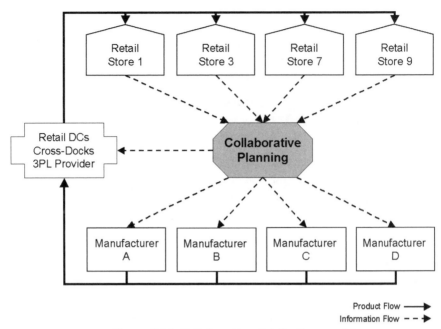

Figure 2.10: Collaborative distribution model.

Such collaborations will make it possible for manufacturers to partner with other manufacturers and deliver to a common customer at a specific store. Transportation volumes for a group of manufacturers could also be combined by store, affording additional economies. For example, imagine a group of ten stores which has a combined volume for one week that adds up to ten trucks. Say there are ten manufacturers involved in the collaboration and each has the equivalent of one full (or nearly full) truck to ship weekly to this group of stores. The Flowcasting system communicates the store orders to all parties involved. Trucks are bulk loaded at the factories and shipped to an RDC or to a third party logistic provider (3PL) location. The trucks are then unloaded and the products are cross-docked to store specific trucks. The stores receive their deliveries on the day requested, and each truck will have a mix of product from each of the ten participating manufacturers.

In large manufacturing companies where products are manufactured in multiple factories, collaboration will be done internally to deliver to a common customer at a specific store. This will entail using a corporate portal, as shown in Figure 2.11.

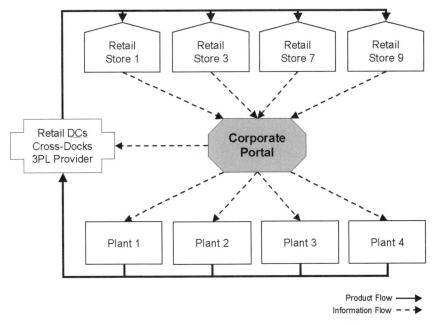

Figure 2.11: Corporate portal model for large manufacturers.

Making It Happen: The Flowcasting Team of the Future

For Flowcasting to succeed, retailers, wholesalers, and manufacturers will need to create Flowcasting teams. The teams' mandate will be to put new business processes in place. These new business processes will support dynamic models of complete product flow from the time products leave factories to the time it ends up on the store shelves. In other words, a whole new world of communications and collaboration will evolve. Retailers will create data repositories, as Wal-Mart and K-Mart did when they created Retail Link and Workbench. These retailer data repositories will contain:

- daily POS, daily store, and DC on hand balances and in transits
- daily store and DC cycle count adjustments
- replenishment lead-times
- minimum store shelf and DC safety stock quantities
- minimum store and DC ordering quantities
- shipping schedules

- new store openings
- new product introductions
- product deletions

Retailer data will flow daily from their repository into the Flowcasting systems, which will contain distribution patterns (factory to MDC to RDC to store, for example) for every product found on retail store shelves. Flowcasting will use the distribution patterns to model the total product flow from factories to store shelves, thus serving as a bridge between the retailer and the wholesaler or manufacturer's ERP system. Figure 2.12 offers a preview of the information flow.

The Composition and Role of Flowcasting Teams

We anticipate that Flowcasting teams will consist of a retailer team and a supplier team. The retailer team will include representatives

The New Flowcasting World of Communications

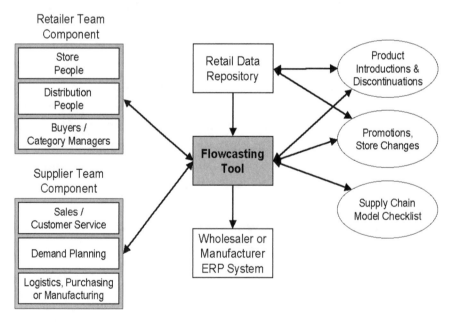

Figure 2.12: Communication patterns in a Flowcasting environment.

from the stores, distribution, category management and purchasing. If the supplier is a wholesaler, the team will include representatives from sales, customer service, demand planning, logistics, and purchasing. And if the supplier is a manufacturer, the team will be made up of representatives from sales, customer service, demand planning, logistics, and manufacturing.

The Flowcasting teams will have two roles. The first will be making sure that foundational data is accurate, complete, and up-to-date. By foundational data, we mean the data repository mentioned previously. It consists of daily POS, inventory balances, lead-times, shelf configurations, safety stocks, MOQs, and shipping schedules.

Specific team members will continually monitor and update the pool of foundational data as business conditions change. The updating will be critical; if the goal is to create accurate models of the way a company wishes to do business, the foundational data must mirror the current environment as well as the rules and schedules used to manage the business on a day-to-day basis.

The second role of the flowcasting team will be to jointly develop and agree upon (the retailer with the wholesaler or manufacturer) store-level sales forecasts that also include promotion planning, product introductions, and product discontinuations.

Finally, Flowcasting teams will act as a buffer for the new business paradigm. You can't overhaul the data structure of a retail supply chain overnight anymore than you can turn an aircraft carrier on a dime. There will be pockets of resistance as well as the normal fears of change that accompany the introduction of new ways of doing business, no matter how much better the outcome may be. Part of the methodology entails preparing people for change. And change there will be! The enormous visibility provided by Flowcasting will be the precursor to the demise of forward buys and product diversions. In addition, over time we will see the reduction of back rooms in retail stores, and a reduction in the number of warehouses and distribution centers across retail supply chains.

Summary

In this chapter, we demonstrated the power of Flowcasting, a time-phased system for planning the flow of product throughout the entire retail supply chain. Key points include the following:

1. True uncertainty only exists at the final point of sale: the retail store. Uncertainty can be eliminated by Flowcasting all product movement throughout the supply chain, beginning at the retail store.
2. Flowcasting provides unparalleled supply chain modeling capabilities, made possible by dependent demand. Flowcasting introduces new opportunities to plan capacities for people, space, and equipment from the same numbers used to purchase and replenish products into retail DCs. The flowcasting projections from Flowcasting can be converted into desired currencies as well as into units of capacity for people, space, and equipment, thereby providing a much-needed bridge between manufacturing and retail trading partners.
3. Flowcasting introduces new approaches to demand management and resource planning in a retail company. It enables a retailer to operate the business from a single set of numbers.
4. In the future, Flowcasting teams will introduce new business practices and processes that will ultimately transform how retailers, wholesalers, and manufacturers interact to achieve improved customer service and greater profitability.

This concludes Section 1 of this book. In the second section, we'll focus on the details of Flowcasting and explain how Flowcasting is used in actual retail settings. You'll quickly see that Flowcasting is far more than a theoretical construct. It's here. And companies are using it to gain a competitive advantage, today.

Section 2:
Flowcasting the Retail
Supply Chain:
From Store to Factory

C H A P T E R   3

It All Begins at the Store
The Only Forecast You'll Ever Need

In the previous chapters we introduced a revolutionary concept: forecasting can be done at the retail store level, and the results of a store-level forecast can be used to drive the entire supply chain in a time-phased manner. The results of such Flowcasting are impressive, and can include massive lead time reductions (70 percent or more for some hard lines), a doubling of inventory turns, and major reductions (30 to 50 percent) in inventory investment. And these benefits accrue while *improving* customer service levels to as high as 99 percent. Because Flowcasting is a completely different approach, the "service/inventory tradeoff" of old no longer applies. Simply put, there can be major improvements in both.

In the next three chapters, we'll take a closer look at how the numbers all "foot" – how the bottom line numbers of the retail store forecast become the top line inputs to the DC forecasts, and how the bottom line DC forecasts become inputs to forecasts at the manufacturing plants. This chapter focuses on where the forecasting all starts -- the retail store. Before we delve into the specifics of forecasting at the retail store, it's important to understand how the fundamental nature of operational forecasting changes in a Flowcasting environment. While the basic act of forecasting remains the same – using current data and history to predict the future based on patterns – in a Flowcasting environment, there is a fundamental shift regarding which customer is being forecasted.

Rethinking Forecasting: Meet The "New" Customer

In today's supply chains, the first big challenge in operational forecasting is to answer the question "Who's my customer?" The common sense answer, of course, is "My customer is the end consumer -- the end consumer is the reason I'm in business." In reality, most partners in an extended supply chain (especially those who are upstream from the store) have split loyalties. As much as they'd like to devote all of their forecasting energy to understanding the end consumer, the fact remains that consumers don't buy from manufacturers -- distributors do. A factory's activity is driven directly by activities in the manufacturing DCs. Likewise, the activity in a retail distribution center is driven by the store's ordering behavior. In short, the various partners in the supply chain must create their own forecast because, practically speaking, the answer to the question, "Who's my customer?" is different for each of them (see Figure 3.1).

Trading Partner	Who is the Customer?	What Does the Trading Partner Need to Forecast?
Retail Store	The Consumer	Consumer's future POS purchases
Retail DC	The Retail Store	Retail Store's future orders
Distributor	The Retail DC	Retail DC's future orders
Manufacturer	The Distributor	Distributor's future orders

Figure 3.1: Forecasting in a traditional retail supply chain.

In a traditional retail supply chain, each partner has its own inventory, lead-time offsets, policies, and constraints. As a result, everybody spends a great deal of time and effort trying to forecast the demands of the immediate customers. This leaves little time to really think about the end consumers, because the link to them is indirect at best. As much as a manufacturer would like to stay on top of store-level demand for their products in real time, the fact of the matter is that the orders that will fulfill consumer demand in a few weeks need to be shipped to the DCs today -- that's the split loyalty. The manufacturer is forced to try to forecast the needs of its DCs and its customers DCs explicitly, just to keep the supply chain running.

By contrast, in a Flowcasting environment, all of the forecasting focus is squarely on the end consumer. By modeling the "chain reaction" of demand from the store shelf back to the factory floor, it's no longer necessary to forecast the needs of the next supply chain partner/customer. The reason for this is that the visibility afforded by a Flowcasting process allows us to answer the question "Who is the customer?" separately from "Where to ship?" (see Figure 3.2).

Trading Partner	Who is the Customer?	Where to Ship?	What Does the Trading Partner Need to Forecast?
Retail Store	The Consumer	The Consumer	Consumer's future POS purchases
Retail DC		The Retail Store	NOTHING
Distributor		The Retail DC	
Manufacturer		The Distributor	

Figure 3.2: How Flowcasting separates demand from supply.

Flowcasting provides high-quality projections that can be translated and rolled up to any level in the supply chain. All product flow needs are unambiguously scheduled around the consumer, and all partners' inventory, lead-time offsets, policies, and constraints are explicitly modeled around projected consumer demand. The net result is that a great deal of unnecessary forecasting is eliminated, as shown in Figure 3.3. This, in turn, means that individuals responsible for creating forecasts can work on more value-added activities within their areas of expertise, rather than spending time trying to predict the future.

If you're skeptical about whether forecasting can really take place at the retail store level, consider this: there has always been forecasting at the retail store level -- it just hasn't been articulated. There's a reason that a retail store orders 10 units of an item and not 100 units when it's time to replenish the shelves for that item. The decision comes from "knowing" the product, the season, and other

Person or Group	Unnecessary Forecasting Activity	What They Could be Doing Instead of Forecasting
DC Replenishment Analysts	Forecasting retail store demand and replenishing DC inventory	Working with suppliers to improve shipment quality and reduce lead-times
Distribution Center Managers	Forecasting throughput and space requirements to handle future volume	Working on inventory accuracy Streamlining layout and work flow
Transportation Managers	Forecasting labor and equipment needs	Analyzing lanes and routes Strengthening partnerships with common carriers
Supplier's Sales Force	Booking orders and predicting customer needs	Selling Finding new markets Managing customer relationships
Retail Buyers	Forecasting future purchases from suppliers for negotiations	Finding new products Researching consumer tastes
Budget Analysts	Forecast sales and purchases for cash flow and margin analysis	Scenario analysis for cash usage and short term investment products

Figure 3.3: Some of the forecasting activities that can be eliminated by Flowcasting.

critical factors. The problem is that, until recently, even if people could articulate their forecasting rationale, there was simply no way to practically do so for every item in the store on a fifty-two week horizon. In other words, the problem hasn't been particularly complex, just very large. With low-cost computing power readily available, and software that can efficiently crunch millions of SKUs, the size issue becomes a technicality. This brings us to the central issue of this chapter: just how do you forecast at the retail store level?

Of Plans and Forecasts

Before delving into the actual steps used to forecast at the retail store level, let's review the context in which forecasting takes place. In Chapter 2, we outlined a series of high-level business processes that all retailers perform to one degree or another (see Figures 3.4 and 3.5). Company business plans are developed in dollars. Next, overall merchandise category strategies are developed that support the business plan. These high-level plans are then translated into supply chain demand plans -- product specific projections of what we *expect consumers to buy*.

In most retail organizations, these plans are created in the aggregate and are totally disconnected from day to day operations. In

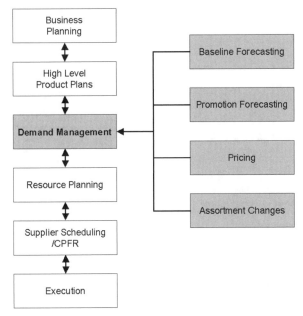

Figure 3.4: Demand Management components of a Flowcasting system.

a Flowcasting world, Demand Management activities (Baseline Forecasting, Promotion Forecasting, Pricing and Assortment Changes) take place at the most atomic level, where the only true demand exists -- by product by store in units. As a result we can take our product/store level forecasts and aggregate them to the category, region, or national levels in any unit of measure desired. Therefore, Flowcasting makes it possible for a retail organization to work from one set of numbers and drive the entire supply chain.

After the product/store level demand plans have been created and projected well out into the future, all of the resources employed from the point of manufacture to the final point of sale (including inventory, labor, space, equipment, and cash) are aligned to the ultimate purpose of satisfying consumer demand -- from the retail store shelf right back to the factory.

The remainder of this chapter will illustrate how a basic demand plan for a single item at a single store feeds into a store level replenishment plan for that item. Subsequent chapters will build on this illustration and fully explore the other aspects of Demand

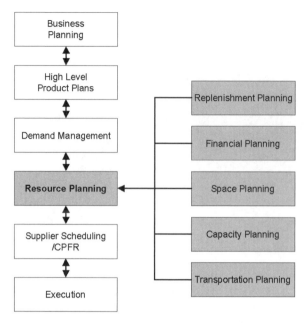

Figure 3.5: Resource Planning components of a Flowcasting system.

Management and Resource Planning at all echelons of the retail supply chain.

As you read on, you will find the logic of Flowcasting to be very simple, intuitive, and easy to understand. And as your level of understanding deepens, you will learn to appreciate just how powerful it can be to plan the entire retail supply chain with a single store-level consumer forecasting process.

Retail Store-Level Forecasting in Action

While there are numerous specific software systems available to help you with the forecasting process, you'll need to carry out five basic steps to build a time-phased projection that can be used to drive the entire retail supply chain:

    Step 1: Get your foundational data in order

    Step 2: Forecast consumer demand at the store shelf

    Step 3: Plan the first store replenishment

    Step 4: Plan future store replenishments

    Step 5: Calculate planned orders to support the
            arrival-based plan

Each step is described in detail below.

Step 1: Get Your Foundational Data in Order

The old saw, "garbage in, garbage out," rings true with Flowcasting and any enterprise business process. For Flowcasting to generate a single forecast that can be used to drive the entire supply chain, it's critical to have the right data in the right form at the right time. In other words, the foundational data must be in good order, and should include:

- Daily POS
- Daily store and DC on hand balances and in transits
- Stores' and DCs' replenishment lead-times
- Minimum store shelf displays and DC safety stock quantities
- Minimum store and DC ordering quantities
- Shipping and receiving schedules

Daily POS

Most retailers today use barcode scanners to track daily sales by item. Ideally, an historical archive of two to three years' worth of scan data should be available as inputs to the Flowcasting process. The data should be tracked by product and by store, in daily or weekly time periods. Also, each item would be scanned discretely by size, color, flavor, and other key replenishment attributes.

Daily Store and DC On Hand Balances and In Transits

Every stocking location – whether at the retail store or the DC -- must have a system-calculated perpetual inventory balance that factors in all sales, receipts, and inventory count adjustments. Ideally, the system-calculated inventory balance at any location will be 95 percent accurate[2] or higher when compared to a physical count. In transits are quantities that are already in route; that is, they have left

---

2 The accuracy measure is stocking location specific. 95 percent accuracy means that the system calculated inventory balance at item/location level matches (within a reasonable tolerance) the physical count 95 times out of 100. See Appendix B for more information on how to achieve high levels of inventory record accuracy.

the source, but have not yet been received into stock at the destination.

Replenishment Lead-Times

For each product, source location, and destination location, the repository should store the elapsed time from the time an order is received at the source until the time the product is received at the destination. For example, if a retail store can get a delivery 3 days after placing an order on its DC, then the lead-time between the store and DC is 3 days. Similarly, if the DC can get a delivery 10 days after placing an order with a supplier, then that is the lead-time between these points.

Minimum Store Shelf Display and DC Safety Stock Quantities

In either case, for each product/location, this represents the lowest level to which you would ever want your inventory balance to fall, in units. At store level, this may mean the minimum amount of stock required for the display to be attractive. For example, if it's desirable to have a minimum of 4 facings at least 2 units deep for a particular product at all times, then the minimum shelf display quantity[3] for that product would be 8 units. At the RDC level, attractiveness is not an issue. Instead, safety stock would be used to hedge against variability in the demand from the stores.

Minimum Store and DC Ordering Quantities

For each product at each location, the minimum order quantity represents the smallest amount of product that will be ordered, in selling units. A retail store, for example, may sell items individually to consumers, but order cases of 12 units from the RDC. When the RDC orders from the MDC, however, it may do so in pallet or truckload quantities for the same item to maximize efficiency. For simplicity in

---

3 In a majority of cases, the minimum required mathematical safety stock (based on demand variability) to maintain a 95 percent service level at the retail store shelf is significantly less than the minimum display requirements calculated by shelf management systems. Flowcasting makes this information highly visible and, over time, retailers will have opportunities to work with suppliers to reduce manufacturing packs by exploring repackaging and remerchandising opportunities.

the upcoming examples, we assume that each location also orders in multiples of the minimum ordering quantity, but in practice it's not uncommon to have multiples set differently from the order minimums.

Shipping and Receiving Schedules

Many locations may only have specific days when they are open for shipping or receiving. This information is required to make sure that product movements are planned to happen only on the days these activities are allowed. For example, while a retail store may be open for business 7 days a week, its receiving crew may be on duty only Tuesday and Thursday mornings. Similarly, DCs may ship or receive product only Monday through Friday, at non-peak times. Holidays and shutdowns should also be incorporated into the schedules. Again, for simplicity in our examples, we only focus on receiving schedules, but shipping schedules can be used as well.

This information may come from a variety of sources (e.g., on hand balances and in transits may come from the ordering system, whereas the shipping and receiving schedules may reside with the transportation department), but it represents a minimum requirement for getting a Flowcasting process running. If you don't already have this information available to run your current replenishment process, then this is the first thing to work on.

Step 2: Forecast Consumer Demand at the Store Shelf

For purpose of illustration, let's consider the task of forecasting demand for a single item in a single store. Our goal is to predict how many units of that product we will sell in that store each day for the next 52 weeks. The demand forecast will consist of three components:

- The baseline forecast stream is a forecast of what you would expect to sell on an ongoing basis.
- The promotional forecast stream contains forecasts of expected demand increases (or decreases) due to promotional activity.
- The local judgment stream contains forecasts of expected demand increases (or decreases) due to local events.

The Baseline Forecast Stream

The first step in creating a baseline forecast stream is to retrieve 2 or 3 years' worth of POS history from the foundational data repository for the item/store being forecasted. If this data is stored in daily time periods, it is aggregated to weekly time periods.

Once the weekly POS history stream is created, it can be fed into pattern-based time series forecasting software[4] that:

1. Filters out the impact of any unusual historical demand periods, such as those caused by past promotions, large special orders, out-of-stocks, and weather-related events
2. Determines if there is a positive or negative sales trend
3. Detects a repeating pattern over a one-year business cycle caused by the inherent influence of changing seasons on that item/store combination
4. Develops a computational model that will project the historic pattern (including trend and seasonality) 52 weeks or more into the future

As illustrated in Figure 3.6, the software generates a weekly forecast of "what would normally happen" in the absence of the effect of promotions and special events.

Most time series forecasting systems also allow users to override the calculations if the trend or seasonality doesn't seem reasonable based on assumptions about future market conditions. In general, the more good POS history data that's available, the less the planner will need to intervene.

But what if an item has been recently introduced and no POS history exists? A common approach in this instance is to simply copy history from a similar item, with a volume scaling factor applied, if necessary.

It's important to reiterate that the baseline forecast stream modeled from history only exists at the product/store level. Because

---

4 Many forecasting packages of this type exist on the market. While they can vary in complexity and user functionality, they all have some method of performing these basic calculations.

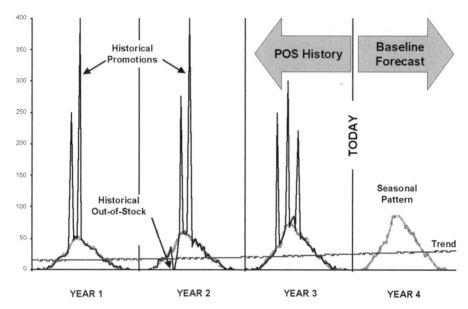

Figure 3.6: Illustration of how a baseline forecast stream is generated from POS history.

we are working solely with pure end consumer demand at the store shelf, there will be specific forecasting rules and guidelines that will apply (see Appendix D for more details).

The Promotional Forecast Stream

A baseline forecast provides an initial forecast every week for a year into the future. Because it's computer generated, it takes little effort to produce all the numbers. To the extent that future trends and seasons will unfold in a similar way as the past, the baseline forecast is a good start. In the case of promotions, however, we know in advance that the future will be different from the past. This is where human intervention is required.

In the example in Figure 3.6, we have promoted the item on different schedules in each of the prior 3 years and will be promoting it again this year. Once the details about the upcoming promotions have been decided, then a forecast can be created. Most retailers plan promotions in the following way for any given item (promotional planning will be covered in more detail in Chapter 6):

1. Finalize the overall promotional plan (schedule, pricing, advertising, etc.) for the item.

2. Review and analyze the POS sales results from past promotions for the item.
3. Develop new promotional consumer forecasts for the item, ideally in collaboration with suppliers and a sampling of store managers.
4. Allocate the forecast to participating stores, based on each store's volume contribution by item or category.

Once this planning process has been completed, the item/store promotional forecasts are overlaid onto the baseline forecast, as shown in Figure 3.7.

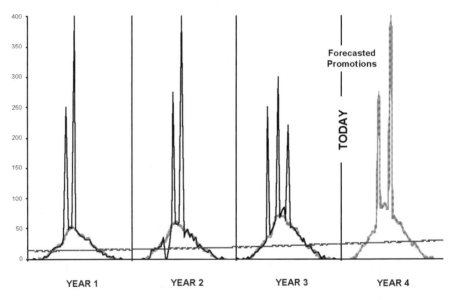

Figure 3.7: Illustration of an integrated baseline and promotional forecast.

The Local Judgment Stream

Like the promotional forecast stream, local judgment is a change to the baseline forecast based on knowledge that the future will be different from the past. The difference is that this information is supplied at the local level, rather than derived from a national or regional number. Examples of local judgment would include in-store specials, markdowns, and community events. These are specific to a particular item in a particular store or group of stores and therefore only known at the item/store level.

Putting It All Together

Once the baseline forecast stream has been appropriately modified to reflect what is planned in the future, we will have a complete picture of what we expect our POS sales to be for the item/store each week for a year into the future (see Figure 3.8).

	Wk 1	Wk 2	Wk 3	Wk 4	Wk 5	Wk 6	Wk 7	...	Wk 52
Baseline Forecast	12	14	18	22	25	33	38	...	9
Promotional Forecast					250			...	
Local Judgment		15						...	
Total Forecast	12	29	18	22	275	33	38	...	9

Figure 3.8: Expected POS sales.

Creating Daily Forecasts

Recall earlier that our goal was to predict how many units of that product we will sell in that store each day for the next several weeks. We've generated the weekly numbers by using a baseline forecast and factoring in promotional plans and local market knowledge. The last step is to take our total weekly forecast numbers and allocate them to each day within the week. This can be done in many ways, but a simple and sensible approach is to apply daily percentages based on how sales and traffic generally unfold in the particular store. For example, a store that is open 7 days a week may have an overall sales and traffic profile in any given week similar to the one shown in Figure 3.9:

Monday	Tuesday	Wednesday	Thursday	Friday	Saturday	Sunday
5%	10%	12%	13%	15%	25%	20%

Figure 3.9: Sample weekly traffic profile.

In this store, 45 percent of the weekly sales happen on the weekend. Monday is the lightest day in the week, representing only 5 percent of total weekly sales.

By applying this simple logic to the total forecast derived earlier (see Figure 3.8), we can generate the daily sales projection shown in Figure 3.10:

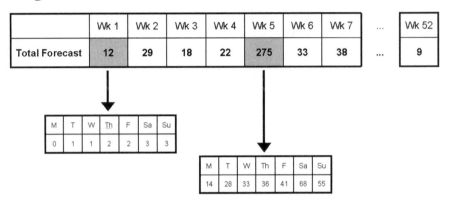

Figure 3.10: Converting weekly forecasts into daily projections.

Now that we have a daily demand forecast for this item/store, we are ready to plan the rest of the supply chain for this item. As will be demonstrated in the remainder of this book, this forecast will drive all other planning activity in the supply chain -- it's the only forecast you will ever need.

At this point, you may be wondering about the amount of effort that will be required on the part of Flowcasting teams to manage a store-level forecasting process -- particularly when we extend the example to include hundreds of stores and thousands of products across a year-long time horizon.

What makes it possible is the fact that properly designed Flowcasting tools will do most of the "grunt work" (generating a 52-week mathematical baseline forecast from POS history) after they have been initially set up. In addition, the people responsible for forecasting within the Flowcasting teams will work by exception, only reviewing forecasts that are tracking out of tolerance. And finally, as you will see in the following chapters, this one forecasting process at store level completely replaces all other forecasting activities in the extended supply chain -- not only for replenishment purposes, but for capacity planning, resource scheduling, and budgeting as well.

Step 3: Plan the First Store Replenishment

When trying to determine what a given store will need to order, a forecast is a good start. After all, you need to know how much of an item you're going to sell before you can decide how much to replenish! But replenishment decisions aren't based solely on a sales forecast. You need additional store/item information, including:

- Current on hand balance and in transits
- Replenishment lead-time from RDC to store
- Minimum store shelf display quantity (time-phased, if necessary[5])
- Minimum store ordering quantity
- Store receiving schedule

Let's step through the process by first organizing our information in an example (see Figure 3.11).

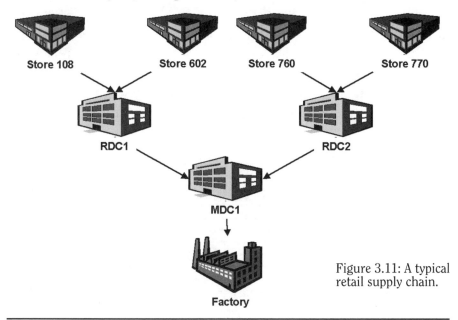

Figure 3.11: A typical retail supply chain.

---

5 An example illustrating the use of time-phased minimum display quantities is shown in Figure 3.12.

The remainder of this chapter will illustrate how the flow of demand, supply, and inventory for a particular product between store 108 and RDC1 can be planned for the next 52 weeks using a single forecast of demand at store level. (In Chapters 4 and 5, this illustration will be extended all the way back to the factory, and Appendix A will show how this same planning process can be applied to other network configurations, such as web retailing, direct-to-store/VMI , and centralized distribution.)

Figure 3.12 shows the results of retrieving the following key information from the foundational data repository pertaining to product 01234567 in store 108:

- The current on hand balance
- The minimum store ordering quantity
- The store's receiving schedule
- The replenishment lead time from order to receipt from RDC1
- The planned minimum display quantities, time phased into the future
- The open in transits that are en route from RDC1

In addition, we have generated a total forecast of demand for this item/store over the next year as described in Step 2. We now have all the information we'll need to plan a year's worth of replenishments to the store from RDC1.

Notice that the minimum display quantity will increase to 48 units on day 7 and drop back down to 12 units on day 14. That is

PRODUCT: 01234567 – Deluxe Widget

LOCATION: Store 108

Current On Hand Balance:	18 units
Minimum Store Ordering Quantity:	12 units
Store Receiving Schedule:	Monday, Wednesday and Friday only
Replenishment Lead-Time from RDC1:	2 days

	Days																		
	1	2	3	4	5	6	7	8	9	10	11	12	13	14	15	16	17	...	364
	M	T	W	Th	F	Sa	Su	M	T	W	Th	F	Sa	Su	M	T	W	...	Su
Total Forecast	1	2	3	3	3	6	4	14	28	33	36	41	68	55	2	3	3	...	6
Min Display Qty	12	12	12	12	12	12	48	48	48	48	48	48	48	12	12	12	12	...	12
In Transits		12																...	

Figure 3.12: Total forecast and basic replenishment information for an item/store.

because the item will be on promotion and an end aisle display of 36 facings will be used in conjunction with the normal 12 facing shelf slot. On day 7, we are planning to set up our end aisle display one day in advance of the start of the sale. On the last day of the sale (day 14), we plan to empty our end aisle display for this item, so we revert back to our standard 12 facing shelf.

Determining When More Inventory Is Needed

We now have enough information to figure out when we need the first replenishment to arrive at the store (see Figure 3.13). We can do so by taking our Current On Hand Balance and subtracting our Total Forecast for each day, until we ascertain the day that we'll drop below our Minimum Display Quantity. This is accomplished through the use of Projected On Hand, which takes the known current on hand balance and, similar to a bank account, simulates what the future balances will be based on when inventory will be deposited (supplied) or withdrawn (demanded) at the location.

PRODUCT: 01234567 – Deluxe Widget
LOCATION: Store 108

Current On Hand Balance:	18 units
Minimum Store Ordering Quantity:	12 units
Store Receiving Schedule:	Monday, Wednesday and Friday only
Replenishment Lead-Time from RDC1:	2 days

	Days																		
	1	2	3	4	5	6	7	8	9	10	11	12	13	14	15	16	17	...	364
	M	T	W	Th	F	Sa	Su	M	T	W	Th	F	Sa	Su	M	T	W	...	Su
Total Forecast	1	2	3	3	3	6	4	14	28	33	36	41	68	55	2	3	3	...	6
Min Display Qty	12	12	12	12	12	12	48	48	48	48	48	48	48	12	12	12	12	...	12
In Transits		12																	
Projected On Hand	17	27	24	21	18	12	8												

Figure 3.13: Determining when more inventory is needed.

In Figure 3.13, you can see that our current on hand balance is 18 units. On day 1, we are forecasting that we will sell 1 unit, leaving us with a Projected On Hand of 17 units at the end of that day.

Our forecast is to sell an additional 2 units on day 2, but we also have an in transit quantity of 12 units that's expected to arrive on that day from RDC1. Therefore, our projected on hand at the end of day 2 is 17 − 2 + 12 = 27 units, and so on. Using this logic, we can see that our projected on hand will drop below our minimum display quantity on day 7, if more stock does not arrive on, or before, this day. So now we also know than on, or before, day 7, we will need to schedule a Planned Arrival of stock into store 108.

Determining How Much Inventory Is Needed

We now know that we need more product to arrive by day 7. We have also determined that our projected on hand on that day will be 8 units, which is a shortfall of 40 units below our minimum display quantity of 48 on that day. Therefore, the quantity we need to arrive on the 7th day is 40 units, which will ensure that we don't drop below the minimum display quantity. However, our store only orders this product in cases of 12 (the minimum ordering quantity), so we have to round up our quantity to 48 units (see Figure 3.14).

PRODUCT: 01234567 – Deluxe Widget
LOCATION: Store 108

Current On Hand Balance:	18 units
Minimum Store Ordering Quantity:	12 units
Store Receiving Schedule:	Monday, Wednesday and Friday only
Replenishment Lead-Time from RDC1:	2 days

	Days																		
	1	2	3	4	5	6	7	8	9	10	11	12	13	14	15	16	17	...	364
	M	T	W	Th	F	Sa	Su	M	T	W	Th	F	Sa	Su	M	T	W	...	Su
Total Forecast	1	2	3	3	3	6	4	14	28	33	36	41	68	55	2	3	3	...	6
Min Display Qty	12	12	12	12	12	12	48	48	48	48	48	48	48	12	12	12	12		12
In Transits		12																...	
Projected On Hand	17	27	24	21	18	12	66												
Planned Arrivals							48												

Figure 3.14: Determining how much inventory is needed.

In Figure 3.14, we can see that if we plan for 48 units to arrive on the 7th day, our projected on hand will again be above our minimum display quantity.

Our store, however, is only open for receiving on Mondays, Wednesdays, and Fridays (as indicated by the white boxes). Since we will drop below our minimum display quantity on the 7th day, we must plan our arrival of 48 units on the first available receiving day *before* our needed arrival date. This would be on day 5 (see Figure 3.15).

PRODUCT: 01234567 – Deluxe Widget

LOCATION: Store 108

Current On Hand Balance:	18 units
Minimum Store Ordering Quantity:	12 units
Store Receiving Schedule:	Monday, Wednesday and Friday only
Replenishment Lead-Time from RDC1:	2 days

	Days																		
	1	2	3	4	5	6	7	8	9	10	11	12	13	14	15	16	17	...	364
	M	T	W	Th	F	Sa	Su	M	T	W	Th	F	Sa	Su	M	T	W	...	Su
Total Forecast	1	2	3	3	3	6	4	14	28	33	36	41	68	55	2	3	3	...	6
Min Display Qty	12	12	12	12	12	12	48	48	48	48	48	48	48	12	12	12	12		12
In Transits		12																	
Projected On Hand	17	27	24	21	66	60	56												
Planned Arrivals					48														

Figure 3.15: Scheduling the first planned arrival.

Based on our revised arrival date, our projected on hand balance on day 5 has been recalculated as follows:

Projected on hand at end of day 4		21
Forecast for day 5	-	3
Planned arrival on day 5	+	48
Projected on hand at end of day 5		66

In bank account fashion, the projected on hand has been recalculated for days 6 and 7 as well, based on the new schedule.

Step 4: Plan Future Store Replenishments

At first blush, the replenishment approach we've just described (subtracting demand from available on hand and in transits) may sound similar to a reorder point system. The key differentiator between a standard reorder point system and the initial calculation in a Flowcasting system is the calculation and tracking of the projected on hand (projected time-phased inventory balance) as described in the previous step.

It is the projected on hand that allows us to extend the replenishment logic for as far out into the future as a forecast exists and to continually critique open purchase orders (in transits) and re-plan future planned arrivals. Instead of merely knowing what will be on the next order, we now have a planning system that will tell us for *each and every day over the next year*:

- How much we plan to sell
- How much we will need to order
- How much inventory we will have on hand

In addition, retailers need only one system to plan the flows of inventories, replenishments, and purchases for all stores and RDCs -- rather than one system for the stores and another for the RDCs. This will be covered in greater detail in Chapter 4.

To illustrate the power of keeping track of our projected on hand balance, consider where we left off in Figure 3.15. We have only calculated our plans out until the end of the 7th day, but there's no need to stop there. Since we are keeping track of our projected on hand day by day, we can extend our replenishment logic out as far as the forecast allows. Starting with our projected on hand of 56 units at the end of day 7, we can simply pick up from where we left off.

If we have calculated a projected on hand of 56 units at the end of day 7, and we think we will sell 14 units on day 8, we'll have only 42 units left over at the end of day 8. Furthermore, the store won't be able to receive any product on day 9, so we need to cover an addi-

PRODUCT: 01234567 – Deluxe Widget

LOCATION: Store 108

Current On Hand Balance:	18 units
Minimum Store Ordering Quantity:	12 units
Store Receiving Schedule:	Monday, Wednesday and Friday only
Replenishment Lead-Time from RDC1:	2 days

	Days																		
	1	2	3	4	5	6	7	8	9	10	11	12	13	14	15	16	17	...	364
	M	T	W	Th	F	Sa	Su	M	T	W	Th	F	Sa	Su	M	T	W	...	Su
Total Forecast	1	2	3	3	3	6	4	14	28	33	36	41	68	55	2	3	3	...	6
Min Display Qty	12	12	12	12	12	12	48	48	48	48	48	48	48	12	12	12	12	...	12
In Transits		12																...	
Projected On Hand	17	27	24	21	66	60	56	42	14										
Planned Arrivals					48														

Figure 3.16: Determining the timing of the second replenishment.

tional 28 units of sales, which will put our projected on hand balance at 14, as illustrated in Figure 3.16.

As Figure 3.16 shows, the arrival on day 8 needs to be at least 34 units, in order to ensure our projected on hand is at least 48 at the end of day 9 (see Figure 3.17).

PRODUCT: 01234567 – Deluxe Widget

LOCATION: Store 108

Current On Hand Balance:	18 units
Minimum Store Ordering Quantity:	12 units
Store Receiving Schedule:	Monday, Wednesday and Friday only
Replenishment Lead-Time from RDC1:	2 days

	Days																		
	1	2	3	4	5	6	7	8	9	10	11	12	13	14	15	16	17	...	364
	M	T	W	Th	F	Sa	Su	M	T	W	Th	F	Sa	Su	M	T	W	...	Su
Total Forecast	1	2	3	3	3	6	4	14	28	33	36	41	68	55	2	3	3	...	6
Min Display Qty	12	12	12	12	12	12	48	48	48	48	48	48	48	12	12	12	12	...	12
In Transits		12																
Projected On Hand	17	27	24	21	66	60	56	78										
Planned Arrivals					48			36										

Figure 3.17: The second planned arrival.

But since we order in multiples of 12, the arrival in day 8 needs to be rounded up to 36. As a result, our projected on hand at the end of day 8 is now 78 units.

In like fashion, the remainder of the forecast horizon can be planned (see Figure 3.18):

PRODUCT: 01234567 – Deluxe Widget

LOCATION: Store 108

Current On Hand Balance:	18 units
Minimum Store Ordering Quantity:	12 units
Store Receiving Schedule:	Monday, Wednesday and Friday only
Replenishment Lead-Time from RDC1:	2 days

	Days																		
	1	2	3	4	5	6	7	8	9	10	11	12	13	14	15	16	17	...	364
	M	T	W	Th	F	Sa	Su	M	T	W	Th	F	Sa	Su	M	T	W	...	Su
Total Forecast	1	2	3	3	3	6	4	14	28	33	36	41	68	55	2	3	3	...	6
Min Display Qty	12	12	12	12	12	12	48	48	48	48	48	48	48	12	12	12	12	...	12
In Transits		12																
Projected On Hand	17	27	24	21	66	60	56	78	50	89	53	144	76	21	19	16	13	...	16
Planned Arrivals					48			36		72		132						

Figure 3.18: A 52-week arrival-based plan.

Notice that, at no point, does the projected on hand dip below the minimum display quantity. We've now worked out each and every time stock will need to arrive at store 108 for the next year.

Step 5: Calculate Planned Orders to Support the Arrival-Based Plan

Now that we have determined when inventory will need to arrive at the store, it's a simple matter to determine when orders will need to be placed on RDC1 to meet the plan. This is where the replenishment lead-time comes into play.

If it takes 2 days for product to arrive at the store after it has been ordered from RDC1, then we simply need to subtract 2 days from each store's arrival date to determine when it will need to be ordered in the future (see Figure 3.19).

PRODUCT: 01234567 – Deluxe Widget

LOCATION: Store 108

Current On Hand Balance:	18 units
Minimum Store Ordering Quantity:	12 units
Store Receiving Schedule:	Monday, Wednesday and Friday only
Replenishment Lead-Time from RDC1:	2 days

	Days																		
	1	2	3	4	5	6	7	8	9	10	11	12	13	14	15	16	17	...	364
	M	T	W	Th	F	Sa	Su	M	T	W	Th	F	Sa	Su	M	T	W	...	Su
Total Forecast	1	2	3	3	3	3	4	14	28	33	36	41	68	55	2	3	3	...	6
Min Display Qty	12	12	12	12	12	12	48	48	48	48	48	48	48	12	12	12	12		12
In Transits		12																	
Projected On Hand	17	27	24	21	66	60	56	78	50	89	53	144	76	21	19	16	13	...	16
Planned Arrivals					48			36		72		132						...	
Planned Orders			48			36		72		132								...	

Figure 3.19: A 52-week ordering and arrival-based plan.

In Figure 3.19, if we want 48 units to arrive on day 5, then it will need to be ordered from RDC1 on day 3. The difference represents the 2-day replenishment lead-time between the store and RDC1. If this store were to get shipments from another location (e.g., another RDC or even a manufacturer's MDC) that is further away, steps 1 through 4 (figuring out when stock will need to arrive) would be exactly the same. The only difference is how far in advance the store would need to place orders.

---

6 Once the replenishment lead time is reached, there is only enough time left to get it on the truck at RDC1 and transport it to the store. At this point, the shipment is considered to be en route to the store, so it's too late to change the dates or quantities.

The planned orders will continue to be recalculated until they are within the replenishment lead-time, at which point they will become firm in transits.[6]

Continuous Re-Planning

Of course, not all plans will happen exactly as expected. On any given day, you may sell more than your forecast or you may sell less – and if you get it exactly right, it's probably a coincidence. That's why, in order to Flowcast properly, the foundational data needs to be refreshed daily. On a net change basis[7], if any of the foundational data has changed for the item/store, then the rest of the planning steps will be executed again, resulting in a plan that not only stretches out an entire year, but is *constantly being kept up to date* with the most recent information.

Recall, for example, the plan we just created for Product #01234567 in store 108 (see Figure 3.19). Suppose that on day 1, instead of selling the 1 unit that was forecast, you actually sold 5. In other words, you oversold your forecast by 4 units. Here's what would happen: after day 1 had passed, you would begin a new planning cycle (day 2). Between day 1 and day 2, your Current On Hand Balance would have dropped from 18 units to 13 units. Assuming that the forecast for the next 52 weeks doesn't change overnight (typically the forecast would change weekly if required), the Flowcasting logic would completely refresh the plan as shown in Figure 3.20):

Because the forecast was oversold on day 1, the impact of this change automatically updates the entire 52-week planning horizon, starting now from week 2. In this particular example, the planned arrival on day 8 increased from 36 units to 48 units as a result.

Flowcasting the Entire Supply Chain

So far we have used a simple example of planning a single item in a single store to illustrate the Flowcasting concept. In fact, the same

---

7 Net change planning is what makes huge retail data volumes manageable. The time-phased plans will only change if one of the input variables changes. Therefore, it's only necessary to re-plan product/locations that have experienced a change from one day to the next.

process (on a much larger scale, executed by computer) can be used to plan replenishment projections for the rest of the products and locations in the retail supply chain. This can be done with *no addi-*

PRODUCT: 01234567 – Deluxe Widget

LOCATION: Store 108

Current On Hand Balance:	13 units
Minimum Store Ordering Quantity:	12 units
Store Receiving Schedule:	Monday, Wednesday and Friday only
Replenishment Lead-Time from RDC1:	2 days

	Days																		
	2	3	4	5	6	7	8	9	10	11	12	13	14	15	16	17	18	...	365
	T	W	Th	F	Sa	Su	M	T	W	Th	F	Sa	Su	M	T	W	Th	...	M
Total Forecast	2	3	3	3	6	4	14	28	33	36	41	68	55	2	3	3	3	...	8
Min Display Qty	12	12	12	12	12	48	48	48	48	48	48	48	12	12	12	12	12	...	12
In Transits	12																	...	
Projected On Hand	23	20	17	62	56	52	86	58	85	49	140	72	17	15	12	21	18	...	16
Planned Arrivals				48			48		60		132					12		...	
Planned Orders		48			48		60		132					12				...	

Figure 3.20: A recalibrated 52-week plan after overselling day 1.

tional forecasting beyond the store-level forecast of consumer demand discussed in this chapter!

Summary

We have illustrated how Demand Management and Resource Planning converge at the retail store level in the supply chain, and have discussed some of the key inputs required to make Flowcasting work. We also described a high-level forecasting process used to predict consumer demand at the store level. We demonstrated how, using this forecast, on hand balances, planned arrivals, and planned orders can be time phased into the future. Here are the key points to remember:

1. Every retail supply chain exists to fulfill the demands of the consumer. In a traditional retail model, the consumer buys products from stores, so it only makes sense to focus all Demand Management activities at store level.

2. The first step in making Flowcasting work is to have an up-to-date repository of common demand and logistics data at the store and RDC level, such as: POS history, inventory bal-

ances, lead-times, store shelf display configuration, safety stock, order minimums, and activity schedules.

3. In a Flowcasting environment, all demand forecasting is done only at the store level, in selling units, and by item, by day for several weeks and months into the future. Starting with baseline forecasts generated by a computer, modifications can be made both top-down (for activities such as national promotion and assortment strategies) and bottom-up (for local promotions and events), as required.

4. By using the aforementioned forecasts as a foundation, some simple real-world constraints can be applied to generate time-phased projected flows of arrivals, orders, and inventory balances for the entire forecast horizon for any item at any store.

5. Outside the replenishment lead time, the time-phased planned flows are fluid and are continually updated with fresh information. In this way, new information from consumers is being input directly into the store (and as we'll see later, the entire retail supply chain) to make sure that no plan is more than 24 hours out of date.

The following chapter extends the Flowcasting process to the next echelon in the supply chain. It demonstrates how RDCs can be planned with the same forecast that drives the stores through the simple power of dependent demand.

C H A P T E R   4

Supplying the Stores
Dependent Demand and Replenishment at the Retail DC

To paraphrase the old saw, "no RDC is an island." The RDC's activities are wholly dependent on the needs of the retail stores. Without stores, there would be no need for RDCs to exist. Yet today, most retailers today have one system for replenishing their stores and another for replenishing their RDCs. Flowcasting reconnects the stores and RDCs, as they should be connected. This means more than drawing from a centralized data repository; it means that the final replenishment plans from the stores actually become the top-line inputs for the RDCs. In this way, the forecasts cascade through the first two levels of the supply chain, starting with the only point of true demand: the store shelves.

In this chapter, we'll extend the logic described in Chapter 3 from the store level to the RDC. As in the examples used in Chapter 3, we'll focus on an individual item. Remember, it doesn't matter whether we're forecasting one SKU or 10,000 SKUs; the logic remains the same. The Flowcasting process crunches the numbers and makes the complexity manageable.

Passing the Demand
Before diving into forecasting at the RDC level, we'll review the process of forecasting at the retail shelf level, as described in Chapter

3. In a Flowcasting environment, replenishment demand and supply planning at store level for any given item requires 5 steps:

1. Get your foundational data in order.
2. Forecast consumer demand at the store shelf.
3. Plan the first store replenishment.
4. Plan future store replenishments.
5. Calculate planned orders to support the arrival-based plan.

The output of this activity is a store-level plan for when product needs to be ordered from the RDC to support demand for the next year into the future. Let's return to the fully calculated example from Chapter 3, for store location 108:

PRODUCT: 01234567 – Deluxe Widget

LOCATION: Store 108

Current On Hand Balance:	18 units
Minimum Store Ordering Quantity:	12 units
Store Receiving Schedule:	Monday, Wednesday and Friday only
Replenishment Lead-Time from RDC1:	2 days

	Days																		
	1	2	3	4	5	6	7	8	9	10	11	12	13	14	15	16	17	...	364
	M	T	W	Th	F	Sa	Su	M	T	W	Th	F	Sa	Su	M	T	W	...	Su
Total Forecast	1	2	3	3	3	6	4	14	28	33	36	41	68	55	2	3	3	...	6
Min Display Qty	12	12	12	12	12	12	48	48	48	48	48	48	48	12	12	12	12		12
In Transits		12																	
Projected On Hand	17	27	24	21	66	60	56	78	50	89	53	144	76	21	19	16	13	...	16
Planned Arrivals				48			36		72		132							...	
Planned Orders		48			36		72		132									...	

Figure 4.1: A 52-week ordering plan for product 01234567 in store 108.

If store 108 was the only retail sales venue in the supply chain, life would be simple. But, of course, supply chains are dynamic entities consisting of numerous nodes. For the sake of illustration, we'll expand the model (see Figure 4.2) to include two stores to demonstrate how Flowcasting can tightly integrate retail stores and RDCs within the supply chain.

In Chapter 3, we determined the replenishment needs of store 108 (Figure 4.1). But to compute RDC1's shipping requirements, we'll also need a time-phased plan for another retail node in the sup-

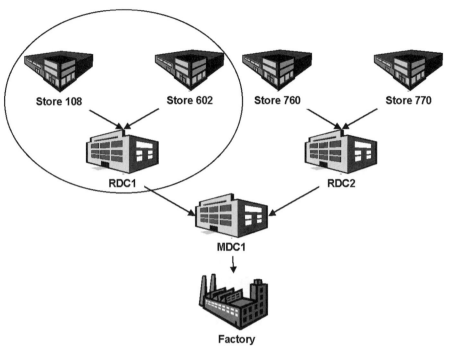

Figure 4.2: Using Flowcasting to integrate retail stores and retail DC.

ply chain, store 602. We can determine store 602's requirements by deploying the same process used to calculate a plan for store 108, but instead using store 602's unique demand forecast, supply constraints, and lead-time:

PRODUCT: 01234567 – Deluxe Widget

LOCATION: Store 602

Current On Hand Balance:	40 units
Minimum Store Ordering Quantity:	24 units
Store Receiving Schedule:	Tuesday, Thursday and Saturday only
Replenishment Lead-Time from RDC1:	3 days

	Days																		
	1	2	3	4	5	6	7	8	9	10	11	12	13	14	15	16	17	...	364
	M	T	W	Th	F	Sa	Su	M	T	W	Th	F	Sa	Su	M	T	W	...	Su
Total Forecast	3	6	7	8	9	15	12	38	76	90	98	112	186	150	2	4	4	...	6
Min Display Qty	24	24	24	24	24	24	96	96	96	96	96	96	96	24	24	24	24	...	24
In Transits																		...	
Projected On Hand	37	31	24	40	31	160	148	110	202	112	230	118	196	46	44	40	36	...	30
Planned Arrivals				24		144			168			216		264				...	
Planned Orders	24		144			168			216		264							...	

Figure 4.3: A 52-week ordering plan for product 01234567 in store 602.

Now that we've calculated the planned orders for the next 52 weeks for stores 108 and 602, it's very easy to determine the demand that RDC1 will need to satisfy over that time period. All we need is the following information:

- Daily DC on hand balances and in transits
- RDC replenishment lead time (from the manufacturer DC)
- RDC safety stock quantities (minimum desired inventory balance)
- RDC minimum order quantities
- RDC shipping and receiving schedules

With that information in hand, we can plan replenishment for RDC1 the same way that we planned replenishment for the stores, with one critical difference: *no additional forecasting will be required to generate a time-phased inventory and replenishment plan for RDC!* Remember, the bottom line numbers from the store replenishment plans cascade to the next level of the supply chain and become the top-line numbers for the RDCs. This makes it possible to determine RDC supply requirements through three easy steps:

Step 1: Calculate RDC shipment projection
Step 2: Calculate arrival-based plan for the RDC
Step 3: Calculate planned orders to support the arrival-based plan

Step 1: Calculate RDC Shipment Projection

By using the Flowcasting process at each store, the work of determining when product will need to ship from RDC1 has already been done. The planned order stream from each store represents how much the stores want shipped and when.

To calculate RDC1's shipment projection, you just need to add up the Planned Orders for each store (see Figure 4.4, which shows the Planned Order lines for stores 108 and 602. The full details for stores 108 and 602 are shown in Figures 4.1 and 4.3, respectively).

	Days																		
	1	2	3	4	5	6	7	8	9	10	11	12	13	14	15	16	17	...	364
	M	T	W	Th	F	Sa	Su	M	T	W	Th	F	Sa	Su	M	T	W	...	Su
Planned Orders - 108			48			36		72		132								...	
Planned Orders - 602	24		144			168		216		264								...	
Total Store Planned Orders	24		192			204		288		396								...	

Figure 4.4: RDC1 shipment projection calculated by summing store planned orders

The total store planned orders line now becomes the dependent demand that RDC1 must satisfy.

Step 2: Calculate Arrival-Based Plan for the RDC

With a demand projection that's been given by the stores, a purchasing plan for RDC1 can now be calculated, through a process similar to the store-level planning described in the previous chapter.

PRODUCT: 01234567 – Deluxe Widget

LOCATION: RDC1

Current On Hand Balance:	250 units
Minimum DC Ordering Quantity:	144 units
DC Receiving Schedule:	Monday to Friday
Replenishment Lead-Time from MDC1:	4 days

	Days																		
	1	2	3	4	5	6	7	8	9	10	11	12	13	14	15	16	17	...	364
	M	T	W	Th	F	Sa	Su	M	T	W	Th	F	Sa	Su	M	T	W	...	Su
Store Planned Orders	24		192			204		288		396								...	
Safety Stock	100	100	100	100	100	100	100	100	100	100	100	100	100	100	100	100	100	...	100
In Transits	144																	...	

Figure 4.5: Dependent demand and basic replenishment data for RDC1.

In Figure 4.5:

- The Minimum DC Ordering Quantity represents the minimum amount that will appear on a purchase order between RDC1 and MDC1. In this case, the volume through RDC1 for product 01234567 is sufficient to order in pallet quantities of 144 units.
- The DC Receiving Schedule describes when the receiving department is open for business at RDC1 (also denoted by the white boxes in the Planned Arrivals line).
- The Replenishment Lead-Time from MDC1 represents the

amount of time required for product to be received into stock at RDC1 after a purchase order has been created on MDC1.

- The Store Planned Orders line represents the sum of the Planned Orders line for all stores that are serviced from RDC1. This is dependent demand that is used in place of a shipment forecast for RDC1.
- The Safety Stock line represents the minimum level of inventory for this item that we want to hold at RDC1 to cover for demand uncertainty.

The terminology is slightly different, but the process is the same for calculating an arrival-based plan for an RDC:

Starting with a current on hand balance of 250 units, we'll determine when the projected on hand is planned to fall below the safety stock. This is the date when the first planned arrival is needed (day 6, in our example, as shown in Figure 4.6).

PRODUCT: 01234567 – Deluxe Widget

LOCATION: RDC1

Current On Hand Balance:	250 units
Minimum DC Ordering Quantity:	144 units
DC Receiving Schedule:	Monday to Friday
Replenishment Lead-Time from MDC1:	4 days

	Days																		
	1	2	3	4	5	6	7	8	9	10	11	12	13	14	15	16	17	...	364
	M	T	W	Th	F	Sa	Su	M	T	W	Th	F	Sa	Su	M	T	W	...	Su
Store Planned Orders	24		192			204		288		396								...	
Safety Stock	100	100	100	100	100	100	100	100	100	100	100	100	100	100	100	100	100	...	100
In Transits	144																	...	
Projected On Hand	370	370	178	178	178	-26												...	
Planned Arrivals																			

Figure 4.6: Determining when the first arrival is needed at RDC1.

As you can see, if no stock arrives on, or before, day 6, the inventory at RDC1 will drop to -26 units. Since our safety stock should be 100 units, 126 units will be required. That number will be rounded up to 144 units, the minimum ordering quantity.

One other factor must be taken into account: RDC1 is not open for receiving on day 6, which means that the first arrival of 144 units will need to be scheduled for day 5, the first available date prior to when the arrival is actually needed. Figure 4.7 below summarizes this simple logic:

PRODUCT: 01234567 – Deluxe Widget
LOCATION: RDC1

Current On Hand Balance:	250 units
Minimum DC Ordering Quantity:	144 units
DC Receiving Schedule:	Monday to Friday
Replenishment Lead-Time from MDC1:	4 days

	Days																		
	1	2	3	4	5	6	7	8	9	10	11	12	13	14	15	16	17	...	364
	M	T	W	Th	F	Sa	Su	M	T	W	Th	F	Sa	Su	M	T	W	...	Su
Store Planned Orders	24		192		204			288		396								...	
Safety Stock	100	100	100	100	100	100	100	100	100	100	100	100	100	100	100	100	100	...	100
In Transits	144																		
Projected On Hand	370	370	178	178	322	118													
Planned Arrivals					144														

Figure 4.7: Scheduling the first arrival at RDC1 to maintain projected on hand above safety stock.

By calculating and tracking the projected on hand at RDC1, we have the ability to continue planning forward for as far out as we have Store Planned Orders. Figure 4.8 below illustrates a 52-week arrival based plan for RDC1:

PRODUCT: 01234567 – Deluxe Widget
LOCATION: RDC1

Current On Hand Balance:	250 units
Minimum DC Ordering Quantity:	144 units
DC Receiving Schedule:	Monday to Friday
Replenishment Lead-Time from MDC1:	4 days

	Days																		
	1	2	3	4	5	6	7	8	9	10	11	12	13	14	15	16	17	...	364
	M	T	W	Th	F	Sa	Su	M	T	W	Th	F	Sa	Su	M	T	W	...	Su
Store Planned Orders	24		192		204			288		396								...	
Safety Stock	100	100	100	100	100	100	100	100	100	100	100	100	100	100	100	100	100	...	100
In Transits	144																		
Projected On Hand	370	370	178	178	322	118	118	118	118	154	154	154	154	154	154	154	154	...	148
Planned Arrivals					144			288		432									

Figure 4.8: A 52 week arrival based plan for RDC1.

Step 3: Calculate Planned Orders to Support the Arrival-Based Plan

As in the case of planning for the retail stores used in our ongoing example, the bulk of the planning activity for RDC1 has been dedicated to determining when supply needs to arrive in order to support the dependent demand. We know that the replenishment lead-time (from order to receipt into stock) is 4 days between RDC1 and MDC1. We can, therefore, create RDC planned orders from the planned arrivals by offsetting the planned arrival dates ahead by the lead-time of 4 days, as illustrated in Figure 4.9.

PRODUCT: 01234567 – Deluxe Widget

LOCATION: RDC1

Current On Hand Balance:	250 units
Minimum DC Ordering Quantity:	144 units
DC Receiving Schedule:	Monday to Friday
Replenishment Lead-Time from MDC1:	4 days

	Days																			
	1	2	3	4	5	6	7	8	9	10	11	12	13	14	15	16	17	...	364
	M	T	W	Th	F	Sa	Su	M	T	W	Th	F	Sa	Su	M	T	W	...	Su
Store Planned Orders	24		192		204		288		396									...	
Safety Stock	100	100	100	100	100	100	100	100	100	100	100	100	100	100	100	100	100	...	100
In Transits	144																	...	
Projected On Hand	370	370	178	178	322	118	118	118	118	154	154	154	154	154	154	154	154		148
Planned Arrivals					144			288		432									
Planned Orders	144			288		432										144			

Figure 4.9: A 52 week ordering and arrival based replenishment plan at RDC1.

As Figure 4.9 shows, on day 1, RDC1 will need to order 144 units from MDC1 to ensure that it arrives on day 5, and so on through the year.

We now have a complete 52-week plan for RDC1, including planned store demand, projected on hand balances, planned arrivals into stock, and planned ordering activity. All three were determined without having to forecast requirements at RDC1. Put another way, the item/store level forecast of consumer demand that we created in Chapter 3 is now directly driving two full echelons of the supply chain.

Whether you use a Flowcasting business process or not, there is a chain reaction of demand from consumers through to the factories. Consumer buying behavior directly impacts store replenishment which, in turn directly impacts RDC replenishment. By modeling this reality explicitly, not only does the amount of energy required for forecasting decrease, but the plans will be far more accurate as well.

The Chain Reaction of Demand

Because the store and DC echelons are being planned in an integrated fashion by using dependent demand -- and all within the same system – the impact of changing the single input variable (the consumer demand at store level) will be clear at both the stores and the RDC. For example, starting in week 1, our integrated plans for stores 108 and 602 and RDC1 would be as shown in Figure 4.10.

By using time-phased planning, the complete chain of events that needs to take place to satisfy consumer demand is simulated in advance. If the forecast is oversold or undersold at store level, the entire 52-week plans are recalculated and shared with RDC1, which in turn recalculates its planned orders to MDC1. At any time, the impact of yesterday's POS sales at store level will be reflected in today's plans at both the stores and the RDCs.

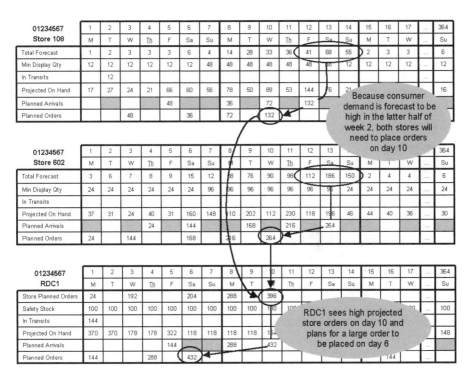

Figure 4.10: The chain reaction of demand from consumers to retail stores to the RDC.

What If: Re-Mapping Demand to Supply

Flowcasting makes timely, robust planning feasible and practical, and gives all trading partners in a retail supply chain a powerful tool for predicting and meeting demand in a cost effective way. That ability makes Flowcasting an essential tool for managing in the real world, where change is a constant and it's often necessary to make decisions "on the fly." For example, with traditional means of managing supply chains, hours of laborious analysis, reforecasting and order reallocation are required to facilitate network changes. With Flowcasting, such activities can be done effortlessly simply by updating the system with the new information.

Think about the model of the supply chain that we have been building in this chapter and the previous chapter. It extends from the retail store shelf to the retail DC. Because the model begins with a forecast of consumer demand at the store shelf, downstream dependent demand can be re-directed through different network configurations as business needs dictate.

Suppose that an analysis of the network reveals that transportation and inventory costs would be better optimized if, say, store 760 were supplied from RDC1, as illustrated in Figure 4.11.

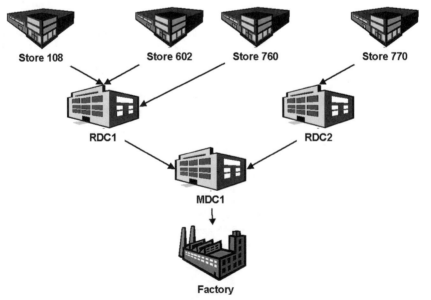

Figure 4.11: A network change resulting in store 760 being replenished from RDC1.

In a traditional supply chain environment (without Flowcasting), the impact of this network decision would be significant for the following reasons:

- Historical demand for RDC1 prior to the network change would be understated, as it would not include orders from store 760. Historical demand for RDC2 similarly would be overstated, as it would include past orders from store 760. As a consequence, it would be necessary to restate demand history for both RDC1 and RDC2 for every product impacted by the change and reforecast at both places as well.
- It would be necessary to revise existing promotional shipment forecasts that were entered into RDC1 and RDC2 before the network change.
- Because of the changes in demand rate, it would be necessary to adjust inbound orders created before the network change for RDC1 and RDC2.

When you consider that every product in store 760 would be affected by this change, this could represent days of work, not to mention the potential for making many errors.

By contrast, in a Flowcasting environment, it's simple enough to re-plan the entire supply chain following a network change. That's because a) there is a single demand forecast -- the one showing consumer demand at the store shelf and b) the network change is only a supply decision that does not impact demand and therefore requires no change to the forecast.

Basically, all that's required is to map store 760's planned orders to RDC1, as shown in Figure 4.12

	Days																		
	1	2	3	4	5	6	7	8	9	10	11	12	13	14	15	16	17	...	364
	M	T	W	Th	F	Sa	Su	M	T	W	Th	F	Sa	Su	M	T	W		Su
Planned Orders - 108			48			36		72		132								...	
Planned Orders - 602	24		144			168		216		264								...	
Planned Orders - 760		12		36					216			36				36		...	
Total Store Planned Orders	24	12	192		36	204		288	216	396		36				36		...	

Figure 4.12: RDC1 shipment projection revised to include planned orders from store 760.

With demand re-mapped to a new network path, all that we need to do is recalculate the plan for RDC1 (and RDC2) using the new streams of Store Planned Orders and the procedures described in Steps 2 and 3 earlier in this chapter. Figure 4.13 shows a revised replenishment plan using this approach.

PRODUCT: 01234567 – Deluxe Widget

LOCATION: RDC1

Current On Hand Balance:	250 units
Minimum DC Ordering Quantity:	144 units
DC Receiving Schedule:	Monday to Friday
Replenishment Lead-Time from MDC1:	4 days

	Days																		
	1	2	3	4	5	6	7	8	9	10	11	12	13	14	15	16	17	...	364
	M	T	W	Th	F	Sa	Su	M	T	W	Th	F	Sa	Su	M	T	W	...	Su
Store Planned Orders	24	12	192		36	204		288	216	396		36				36		...	
Safety Stock	100	100	100	100	100	100	100	100	100	100	100	100	100	100	100	100	100	...	100
In Transits	144																	...	
Projected On Hand	370	358	166	166	418	214	214	214	142	178	178	142	142	142	142	106	106		128
Planned Arrivals					288			288	144	432						144			
Planned Orders	288			288	144	432						144							

Figure 4.13: Revised replenishment plan for RDC1 using new store planned orders stream.

Once a decision has been made to change the network, it can be implemented in a matter of minutes -- not days or weeks -- and the entire supply chain will be updated accordingly.

The ability of a Flowcasting system to map demand at will vastly simplifies other supply chain challenges as well, including:

- Adding new RDCs to the network or removing existing RDCs from the network
- Opening new stores, or closing existing stores
- Temporarily re-directing demand to alleviate overstocks
- Simulating the short-term operational impact of planned network changes at every node
- Planning direct-to-store deliveries or VMI programs with suppliers
- Carrying out multi-echelon replenishment (ordering in bulk into one RDC from overseas, then breaking up the order for shipments to other RDCs for distribution to stores)

Again, this remarkable level of flexibility is made possible through *less* forecasting, not more.

It's clear that Flowcasting can vastly streamline and simplify a retail enterprise. But to realize the full benefit of Flowcasting, the process must be extended from the retail shelves all the way back to the factory. Since most retailers rely on other entities (with their own separate planning systems) to manufacture the products they sell, a standardized form of communication is required to manage the myriad supplier relationships within a Flowcasting environment. The vehicle for doing so is called "supplier scheduling."

Supplier Scheduling

The output of the Flowcasting process at RDC1 (and any other RDCs) is a projection of what suppliers must sell and ship to the retailer, 52 weeks into the future (i.e., a stream of Planned Orders). By sharing the Planned Orders with wholesalers and manufacturers, *the retailer can eliminate the need for these suppliers to forecast what the retailer is going to buy* – information about demand is disseminated and refreshed daily as conditions change in retail stores and RDCs.

Flowcasting also not only reduces forecasting efforts, but it provides vastly superior forecast quality at the downstream echelons. Less effort is required because the entire supply chain is planned with the consumer demand forecast at the store shelf. The forecast quality is superior, because every constraint and inventory pool upstream from the consumer is considered in the projection -- there's no need to guess the demand at each echelon of the supply chain.

The sharing of planned orders is commonly known in manufacturing and distribution circles as Supplier Scheduling, and will be discussed in more detail in Chapter 5. Even without further discussion, it should be obvious that supplier scheduling represents a radical departure from the way retailers, wholesale distributors, and manufacturers have traditionally conducted business.

Summary

In this chapter, we extended the Flowcasting business process from the retail store to the RDC echelon in the supply chain. We demonstrated that planning replenishment at the RDC is very similar to planning for demand at a retail store. Here are the key points to remember about managing in a Flowcasting environment:

1. There is only one echelon in the supply chain where consumption occurs. Until a product is taken from the store shelf, all other inventory movements prior to that point are simply value-added transfers that are dependent on the store-level consumption. Hence the term "dependent demand" for consumer demand that will cascade through the supply chain.

2. As long as all of the retail stores serviced by an RDC are calculating and sharing planned orders, the RDC receives its demand plan "for free" -- no additional forecasting is required beyond the store level consumer demand forecast discussed in Chapter 3.

3. While the terminology is different, the Flowcasting technique used at the RDC is the same as that used in the store. This entails:
   i. Determining when supply must arrive to satisfy the demand
   ii. Offsetting the arrivals by the replenishment lead-time to determine when product needs to be ordered from the next echelon in the supply chain.

4. Because dependent demand (in the form of store planned orders) is being shared between the retail stores and the RDC, the impact of changes in consumer demand at the store shelf can be seen at the retail stores and the RDC -- virtually in real time.

5. The shared 52-week replenishment plans at the stores and DCs are not static. Every day, the information is updated, and the chain reaction of demand is cascaded downstream and recalculated for the next 52 weeks into the future.

6. Once store-level consumer demand forecasts exist, demand can be flexibly mapped and re-mapped to support any supply network configuration with minimal effort.

7. The sharing of highly relevant and directly actionable information with suppliers will allow retailers, wholesalers, and manufacturers to eliminate unnecessary forecasting from the supply chain. This, in turn, will not only reduce costs and improve supply chain dynamics, but it will completely transform business relationships for the better.

The next chapter moves the Flowcasting process outside the retailer's domain and into the supplier's distribution and manufacturing processes. It shows that through supplier scheduling, the benefits of sharing dependent demand are not confined within organizational boundaries.

C H A P T E R   5

Supplying the Retailer
Wholesale Distribution and Production Scheduling

So far, we've seen how Flowcasting links retail stores and RDCs through a single store-level forecast. The key is dependent demand, which specifies how much product must be shipped and when is the product needed, taking into account all relevant constraints. That information is "actionable" at every node in the retail supply chain, which means that the dependent demand can be used directly by the next partner upstream, with no translation or interpretation necessary.

In this chapter, we'll describe how dependent demand can extend beyond the retailer's organization (stores and RDCs) and transform business relationships and planning processes with wholesale distributors, manufacturers and raw material suppliers. It will also describe how manufacturers that utilize ERP systems can internalize Flowcast-generated dependent demand provided by key customers. If all this seems like a tall order, bear in mind that Flowcasting reduces uncertainty between nodes in the supply chain. And the more you can reduce uncertainty, the less the need for individual nodes to guess (forecast) what's needed today, tomorrow, and a year out.

Flowcasting for Upstream Supply Chain Partners

Recall how, taking the Store Planned Orders (dependent demand) from store 108 and store 602 as givens, we were able to Flowcast planned orders from RDC1 on MDC1 (See Figure 5.1).

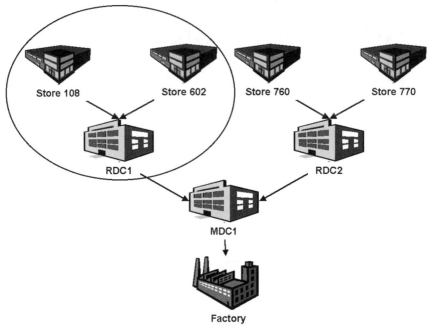

Figure 5.1: The network elements of RDC1's product flow plan.

The completed product flow plan for RDC1 based on this network is shown in Figure 5.2.

PRODUCT: 01234567 – Deluxe Widget

LOCATION: RDC1

Current On Hand Balance:	250 units
Minimum DC Ordering Quantity:	144 units
DC Receiving Schedule:	Monday to Friday
Replenishment Lead-Time from MDC1:	4 days

	Days																		
	1	2	3	4	5	6	7	8	9	10	11	12	13	14	15	16	17	...	364
	M	T	W	Th	F	Sa	Su	M	T	W	Th	F	Sa	Su	M	T	W		Su
Store Planned Orders	24		192			204		288		396									
Safety Stock	100	100	100	100	100	100	100	100	100	100	100	100	100	100	100	100	100	...	100
In Transits	144																		
Projected On Hand	370	370	178	178	322	118	118	118	118	154	154	154	154	154	154	154	154	...	148
Planned Arrivals					144			288		432									
Planned Orders	144			288	432											144			

Figure 5.2: A 52-week flow plan at RDC1.

But as we can see from Figure 5.1, a planned order stream also needs to be created for RDC2 so that MDC1 can have complete visibility into its dependent demand. To do so, we need to create a Flowcasting plan for RDC2 in addition to the one for RDC1. First, we collect and sum the planned order streams from the stores that are serviced by RDC2 (see Figure 5.3):

	Days																		
	1	2	3	4	5	6	7	8	9	10	11	12	13	14	15	16	17	...	364
	M	T	W	Th	F	Sa	Su	M	T	W	Th	F	Sa	Su	M	T	W	...	Su
Planned Orders – 760		12			36				216			36				36		...	12
Planned Orders – 770	48		12		24			216		360					12		12	...	
Total Store Planned Orders	48	12	12		60			216	216	360		36			12	36	12	...	12

Figure 5.3: Calculating total dependent demand at RDC2.

As in the case of RDC1, the total store planned orders stream now becomes the "top line" of RDC2's time-phased plan. With RDC2's replenishment data, the Flowcasting process can be employed to produce a complete product flow plan for RDC2 (Figure 5.4):

PRODUCT: 01234567 – Deluxe Widget

LOCATION: RDC2

Current On Hand Balance:	160 units
Minimum DC Ordering Quantity:	144 units
DC Receiving Schedule:	Monday to Friday
Replenishment Lead-Time from MDC1:	2 days

	Days																		
	1	2	3	4	5	6	7	8	9	10	11	12	13	14	15	16	17	...	364
	M	T	W	Th	F	Sa	Su	M	T	W	Th	F	Sa	Su	M	T	W	...	Su
Store Planned Orders	48	12	12		60			216	216	360		36			12	36	12	...	12
Safety Stock	50	50	50	50	50	50	50	50	50	50	50	50	50	50	50	50	50	...	50
In Transits																		...	
Projected On Hand	112	100	88	88	172	172	172	100	172	100	100	64	64	52	160	148	148	...	70
Planned Arrivals					144			144	288	288					144				
Planned Orders			144		144	288	288						144						

Figure 5.4: A 52-week flow plan at RDC2.

With RDC2 now calculating planned orders in addition to RDC1, we can continue the chain reaction of demand down to MDC1. In the same way that the RDCs calculate their dependent demand by summing store planned orders, MDC1 can calculate its dependent demand by summing up planned orders from RDC1 and RDC2 (in our example RDC1 and RDC2 are the only two customers of MDC1 -- see Figure 5.5):

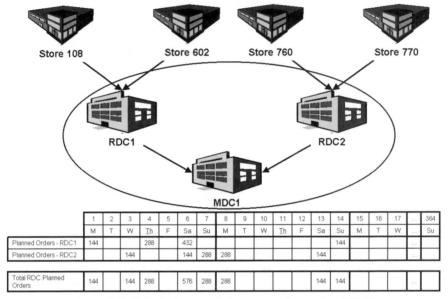

Figure 5.5: Calculating total dependent demand at MDC1.

Once again, this dependent demand stream from the RDCs becomes the enabler for the Flowcasting process in MDC1[8]. With a dependent demand stream given to it, MDC1 is simply another distribution node that can be planned in exactly the same way as RDC1 and RDC2 (see Figure 5.6).

PRODUCT: 01234567 – Deluxe Widget

LOCATION: MDC1

Current On Hand Balance:	400 units
Minimum DC Ordering Quantity:	576 units
DC Receiving Schedule:	Seven days a week
Replenishment Lead-Time from Factory:	5 days

	Days																		
	1	2	3	4	5	6	7	8	9	10	11	12	13	14	15	16	17	...	364
	M	T	W	Th	F	Sa	Su	M	T	W	Th	F	Sa	Su	M	T	W	...	Su
Store Planned Orders	144		144	288		576	288	288					144	144				...	
Safety Stock	250	250	250	250	250	250	250	250	250	250	250	250	250	250	250	250	250	...	250
In Transits	576																	...	
Projected On Hand	832	832	688	400	400	400	688	400	400	400	400	400	256	688	688	688	688	...	400
Planned Arrivals						576	576							576				...	
Planned Orders	576	576						576									576	...	

Figure 5.6: A 52-week flow plan at MDC1.

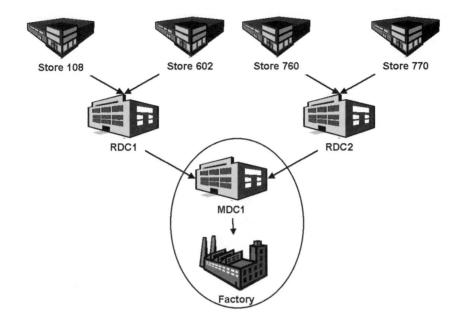

Figure 5.7: Integrating MDC1 with the factory.

The Planned Orders line in MDC1's plan can then be given to the factory to plan production as shown in Figure 5.7. While the factory is the last trading partner in the supply chain, the Planned Orders generated by the Flowcasting system will still drive a number of processes within the manufacturer's operation -- think of them as "sub-nodes" driven by dependent demand. We'll now turn our attention to the processes affected by Flowcasting within the factory.

While the stores, RDCs, and MDC all redistribute finished goods, it is the factory that sits at the end of the retail supply chain, charged with the responsibility of producing the products that will eventually reach the consumers' hands. Rather than passing a stream

---

8 Our example assumes that MDC1 is a distribution center of the manufacturing company, but this need not be the case. MDC1 could also represent a third-party wholesaler/distributor that sits between the manufacturer and the retailer. Because each node in a Flowcasting supply chain produces the same type of universally actionable information (how much is needed and when must it ship), it does not matter how many different organizations are involved in getting the product from the factory to the store shelf.

of planned orders to the next node in the retail supply chain, the factory instead takes its dependent demand from MDC1 and produces a Recommended[9] Master Production Schedule (MPS)[10].

The now familiar Flowcasting method of planning supply to meet demand is no different for a factory than it was in the retail stores or distribution centers discussed in Chapters 3 and 4. The only difference is a change in terminology, specifically:

- "Manufacturing Lot Size" represents the amount of product that is made in a single production run and is used instead of "Minimum DC Ordering Quantity."
- "Manufacturing Lead Time" represents the amount of time needed to produce a single lot and is used instead of "Replenishment Lead Time."
- "Work in Process" represents product that has begun a production run but not yet finished. It is used in place of "In Transits."
- "MPS Available" represents when finished goods are needed to be available off the production line and is used instead of "Planned Arrivals."
- "MPS Start" represents when production needs to begin in order to have finished goods available by the MPS Available date and is used instead of "Planned Orders."

Because the factory in our example runs lean, it only produces what it needs to ship, and no safety stock is planned.

Assume for purposes of this example that the recommended MPS is feasible (we have an agreed-to level of production for a specific product stated in specific times and quantities and both required

---

9 We say "Recommended" because the determination of what needs to be produced, how much, and when, involves the need to plan required labor and equipment capacities as well as materials needed to support production. This planning requires a balancing act between the availability of both materials and capacities. Consequently, human beings are required to create this critical balance and maintain it through a master schedule policy supported by executive management.

10 The subject of Master Production Scheduling is extremely important but is beyond the scope of this book. Over the years, the accumulated body of knowledge on MPS has been well documented. The American Production & Inventory Control Society (APICS) is an excellent resource for information on MPS and related topics.

materials and capacities are or can be made available). With the MPS stated and agreed upon within a given planning horizon, the purchasing department within the factory knows when production runs for the 01234567 Deluxe Widget are planned to start. By taking this projection and multiplying it through the bill of material (BOM) for the Deluxe Widget, the factory can plan its purchases of the raw materials that will be necessary to support the master production schedule .

For example, suppose that a finished 01234567 Deluxe Widget is comprised of the following components:

- 6 oz. blue plastic pellets
- 1.5 ft. nylon tubing
- 3 metal washers
- 1 packages boxes

That means each production run of 576 Deluxe Widgets will require the following:

- 216 lbs (3,456 oz.) blue plastic pellets
- 864 ft. nylon tubing
- 1,728 metal washers
- 576 packages of boxes

With the quantities and timing provided by the "MPS Start" line as shown in Figure 5.8 and the conversion table provided by the

PRODUCT: 01234567 – Deluxe Widget

LOCATION: Factory

Current On Hand Balance:	0 units
Manufacturing Lot Size:	576 units
Factory Operating Schedule:	Seven days a week
Manufacturing Lead-Time:	1 day

	Days																		
	1	2	3	4	5	6	7	8	9	10	11	12	13	14	15	16	17	...	364
	M	T	W	Th	F	Sa	Su	M	T	W	Th	F	Sa	Su	M	T	W	...	Su
MDC Planned Orders	576	576							576								576	...	
Safety Stock	0	0	0	0	0	0	0	0	0	0	0	0	0	0	0	0	0	...	0
Work in Process	576																	...	
Projected On Hand	0	0	0	0	0	0	0	0	0	0	0	0	0	0	0	0	0	...	0
MPS Available		576							576								576	...	
MPS Start	576							576								576		...	

Figure 5.8: A 52-week recommended master production schedule (MPS) at the factory.

MASTER PRODUCTION SCHEDULE

	1	2	3	4	5	6	7	8	9	10	11	12	13	14	15	16	17	...	364
	M	T	W	Th	F	Sa	Su	M	T	W	Th	F	Sa	Su	M	T	W	...	Su
Deluxe Widgets		576							576								576	...	

BILL OF MATERIAL

RAW MATERIAL DEPENDENT DEMAND

	1	2	3	4	5	6	7	8	9	10	11	12	13	14	15	16	17	...	364
	M	T	W	Th	F	Sa	Su	M	T	W	Th	F	Sa	Su	M	T	W	...	Su
Blue Plastic Pellets (lbs)		216							216								216	...	
Nylon Tubing (ft)		864							864								864		
Metal Washers (ea)		1728							1728								1728		
Package Box (ea)		576							576								576	...	

Figure 5.9: Using the MPS and BOM to drive dependent demand for
raw material components.

BOM, we now know when raw materials and packaging supplies will
be needed by the factory to produce the Deluxe Widgets[11] (see Figure
5.9).

We have now closed the loop by creating a 52-week plan of
demand, supply, and inventory for every retail store, distribution center, and factory in the supply chain. And remember, all of these plans
were generated *without any forecasting beyond the forecast we created at store level in Chapter 3.*

While everything that has been described from the beginning of
Chapter 3 until now may seem intuitive, it is assumed that the communication links between nodes have already been firmly established. Between retail stores and RDCs, communication is relatively
easy to set up, since all of these nodes are generally a part of the same
company. Within the retailer's organization a single, self-contained
system would be used to plan both the stores and the RDCs simultaneously.

---

11 In a factory that produces several products sharing some (or all) of their raw
materials or component parts in different proportions, the MPS will need to be
exploded through all bills of material before a purchasing plan can be calculated.

When it comes to the manufacturing and wholesale distribution activities, however, multiple organizations come into play as shown in Figure 5.10. At the beginning of this chapter, we stated that the process must not end with the retailer; for Flowcasting to become a reality and change the way retailers and their suppliers do business, the information must extend from the point of sale back to the procurement of raw materials at the factory. But when organizational lines are drawn between functions in the supply chain, it becomes necessary to have a standardized, efficient way of sharing actionable information. In order to plan the supply chain seamlessly (that is, as if those organizational lines didn't exist), retailers need to speak the language of their suppliers, and vice-versa. This can be accomplished through a process called "supplier scheduling," which is the topic of the next section.

Supplier Scheduling

Without the Flowcasting process, the manufacturer must independently determine the items and quantities it must ship out to meet the retailer's demands. Specifically, it must figure out which

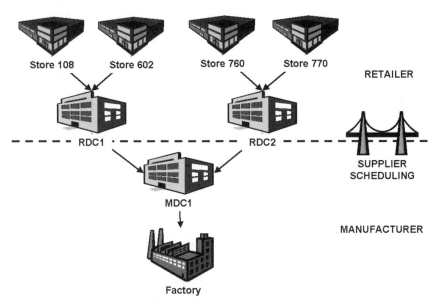

Figure 5.10: Typical lines of ownership and the role of supplier scheduling in the retail supply chain.

days it must ship on and the location is must ship to, several weeks or even months into the future. This is done today at great time and expense through key account sales forecasting and order booking.

But as we've already seen, planned order streams can be effort-lessly calculated at any level in the supply chain with a Flowcasting business process. And no matter where you look in the supply chain, planned orders always represent the same thing: which items need to ship, the quantities needed, and the specific ship dates and locations, 52 weeks into the future. Flowcasting answers all of these questions -- what, where, how much, and when, at the required level of detail. And the information produced at one echelon in the supply chain requires no additional interpretation by the next.

In a Flowcasting world, the demand requirements on the sup-plier have already been scheduled within the retailer's planning process (hence, the term "supplier scheduling"). The ramifications of having this information on tap are highly significant for all suppliers:

- No longer will manufacturers need to guess about what their retail customers will need; the retailers will tell them what they are planning to buy and when for the next several months, thereby eliminating the need for manufacturers to forecast sales and shipments for key accounts. This will serve to completely redefine the role of the manufacturer sales rep (see Appendix H).

- No longer will manufacturers be blindsided by demand shocks that increase in urgency and severity as they ripple through the supply chain over a period of several weeks. The moment something unexpected happens at the retail shelf, the chain reaction of demand is refreshed, and all trading partners in the supply chain (including the manufacturer) can see the precise impact on their operations the very next day.

- No longer will manufacturers need retailers to lock in their orders weeks or months in advance as a buffer against forecast error. By virtue of the fact that retailers explicitly state their intentions many weeks into the future, demand uncertainty for the manufacturer is drastically reduced, if not eliminated completely. Buffer can be stripped out of lead-times, allowing postponement of product flow until the last possible moment. In a Flowcasting environment, the ordering lead-time between retailers and manufacturers represents only the time required for picking, packing, loading and shipping to the destination.

- No longer do retailers and manufacturers behave as independent fiefs with disparate planning approaches. The fact that all entities use the same Flowcasting process means that the lines between retailer, wholesaler, and manufacturer dissolve; for satisfying demand, they act as one entity with the sole purpose of getting product into the hands of consumers. Transfers of product ownership are appropriately treated as mere administrative formalities.

- No longer are supply issues uncovered and discussed when it's too late to do anything about them. Implicit in the act of sharing supplier schedules for joint planning is the notion that silence implies agreement. In other words, in exchange for keeping the supplier schedules up-to-date and accurate, the retailer can expect the supplier to use this information, internalize it and spot potential supply problems while there's still an opportunity for contingency planning. Flowcasting teams (with representative from both the retailer and the supplier) will solve potential problems rather than react to problems that have already happened.

Supplier Scheduling Redefines Business Relationships

Supplier scheduling is far more than a process for efficiently moving data among trading partners. It represents a drastic transformation of the way the trading partners work together and do business. Over time, familiarity and trust breeds efficiency between supply chain partners, thereby eliminating the need for retailers to constantly change supply sources on the basis of who offers the lowest price this week. With the shared Flowcasting information in hand, the trading partners can turn to other opportunities for lowering costs, such as renegotiating order minimums, reducing lead-times, and reducing inventory along the entire extended retail supply chain.

When partners share projections in the form of supply schedules, legal purchase transactions become "non events." At the end of every day, any planned orders that are within the lead-time release horizon could be sent to the retailer's transaction system for automatic purchase order creation. Suppliers receive constantly updated schedules from their customers, so by the time the purchase order is received, the product has already been made and just needs to be shipped.

As the long-term retailer/manufacturer relationship strengthens and matures, the need to have a purchase contract for every shipment will diminish. Instead, companies will annually agree on business terms (pricing, order quantities, lead-times, etc.), which will be reflected in the supplier schedules by the retailer. On a day-to-day basis, manufacturers will automatically ship everything that's on the supplier schedules within the agreed-upon lead-time. Tracking numbers may be generated for each shipment, but formal purchase orders will become a thing of the past. At the end of the month, a single statement, detailing the month's shipping activity, will be sent to the retailer for payment.

Simplifying the transactions and removing red tape will enable the retailer and manufacturer to focus on new ways of improving their processes and satisfying customers. (See Chapter 11 for a specific example of supplier scheduling, its financial benefits, and the elimination of purchase orders and invoices.)

Interfacing Supplier Schedules into the Supplier Processes

Our example thus far assumes that each inventory pool in the supply chain will have 100 percent visibility into its immediate customers' demands. For a typical retailer that owns both its stores and RDCs, this is likely to be the case. Between the stores and the RDCs, the supply chain is self contained.

But what about the manufacturers and wholesalers? Most often, a manufacturer will have many different retailers as customers for its products. To the extent that some of these retailers provide supplier schedules and others do not, the manufacturer will be have multiple demand streams:

In Figure 5.11, a distributor/manufacturer supplies product to three different retail customers. Each of these retailers has a different planning approach:

- Retailer A operates in a complete Flowcasting environment. Based on a consumer demand forecast, the stores create a 52-week stream of planned orders. These planned orders become the demand stream at the RDCs which, in turn, create 52 weeks of planned orders. The planned orders from the RDCs are shared with the Distributor/Manufacturer as supplier schedules.

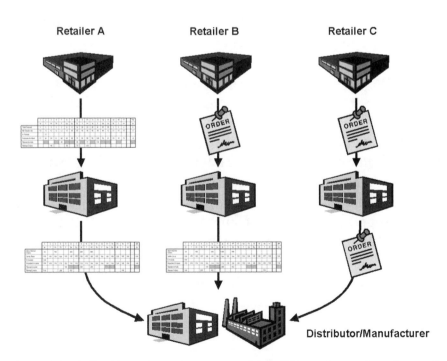

Figure 5.11: A distributor/manufacturer receiving different inputs from its retail customers.

- At the other end of the spectrum, Retailer C uses a traditional ordering strategy at the stores and the RDCs[12]. No visibility exists beyond the next order between any two supply chain entities. The Distributor/Manufacturer is required to forecast Retailer C's demand explicitly.
- Retailer B is in transition to a full Flowcasting environment. Like Retailer C, its stores send only immediate replenishment requests to the RDCs. Like Retailer A, the RDCs produce a stream of planned orders which are, in turn, shared with the MDC/factory as supplier schedules, but the planned order stream is based on a forecast of total demand from the stores, not dependent demand from the stores.

From the Distributor/Manufacturer's point of view, both Retailer A and Retailer B are sending the same type of actionable time-phased information. However, Retailer A's supplier schedules will be of much higher quality, because all inventory and constraints are being considered at the lowest level of granularity (from the store shelf back). Retailer A has virtually removed uncertainty from the most important supply chain echelon.

So, how can a Distributor/Manufacturer benefit from Flowcasting, given the "mixed bag" of information it will receive from its retail customers (that is, some retailers provide supplier schedules and others don't)?

As Figure 5.11 shows, Retailer A and Retailer B both share supplier schedules (of differing quality). Therefore, the Distributor/Manufacturer no longer needs to forecast these accounts. Instead, the only forecasting effort required is for Retailer C, who does not share a supplier schedule. The approach for planning MDC1 would include a mixture of summing dependent demand from retailers who provide supplier schedules and forecasting shipments for retailers who do not, as illustrated by the "Total Retailer Demand" line in Figure 5.12.

---

12 At the RDCs, a traditional reorder point strategy would likely be used. At store level, orders may be generated manually based on a visual shelf review or with a simple reorder point system as well.

PRODUCT: 01234567 – Deluxe Widget
LOCATION: MDC1

Current On Hand Balance:	650 units
Minimum DC Ordering Quantity:	576 units
DC Receiving Schedule:	Seven days a week
Replenishment Lead-Time from Factory:	5 days

	Days																		
	1	2	3	4	5	6	7	8	9	10	11	12	13	14	15	16	17	...	364
	M	T	W	Th	F	Sa	Su	M	T	W	Th	F	Sa	Su	M	T	W	...	Su
Retailer A Pl. Orders			144	288		576	288	288					144	144				...	
Retailer B Pl. Orders		288			288			144			288					576		...	
Retailer C Forecast	123	123	123	123	123	123	123	62	62	62	62	62	62	62	96	96	96	...	75
Total Retailer Dmd	123	411	267	411	411	699	411	494	62	62	350	62	206	206	96	672	96	...	75
Safety Stock	250	250	250	250	250	250	250	250	250	250	250	250	250	250	250	250	250	...	250
In Transits	576			576	576													...	
Projected On Hand	1103	692	425	590	755	632	797	303	817	755	405	343	713	507	411	315	795	...	395
Planned Arrivals						576	576		576				576			576	576	...	
Planned Orders	576	576		576				576			576	576						...	

Figure 5.12: Planning MDC1 for a mixed demand stream.

From the manufacturer's point of view, the ideal situation would be for all of its retailer customers to provide supplier schedules that represent 100 percent of their demand, not only for their manufacturing and distribution needs, but for Sales and Operations Planning (S&OP) as well (S&OP will be discussed in more detail in Chapter 11). How likely is this to happen? As Flowcasting gains acceptance within the retail community, more of the manufacturers' demand will be handed to them in the form of supplier schedules. And as this plays out over time, a critical mass will be reached. Manufacturers will begin to transform their businesses from make-to-stock to make-to-order; every activity, from raw material acquisition, selling, and distributing finished goods, will be subject to review and changed for the better. It is not a question of if, but when.

While the inventory and service-level benefits of the Flowcasting approach provide retailers with ample incentive to adopt, suppliers can hasten this adoption by agreeing to protect supply for customers that operate in a Flowcasting environment.

Available To Promise and Protected Supply

When retailers invest in the ability to provide supplier schedules to their partners, they create a true win/win situation. By treating planned orders from retail customers as promised orders, the supplier has a much clearer picture of what can be sold to other customers without harming its long-term relationships with retailers who provide schedules.

A good way to do this is to use Available To Promise (ATP), a capability that ensures quality order promising in a make-to-order business. ATP is an excellent approach for protecting the supply of retailers who provide schedules. In addition, with time-phased information at hand, the ATP calculation can be continually recalculated for as far out as needed to make decisions.

Consider the example in Figure 5.12. We know that Retailers A and B both provide planned order streams to MDC1, while Retailer C does not. We also know that the current on hand balance at MDC1 is 650 units and that in transit quantities and planned arrivals from the factory are scheduled well out into the future. With this information, we are able to do a time-phased cumulative available to promise calculation for deluxe widgets at MDC1.

In Figure 5.13, the Promised Orders line represents the sum of the planned orders from Retailers A and B only. Retailer C is excluded from this calculation because it does not provide a schedule. Since the supplier is forced to forecast its demand, supply will not be protected for Retailer C.

Current On Hand:		Days															
650		1	2	3	4	5	6	7	8	9	10	11	12	13	14	15	...	364
		M	T	W	Th	F	Sa	Su	M	T	W	Th	F	Sa	Su	M	...	Su
Promised Orders			288	144	288	288	576	288	432				288		144	144		
Planned Supply		576			576	576	576	576		576				576				
Available to Promise		794	794	794	1082	1370	1370	1226	1226	1514	1514	1514	1514	1802	1802	1802	...	

Figure 5.13: Calculating cumulative Available To Promise (ATP) at MDC1.

The Planned Supply line represents all scheduled supply, including in transits and planned arrivals in MDC1's Flowcasting plan. The Available To Promise line represents supply that will be available for MDC1 to sell to other customers, after Retailer A and B's demands have been met.

In our example, our current on hand is 650 units and an additional 576 units is in transit, so our Planned Supply on the beginning of day 1 is 1226 units. The next Planned Supply is 576 units, due to arrive on day 4.

Our Promised Orders (that is, supply that has been protected for Retailer A and Retailer B) between now and day 4 is 432 units (288 on day 2 and 144 on day 3). The difference between the Planned Supply and Promised Orders over the next 3 days represents the Available To Promise: 1226 − 432 = 794.

Put another way, if a customer other than Retailer A or Retailer B wants product from MDC1 over the next 3 days, MDC1 can only sell 794 units to that customer, even though they will have 1226 units in supply.

Because the Promised Orders and Planned Supply are calculated over a long time horizon in a Flowcasting environment, the ATP calculation can be extended as far out as is needed. For example, on day 4, additional supply of 576 units is planned, and the Promised Orders are 288 units. The ATP in the previous period was 794 units. So the cumulative ATP on day 4 is 794 + 576 − 288 = 1082, and so on.

The key point is that a Flowcasting relationship between partners requires a high level of trust and co-operation to make it work. If retailers make the necessary investments to provide schedules to suppliers, they will expect a high level of service with no excuses from suppliers. Conversely, if suppliers are to reserve inventory without a firm purchase contract locked in, they expect retailers to follow their schedules.

Flowcasting and CPFR

Those who are familiar with CPFR will recognize the steps that comprise CPFR have been totally institutionalized as part of the day-to-day activities of the Flowcasting business process. Some of the wording may be somewhat different, but the steps and objectives are identical. To recap Chapters 1 through 5, thus far, you have seen how:

1. Flowcasting teams (Retailer and Manufacturer or Wholesaler) have been created.
2. The teams have met, and Collaborative Arrangements and Joint Business Plans are set and agreed upon.
3. Product flow plans (from the factory floor to the store shelf) have been developed and agreed to.

4. Store-level sales forecasts have been created, aggregated, and agreed to.
5. Store and retail DC inventories have been considered.
6. Inventory targets, service-level objectives (required safety stocks), lead-times and minimum ship quantities and transportation requirements have been considered.
7. Resulting supplier schedules have been internalized and integrated (S&OP, DRP, MPS, and ATP) by the manufacturer.
8. Constraints (production, distribution, and transportation) have been identified and resolved, and supplier schedules are now protected for delivery to the retailer.
9. Exception Management and Performance Assessments are ongoing.

The difference between Flowcasting and CPFR is the following: With CPFR, you can have a working arrangement with one or more trading partners and continue to do business as usual with all other trading partners. If you are a retailer, Flowcasting will drive all your forecasting, inventory management, and replenishment activities. If you are a manufacturer, to get the full benefits of Flowcasting you must internalize the processes and integrate them into what we call the four main touch points. The last three touch points below were addressed in this chapter, and the first touch point, Sales & Operations Planning, is covered in Chapter 11:

1. Sales & Operations Planning (S&OP)
2. Distribution Resource Planning (DRP)
3. Master production Scheduling (MPS)
4. Available-to-Promise (ATP)

With a Flowcasting business process in place, trading partners have built a complete product flow model of the way they have agreed to do business inside the computer. This model now resides inside the same system, and both the retailer and the manufacturer or wholesaler have access to this ecosystem. We cannot think of a better way of doing business and have trading partners jointly Collaborate, Plan, Forecast, and Replenish their complete supply chains from the factory floor to the retail store shelf.

Summary

In this chapter, we "closed the loop" by continuing the same Flowcasting process that began in Chapter 3 beyond the walls of the retail organization to their upstream supply partners. We demonstrated that the inventory planning problem can be universally solved with the same planning method, whether the operation is a retail store, a distribution center or a factory. Here are the key points to remember:

1. The concept of dependent demand is not limited to a particular type of trading partners; it's relevant to every echelon in the supply chain.
2. Store-level forecasts of consumer demand can actually drive every planned product movement, from the extraction of raw materials to the production of finished goods through the distribution network and into consumers' hands.
3. Supplier scheduling is the bridge that will connect Flowcasting team members from separate organizations. It represents a fundamental change in the business relationships between retailers and their suppliers.
4. The visibility provided by retailers in the form of supplier schedules requires that retailers and manufacturers act in true partnership -- reducing cycle time and waste, simplifying terms and conditions, and making long-term commitments on the demand and supply side.
5. Each retailer that comes on stream with supplier scheduling is one more key account that the supplier no longer needs to forecast.
6. By respecting supplier schedules from retailer customers that provide them, suppliers can more accurately calculate their Available To Promise over a long time horizon. By pro-

tecting supply in this manner, suppliers can reward retailers for sharing their planning information.

7. When a critical mass of retailers adopt the Flowcasting business model, manufacturers can transform their operations from make-to-stock to make-to-order. For manufacturers with a small number of large customers, this may happen very quickly.

This concludes Section 2 of this book. In the third and final section, the proverbial rubber will "hit the road." The chapters in Section 3 show how Flowcasting can be used to solve some of retail's most common (and most frustrating) challenges: managing promotions, product introductions and discontinuations, seasonal products, slow moving items, and operational and financial planning. Finally, we present a high-level plan for implementing Flowcasting in today's networked retail supply chains.

Section 3:
Solving Business Problems
with Flowcasting

C H A P T E R   6

Promotional Planning
Product When You Want It

In the previous chapters we've illustrated how Flowcasting makes it possible to use a single forecast, generated at the retail store level, to drive scheduling and replenishment planning through each node of the supply chain. We've talked about the many benefits of Flowcasting, too, in terms of reduced inventory, reduced costs, and the ability to conduct effective business simulations. In the following chapters, we'll focus on how Flowcasting can resolve thorny problems that can't be resolved well with traditional "every-node-for-itself" forecasting approaches. This chapter focuses on running profitable promotions. Chapters 7, 8, 9, and 10 will deal with product introductions and discontinuations, seasonal planning, managing slow sellers, and operational planning, respectively.

Promotion Planning Using Flowcasting

For most retailers, promotions are the life blood of the business; yet promotions are also classic "double bind" -- damned if you do, damned if you don't. While they are designed to increase sales and drive traffic to the store, promotions typically result in disappointing financials and frustrated customers; despite best efforts, promotions are often poorly planned and executed throughout the extended retail supply chain. At the same time, to remain competitive in cutthroat business environments dominated by price wars, the pressure is ever great to engage in new promotions.

Numerous studies confirm that retail out-of-stocks during promotions constitute a serious problem. The landmark 1996 Accenture study for Coca-Cola Research Council, for example, demonstrated that, on average, retailers were out of stock 8 percent of the time. Even worse, during promotional periods, that figure skyrockets to 15 percent of the time. The impact on sales and customer satisfaction, of course, is enormous.

What's changed since the Accenture study? Very little, according to recent studies by the Gartner Group and Roland Berger – during promotions, some stores experience stock outs, others swim in excess inventory. The studies also conclude that 75 percent to 90 percent of out-of-stocks result from poor store-level forecasting and ordering practices and an unresponsive supply chain.

As we will show in this chapter, Flowcasting attacks the root causes of both problems head on, giving retailers the ability to drastically reduce out-of-stocks.

Flowcasting is an ideal solution for this dilemma, because store-level forecasts of consumer demand are translated into demand projections for all trading partners in the retail supply chain. The supply chain is linked naturally by cascading dependent demand, and projections based on that demand are recalculated daily as sales happen in each of the retailer's stores. The entire supply chain sees when and where inventory is required to support the promotion on a store-by-store basis, *before* it's needed and while the promotion unfolds. The result is that inventory can be quickly redeployed to avoid stock-outs and lost sales. This is, of course, very different from the way promotions are currently planned and monitored, because store level projections of inventory are not available or re-planned daily.

In this chapter, we'll examine:
1. Using Flowcasting to plan promotions
2. How to minimize out-of-stocks and overstocks
   using postponement
3. How Flowcasting supports store specific promotions

4. How Flowcasting enables continuous collaboration

5. Using the principles of Flowcasting to improve product flow

1. Using Flowcasting to Plan Promotions

In the previous section, we demonstrated the mechanics of Flowcasting using a sample dynamic retail supply chain. In this chapter, and throughout the remainder of this section, we'll simplify the example. In this case, suppose we have a very simple retail supply chain that consists of two stores, an RDC, an MDC, and a factory as depicted in Figure 6.1:

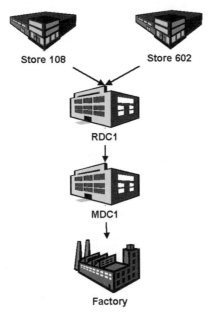

Figure 6.1: Example retail supply chain.

Suppose that a product that regularly sells for $9.99 in both stores is to be sold for $6.99 during a one-week promotion. The initial Flowcasting plan for this item for store 108, in weekly time periods[13], is shown in Figure 6.2:

---

13 Recall from Chapter 3 that the Flowcasting plan was depicted in daily time periods. In our example, we switched to weekly periods because promotions are usually planned several weeks out. Keep in mind that the actual plans are day-by-day; we've simply chosen to display the information in weekly views for ease of demonstration.

PRODUCT: 12345678 – Promoted product

LOCATION: Store 108

Current On Hand Balance:	40 units
Minimum Store Ordering Quantity:	12 units
Store Receiving Schedule:	Monday, Wednesday and Friday only
Replenishment Lead-Time from RDC1:	2 days

	Weeks											
	1	2	3	4	5	6	7	8	9	10	...	52
Forecast - Base	9	11	12	8	7	9	8	7	6	8	...	9
Forecast - Lift											...	
Total Forecast	9	11	12	8	7	9	8	7	6	8	...	9
Min Display Qty	28	28	28	28	28	28	28	28	28	28	...	28
In Transits											...	
Projected On Hand	31	32	32	36	29	32	36	29	35	39	...	40
Planned Arrivals		12	12	12		12	12		12	12	...	
Planned Orders	12	12	12		12	12		12	12		...	

Figure 6.2: Flowcasting plan for a product that will be promoted for store 108.

As you can see, two components of the forecast have been shown: base and lift. The base forecast is the normal forecast that is derived by using historical point of sale data as discussed in Chapter 3. The lift forecast represents how much additional product you expect to sell during the promotion period based on the offer. The forecast total is the sum of the base and promotion, and reflects the total consumer forecast, which in turn will serve as the driver of the entire retail supply chain for this item.

Let's say that the aforementioned promotion will take place in week 6. There are many approaches for determining how much additional product will sell during the promotional period, store by store. Sometimes history can help if the item has been promoted regularly. More often, retailers and suppliers will collaborate to determine the total incremental forecast during the promotion period. Then, using historical sales percentages, this total forecast is allocated to each store. Suppose that store 108 is expected to sell an additional 30 units as a result of the promotion. The resulting Flowcasting plan is depicted in Figure 6.3:

PRODUCT: 12345678 – Promoted product

LOCATION: Store 108

Current On Hand Balance:	40 units
Minimum Store Ordering Quantity:	12 units
Store Receiving Schedule:	Monday, Wednesday and Friday only
Replenishment Lead-Time from RDC1:	2 days

	Weeks											
	1	2	3	4	5	6	7	8	9	10	...	52
Forecast - Base	9	11	12	8	7	9	8	7	6	8	...	9
Forecast - Lift						30					...	
Total Forecast	9	11	12	8	7	39	8	7	6	8	...	9
Min Display Qty	28	28	28	28	28	28	28	28	28	28	...	28
In Transits											...	
Projected On Hand	31	32	32	36	29	38	30	35	29	33	...	40
Planned Arrivals		12	12	12		48		12		12	...	
Planned Orders	12	12	12		48		12		12		...	

Figure 6.3: Flowcasting plan for a product that is promoted for store 108.

The additional promotional forecast of 30 units in week 6 has caused a planned arrival of 48 units to be calculated. Because of the 2 day lead-time, it will be ordered in week 5.

In store 602, the promotional forecast for week 6 was 40 units, and the Flowcasting plan is depicted in Figure 6.4:

PRODUCT: 12345678 – Promoted product

LOCATION: Store 602

Current On Hand Balance:	40 units
Minimum Store Ordering Quantity:	24 units
Store Receiving Schedule:	Tuesday, Thursday and Saturday only
Replenishment Lead-Time from RDC1:	3 days

	Weeks											
	1	2	3	4	5	6	7	8	9	10	...	52
Forecast - Base	11	14	15	13	21	19	18	17	16	18	...	19
Forecast - Lift						40					...	
Total Forecast	11	14	15	13	21	59	18	17	16	18	...	19
Min Display Qty	36	36	36	36	36	36	36	36	36	36	...	36
In Transits											...	
Projected On Hand	29	39	48	59	38	51	57	40	48	54	...	40
Planned Arrivals		24	24	24		72	24		24	24	...	
Planned Orders	24	24	24		72	24		24	24		...	

Figure 6.4: Flowcasting plan for a product that is promoted for store 602.

In this case, store 602 will order 72 units in week 5 to ensure that product arrives in week 6 to support the promotion.

The Flowcasting plan for RDC1 is depicted in Figure 6.5 and is based on the dependent demand from stores 108 and 602:

PRODUCT: 12345678 – Promoted product

LOCATION: RDC1

Current On Hand Balance:	110 units
Minimum DC Ordering Quantity:	48 units
DC Receiving Schedule:	Monday to Friday
Replenishment Lead-Time from MDC1:	4 days

	Weeks											
	1	2	3	4	5	6	7	8	9	10	...	52
Store Planned Orders	36	36	36		120	24	12	24	36		...	
Safety Stock	72	72	72	72	72	72	72	72	72	72	...	72
In Transits											...	
Projected On Hand	74	86	98	98	74	98	86	110	74	74	...	108
Planned Arrivals		48	48		96	48		48			...	
Planned Orders	48	48		96	48		48				...	

Figure 6.5: Flowcasting plan for promoted product at RDC1.

In week 4, RDC1 will need to order 96 units from MDC1 to support the promotion in week 6 for both stores.

The plan for MDC1 is shown in Figure 6.6:

PRODUCT: 12345678 – Promoted product

LOCATION: MDC1

Current On Hand Balance:	200 units
Minimum DC Ordering Quantity:	144 units
DC Receiving Schedule:	Seven days a week
Replenishment Lead-Time from Factory:	5 days

	Weeks											
	1	2	3	4	5	6	7	8	9	10	...	52
RDC1 Planned Orders	48	48		96	48		48				...	48
Safety Stock	108	108	108	108	108	108	108	108	108	108	...	108
In Transits											...	
Projected On Hand	152	248	248	152	248	248	200	200	200	200	...	152
Planned Arrivals		144			144						...	
Planned Orders	144			144							...	

Figure 6.6: Flowcasting plan for promoted product at MDC1.

Based on similar logic, we can calculate the planned orders that MDC1 will need in order to support the promotion. The planned orders from MDC1, in turn, provide the demand forecast for the manufacturing factory (see Figure 6.7).

PRODUCT: 12345678 – Promoted product

LOCATION: Factory

Current On Hand Balance:	440 units
Manufacturing Lot Size:	288 units
Factory Operating Schedule:	Seven days a week
Manufacturing Lead-Time:	7 days

	Weeks											
	1	2	3	4	5	6	7	8	9	10	...	52
MDC1 Planned Orders	144			144							...	144
Safety Stock	216	216	216	216	216	216	216	216	216	216	...	216
Work in Process											...	
Projected On Hand	296	296	296	440	440	440	440	440	440	440	...	252
MPS Available				288							...	
MPS Start			288								...	

Figure 6.7: Flowcasting plan for promoted product at the manufacturing plant.

By applying the logic outlined in Chapter 5, the Flowcasting system would calculate when the factory needs to produce more inventory. The Master Production Schedule (MPS) indicates when production needs to start (MPS – Start) and when production will be finished (MPS -- Available) -- that is, when the product is available for distribution. The linkage between Flowcasting and the MPS is critical for solving one of the root causes of out-of-stocks during promotions: an unresponsive supply chain. Flowcasting eliminates this problem by cascading dependent demand from customer to supplier -- in effect, translating consumer demand into Store demand, DC demand, Factory demand and, ultimately, Master Production Schedules.

In our example, a promotion at store-level in week 6 causes dependent demand to cascade throughout the retail supply chain. RDC1 must plan resources in order to ship 120 units to the stores and, in the same week, receive 96 units to support the promotion. Similarly, MDC1 must plan to ship 96 units in week 4 and receive 144 units in week 2, while the factory must ship 144 units in week 1 (the current week). As sales happen in each store, their plans are re-calculated and translated throughout the entire supply chain so all trading partners can monitor the impact of activities at the retail shelf level.

The basic supply chain linkage that Flowcasting provides is an important foundation for reducing stock-outs and costs, since all trading partners can see and prepare for the impact of promotional volumes. However, to significantly reduce out-of-stocks during promotions (and during non-promotional periods as well), the supply chain must operate in near real-time. That means plans must be calculated and communicated at least daily, especially during promotional periods. Daily replanning is a cornerstone of Flowcasting and provides the opportunity to make decisions as late as possible.

The Power of Postponement

At first blush, the reason for stock-outs during promotions is obvious: the forecasts weren't accurate. Forecast inaccuracy is certainly a contributing factor, but based on the collective experiences of the authors, many retailers actually do a good job of forecasting for promotions, at least in total. The problem is that they often make premature or incorrect decisions about allocating inventory to each store participating in the promotion.

Today, most retailers determine the total forecast for a promotion, then allocate and ship the entire allocation to the stores *before* the promotion even starts. This is a questionable practice, because it's difficult to predict how much product you'll need and where it needs to be deployed. Worse, it's almost impossible to make adjustments if the predictions about store-level inventory allocations turn out to be wrong. Since most promotions last a week and all of the inventory has been deployed, there is no time or available inventory in the RDCs to make mid-course corrections. As a result, some stores do well, some stock out, and the rest are overstocked.

Flowcasting can minimize this inventory deployment problem by allocating only partial quantities to the stores and using early sales information to adjust the supply chain *in mid-promotion*. In other words, Flowcasting enables you to postpone the decision to allocate inventory to the stores until you absolutely must. Most supply chain professionals recognize that this approach always provides the best possible customer service at the lowest possible cost. Before the advent of Flowcasting, however, there was no practical way to apply this philosophy for promotional planning.

Making Mid-Course Corrections -- Early News Is Best

In order to make mid-course corrections, it's necessary to be able to review the Flowcasting plans in daily, rather than weekly, time periods in order to show how re-planning during the promotion week avoids stock-outs by redeploying inventory to where it's needed. This isn't difficult, given that the weekly "views" used in our example so far are actually aggregates of the daily information. Recall the daily percentages for store 108 derived in Chapter 3:

Monday	Tuesday	Wednesday	Thursday	Friday	Saturday	Sunday
5%	10%	12%	13%	15%	25%	20%

Now we can see how the Flowcasting process works prior to the promotion and during the promotional week. Remember that the promotion was planned in week 6 and that the total forecast for store 108 was 39 units.

The Flowcasting plan for the promotional week is shown in Figure 6.8

PRODUCT: 12345678 – Promoted product

LOCATION: Store 108

On Hand Balance, Beginning of Week 6:	29 units
Minimum Store Ordering Quantity:	12 units
Store Receiving Schedule:	Monday, Wednesday and Friday only
Replenishment Lead-Time from RDC1:	2 days

	Days						
	M	T	W	Th	F	Sa	Su
Forecast - Base	0.5	0.9	1.1	1.2	1.4	2.3	1.8
Forecast - Lift	1.5	3.0	3.6	3.9	4.5	7.5	6.0
Total Forecast	2.0	3.9	4.7	5.1	5.9	9.8	7.8
Min Display Qty	28	28	28	28	28	28	28
In Transits							
Projected On Hand	39.0	35.1	42.4	37.3	55.4	45.6	37.8
Planned Arrivals	12		12		24		
Planned Orders	12		24				

Figure 6.8: Daily Flowcasting plan for the promotion week in store 108.

With this daily view of the information, we can see the 48 units that are expected to arrive in week 6 are actually planned in 3 separate arrivals across the week. This is more effective than planning for all 48 units to arrive at the beginning of the week, because as each day passes, the process will re-plan and adjust the planned arrivals based on what is actually happening at the point-of-sale level. If sales are brisker than expected, the Flowcasting system will bring ahead the upcoming planned arrivals and perhaps increase the quantity. Since store 108 can obtain more inventory from RDC1 in 2 days, actual sales during the promotion week will trigger an adjustment in the plan and RDC1 will see this dependent demand change. And since not all the product was shipped to the stores in advance of the promotion, there's an excellent chance that RDC1 will have inventory available to redeploy if the need arises.

There's a saying in forecasting that "early news is best." This means that actual sales are happening and the process is adjusting store-by-store, whether the news is good or bad. Sales may be taking off in store 108, which results in planned arrivals being needed earlier and possibly for larger quantities. In the example above for store 108, the planned arrival for 24 units originally planned for Friday may instead be needed on Wednesday. This would change the plan at the RDC1, since the RDC would now see that this item will need to be shipped two days earlier. But this could be completely offset by Store 602, where sales may be lagging and planned arrivals have been pushed out to a later date.

Replanning happens daily for all stores and RDCs. The entire supply chain sees the net result of adjustments to planned arrivals at all locations. These adjustments are based entirely on sales, thereby ensuring that the supply chain is responsive and is planning based on the latest market information. Since the planning process postponed the decision to ship all of the inventory to the stores in advance, some has been kept in reserve at RDC1 and will now go to Store 108. If you think about the number of stores that a given RDC supplies, you'll appreciate how Flowcasting allows you to provide the highest in-stock position while keeping inventories under control.

In addition, if sales were taking off in a particular store, the Flowcasting system would trigger an exception to re-forecast the remaining days of the promotion for that store and item. For example, suppose that for a given item/store the sales on the first day of the promotion were 75 percent of what was expected for the entire week. The process would alert the planner about this situation, and the planner would re-forecast the remaining days. The revised forecast would cause the replanning of supply. All partners in the supply chain would see the impact of the store's new plan (and any other stores in a similar situation), and their plans would be changed to meet demand. As you can see, a supply chain linked by Flowcasting is tightly connected; the trading partners can respond to the most current demand signals, thereby eliminating one of the root causes of out-of-stocks.

Initial Distributions of Stock

As cited in the studies at the beginning of this chapter, being in stock for promotions has been historically difficult for many retailers. Every time a sale is held, retailers face the risk of alienating their customers. This is especially true if customers make a special trip to get the advertised item, only to be disappointed by an empty shelf when they get there. This risk can be mitigated by shipping an initial distribution quantity of the promotional items to each store. In our example, if 50 percent of the weekly planned arrivals were shipped to the store just before the promotion as an initial distribution quantity, the Flowcasting system would adjust the plan as depicted in Figure 6.9.

PRODUCT: 12345678 – Promoted product

LOCATION: Store 108

On Hand Balance, Beginning of Week 6:	29 units
Minimum Store Ordering Quantity:	12 units
Store Receiving Schedule:	Monday, Wednesday and Friday only
Replenishment Lead-Time from RDC1:	2 days

	Days						
	M	T	W	Th	F	Sa	Su
Forecast - Base	0.5	0.9	1.1	1.2	1.4	2.3	1.8
Forecast - Lift	1.5	3.0	3.6	3.9	4.5	7.5	6.0
Total Forecast	2.0	3.9	4.7	5.1	5.9	9.8	7.8
Min Display Qty	28	28	28	28	28	28	28
In Transits	24						
Projected On Hand	51.0	47.1	42.4	37.3	55.4	45.6	37.8
Planned Arrivals					24		
Planned Orders							

Figure 6.9: Daily Flowcasting plan for a product that is promoted for store 108, including an initial distribution quantity at the beginning of the promotion week.

Notice that an in transit of 24 units is planned to arrive at the store on Monday -- the start of the promotion week -- reflecting the decision to distribute 50 percent of the promotion quantity to the store. By distributing a portion of the store's supply at the beginning of the promotion, the risk of early sales causing a stock out is reduced; it is clear that additional inventory is not currently planned to arrive at the store until Friday.

Keep in mind that this approach is applicable to all stores. The RDCs use all of the stores' up-to-date projections as their dependent demand forecast, then Flowcast and shares their plan with their supplier (MDC1). As a result, the retail supply chain is completely synchronized.

Of course you can choose any initial distribution percentage (e.g., 50 percent, 40 percent, etc.) to send to the store. This would be a management decision on how you would like to execute a promotion, based partially on an assessment of risk. The key is that you are not distributing all the promotion quantity to each store up front. You're deciding on an initial distribution percentage and then letting actual sales help determine where additional inventory is needed. This provides tremendous flexibility; as sales happen at different than expected rates at the various stores, inventory can be quickly moved to where it's needed. The result is increased sales, improved customer service, and reduced costs.

The Power of Continuous Planning

Today, most store-level planning is not done on a continuous basis; processes and systems currently in use do not have the ability to check every item in every location, every day.

Most retailers instead tend to use a "set-it-and-forget-it" approach; that is, forecasts are developed, and inventory is moved to the stores in advance of the promotion with the hope that the deployment decisions were good. But, as mentioned earlier, it's difficult to make correct deployment decisions in advance of the actual promotion. In addition, many items are not (by design) planned daily, but on a 3- to 5-day re-planning cycle instead. For these items, it may be 3 to 5 days before a problem becomes known, at which point it's too late to do anything about it -- you can't fix an out-of-stock retroactively.

The Flowcasting process uses the power of continuous planning to avoid such problems. The resulting reduction in out-of-stocks makes for more satisfied customers. And the level of anxiety and frustration in executing a promotion largely vanishes!

Continuous Collaboration

For a Flowcasting process to work well, collaboration is required between the retailer and the manufacturer, especially in planning and executing promotions. This means a shift in the way that promotions are conceptualized. Traditionally, manufacturers have taken the lead in planning promotions and offering discounted prices to their retail and wholesale customers. However, in recent years, the trend has shifted to a more collaborative environment, with retailers and manufacturers developing joint promotion plans. Collaboration now begins early and continues throughout the promotion and beyond.

Flowcasting takes collaboration between retailers and manufacturers to a new level, enabling trading partners to improve the forecast. For example, a retailer may have some historical data that bears on how well an item sold at a specific discounted price. A supplier might be able to provide sales history of similar promotions in other markets. By combining that information, the trading partners can often generate an improved forecast.

With the inherent connectivity of Flowcasting, all trading partners have visibility into future promotions and the dependent demand they must plan to; this is information that's being constantly kept up-to-date on the basis of what's selling at the cash register. Suppose that four promotions were planned at specific time periods during the upcoming year. The supplier would collaborate with the retailer to build a joint promotion plan, using the product-by-product time-phased plan as a common denominator. Promotional plans would be developed in advance and would not only achieve sales targets, but would also be executable by both manufacturer and the retailer.

In addition, demand projections are shared among suppliers, thereby ensuring constant collaboration. In this context, silence means approval; unless a trading partner indicates otherwise, it's assumed that everyone will be able to satisfy dependent demand upstream. Keep in mind that these demand projections are weeks and months into the future, even for promotions, so most partners have ample time to plan to meet the demand.

For example, when a retailer plans a promotion in a Flowcasting environment, suppliers would see an immediate impact in the planned orders they receive from the retailer. If the promotion exceeds the supplier's capabilities, the supplier and retailer would collaborate on a promotion plan that works. As a supplier, imagine receiving the output of a Flowcasting process from *all* your retail customers. You would have clarity regarding future demand projections, making it easy to determine whether a promotion could be supported. All that needs to be done is to convert demand projections into capacity and resource requirements (discussed in more detail in Chapter 10).

Store-Specific Promotions -- Laser Focused Marketing

It's clear that the Flowcasting approach provides supply chain planners with unprecedented opportunities for improving service and reducing costs. Flowcasting also provides marketers with the opportunity to become laser-focused in planning and executing marketing programs.

This is especially beneficial for planning market specific promotions. Since the Flowcasting process pushes a store-level forecast of consumer demand throughout the entire retail supply chain, store-specific promotions become feasible and easy to plan and execute. For example, in some situations the retailer may decide to change a shelf configuration prior to a promotion. A new aisle display may effectively draw attention to products on sale and, in some cases, drive sales and traffic. Planning for such occurrences is simple if Flowcasting is used to drive the supply chain. In effect, you would simply adjust, in advance, the shelf display for the affected stores. The resulting store-level plans would take these adjustments into account. The shelf display could be increased just prior to the promotion and then reduced as the promotion ended.

Suppose your marketing team wanted to test the impact that a new shelf display will have on the promotion for store 602. At the beginning of the promotion, instead of having 36 units on display, a special section that holds 54 units is created. As the promotion winds down, the shelf will return to its normal display of 36 units. The resulting Flowcasting plan is shown in Figure 6.10.

PRODUCT: 12345678 – Promoted product

LOCATION: Store 602

Current On Hand Balance:	40 units
Minimum Store Ordering Quantity:	24 units
Store Receiving Schedule:	Tuesday, Thursday and Saturday only
Replenishment Lead-Time from RDC1:	3 days

	Days						
	M	T	W	Th	F	Sa	Su
Forecast - Base	3	3	3	3	3	3	3
Forecast – Lift	6	6	6	6	6	6	6
Total Forecast	9	9	9	9	9	9	9
Min Display Qty	54	54	54	54	54	54	36
In Transits	24	24					
Projected On Hand	55	70	61	76	67	58	49
Planned Arrivals				24			
Planned Orders	24						

Figure 6.10: Daily Flowcasting plan for a product using a time-phased shelf change.

Notice that the plan for store 602 has been recalculated and reflects the decision to merchandise the product in a different fashion. During the period where the special shelf configuration was used, additional arrivals are planned. By reducing the shelf configuration from 54 units back to 36 units, you avoid an arrival that would have been planned to keep 54 units in stock.

In addition, given the process plans at store level, virtually any combination of marketing programs can be easily created and executed. For example, a retailer may want to create separate promotional plans for its rural and metropolitan stores. Or perhaps a small group of local stores are hosting a charity event that will drive traffic. The ability of this process to facilitate laser-focused marketing programs can only help drive sales, increase customer loyalty, and reduce costs.

Natural Planning

As we've demonstrated thus far, Flowcasting provides a natural linkage between all nodes in the retail supply chain, so that promotional demand is immediately translated and shared among trading partners. Each node has visibility into the demands they must meet into order to support the promotion. The key point is that promotional forecasting only exists at the store level -- all other demands are calculated.

As actual sales transact or inventory balances change, each node in the supply chain has complete visibility which, in turn, greatly improves planning for promotions. The guessing and re-forecasting at all levels is replaced with up-to-date dependent demand calculations. These calculations become the marching orders for all nodes as they plan and schedule the resources necessary to support the promotion.

In Figure 6.11 below, our retail supply chain is linked from store shelf to factory.

Linking the Retail Supply Chain -- From Factory to Store

As the illustration shows, there is no guesswork as to what will be demanded. There is an old saying in supply chain management: never forecast what you can calculate. Flowcasting gives new meaning to that concept.

Imagine if you were working using a Flowcasting process and planning promotions. As a retail supply chain professional, you would only collaborate with people (suppliers, store personnel, etc.) on one element: real consumer demand. All other demand would be calculated on the basis of a forecast conducted at the store shelf level.

As a supplier, you might also be involved in forecasting consumer demand for a promotion. After that, you would automatically have precise information regarding demand, shipping, inventory, and manufacturing projections related to that promotion, including the timing of all activities. All the guesswork regarding how much to produce and where to deploy it would be eliminated. Your new focus

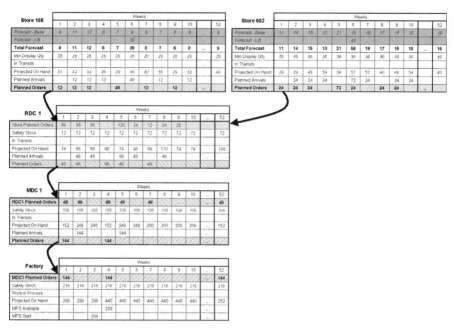

Figure 6.11: Natural linkage of the retail supply chain for promotion planning.

would be on planning the resources needed to support the promotion.

The Flowcasting process provides crystal clear projections of demand. As most retailers use multiple distribution centers to supply their stores, these DCs would plan all of their activities on the basis of dependent demand from the stores they supply. As a result, in a multi-DC environment the Flowcasting process produces demand projections from the supplier to each RDC. Gone are the days when the manufacturer produces and deploys product in advance of the promotion, hoping that their guesses were correct. Instead, trading partners would plan to a single version of the truth: consumer demand.

Summary

In this chapter, we've shown how Flowcasting makes promotional planning far more effective. Here are the key points to remember:

1. Retail out-of-stocks for promotions are, on average, 15 percent. Most stock outs are the result of poor store ordering and an unresponsive supply chain. The Flowcasting process eliminates these root causes, and provides the opportunity to vastly reduce out-of-stocks.

2. Since the Flowcasting process begins at the store level, virtually any kind of promotion can be planned and executed throughout the extended retail supply chain. The ability to plan and execute laser-focused marketing programs makes promotions more targeted and less risky.

3. In most promotions, some stores sell more than expected while others sell less. With Flowcasting, only a portion of the inventory is positioned at the store level. This provides opportunities for re-supplying stores that need more inventory during the promotion.

4. At the manufacturer's end of the supply chain, Flowcasting provides production schedulers with unprecedented visibility into the needs of their customers. They can see changes in demand at the plant only a day or two into the promotion and can adjust their production to provide the right amount of product to the DCs that need it.

5. Flowcasting naturally links all nodes in the supply chain. This takes the guesswork out of determining how much to produce and where to deploy product during promotions.

The next chapter continues to show how Flowcasting simplifies and improves common planning problems in the extended retail supply chain. It will focus on product introductions and discontinuations -- two planning challenges that retailers face on an ongoing basis.

C H A P T E R   7

Product Introductions and Discontinuations
Managing Store by Store

The challenge of planning and replenishing inventory is hard enough during regular business and promotions. When you add the task of managing the introduction of new products and the discontinuation of obsolete or non-performing products, the task seems almost Herculean. To be sure, thousands of new products enter the marketplace every year -- in the food industry alone, some 20,000 new products are introduced every year. Just about every category from electronics to hard goods has experienced an explosion in new product entries as life cycles shorten and innovation (significant, incremental, or purely cosmetic) becomes the platform for gaining a competitive advantage. Of course, many of the "new" items are not new -- they're new versions of existing items or replacements for items being phased out.

So how do retail supply chains manage product introductions and discontinuations? As in the case of promotions, the answer is "not well." Without an effective planning approach, the result is inevitably excess and obsolete inventory, reduced service levels and increased costs. The main cause today is the inability to use product flow (i.e., inventories and shipments) projections, store by store, in order to make good decisions about the timing of future inventory flows throughout the entire supply chain. Flowcasting, as we'll demonstrate in this chapter, addresses this and makes it feasible for retail supply chains to effectively manage the introduction and discontinuation of products.

The Product Lifecycle

All products have a lifecycle. They are introduced, then sales build to a certain level, and continue for some period of time. Eventually, sales taper off until the product no longer sells at a profitable rate, if at all. Figure 7.1 illustrates a generic product sales lifecycle:

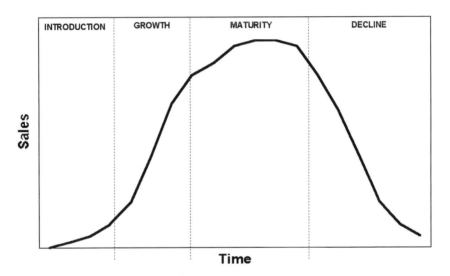

Figure 7.1: Generic product sales lifecycle.

At the start of the lifecycle, sales typically happen at a slower rate and take some time to build up. This is natural, since the product is new to the marketplace and takes time to gain acceptance as a result of advertising, marketing, and word-of-mouth. When the product has reached maturity, its sales will reach a plateau, after which sales begin to slow and the product is eventually discontinued. The amount of time a product spends in each phase of the lifecycle can vary widely by product type. For example, the total lifecycle for most consumer electronics products is weeks or months. For motor oil, it's decades.

Product Introductions -- In With the New

The introduction of new products is critical to consumer goods companies and their extended supply chain partners. Retailers routinely add products to their assortments as a way to drive growth.

To see how Flowcasting facilitates a new product introduction, let's revisit the simplified retail supply chain that we introduced in the previous chapter (see Figure 7.2).

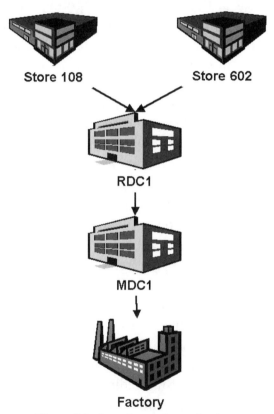

Figure 7.2: Sample retail supply chain.

For simplicity's sake, let's say that a new product will be carried in stores 108 and 602, which are supplied by RDC1. The first challenge concerns forecasting sales of the product. As discussed in Chapter 3, 2 to 3 years of sales history are necessary to produce a good baseline forecast. New products, by definition, have no sales history, so it is necessary to copy sales history from a similar item to the new item. A scaling factor may also be applied; for example, it may be estimated that the new item will have a rate of sale that is only 80 percent of the product from which history is being copied. In some cases, this might also involve merging history from a number of items if the new product is expected to behave like a category or group of products, rather than one specific product.

Once the copied history is in place, we can begin Flowcasting the new item on a 52-week basis for each store as we would for any other item. "But isn't this just guessing?" you might ask. "Aren't we losing the precision of the computer to human judgment?" In fact, this approach provides the best of both worlds. Computers are fabulous at crunching numbers, but only humans can make the judgments about human behavior necessary to create a valid simulation of reality. No computer program (at least no program that currently exists) can intuit the similarities of products or the similarity of a product to a whole category the way humans do. Perhaps even more important is that having people involved and taking ownership ensures that there is accountability in the process of making decisions about how new products will behave -- there's a point at which human instinct supersedes logic and programming routines.

In many cases, forecasting a new product is an excellent opportunity for collaboration between retailer and manufacturer. In all likelihood, the manufacturer has knowledge about how the new product is selling in other markets, or has done research that supports the justification for making the product in the first place. This necessary collaboration makes the forecasting of new products an ideal process for the Flowcasting team, which is comprised of representatives from all participating trading partners. Bear in mind that collaborating on new product introductions doesn't require sophisticated technology; more often than not it can happen over the phone, supported via email and spreadsheets. The goal is to develop the best estimate of how well the new product will sell, using as much information and relevant experience as possible.

Forecasting and Flowcasting the New Product

Once the new item has been "assigned" a sales history, a baseline forecast can be calculated in the same way as it would be for any other product. Although the history has been artificially created, a forecast start date can be applied to the item, so you can actually plan for sales to start 3 or 4 months in the future. This allows the entire supply chain to calculate dependent demand and prepare for delivery of the new product to the store shelf.

The forecast start date indicates the date you expect sales to begin to occur, store by store, depending on the product being introduced. For a "big bang" product introduction, the forecast start date would be the same date across all stores. If the rollout will instead be gradual (perhaps starting with a market test), you may use different start dates for different groups of stores.

In addition to the forecast, the introduction of a new product normally requires that shelf configurations also be determined, store by store. Usually this is done as part of a larger product introduction process, using plan-o-grams or other tools that help to determine appropriate shelf display sizes in specific markets or market types. With Flowcasting, the shelf changes can be planned to occur slightly in advance of sales to allow store personnel time to re-merchandise the shelves to accommodate new product. This future-dated shelf planning highlights an important component of the process -- the separation of demand planning from supply planning.

Typically, a retailer performs demand and supply planning at the same time, by estimating sales and then placing purchase orders with suppliers. It is the job of Flowcasting teams to de-couple this linkage, given the fact that the forecast is independent of the supply plan (see Figure 7.2). Of course, the forecast drives the planned orders, but remember that planned orders are just that -- "planned." Supply decisions -- such as safety stock, lead times, etc. -- are factored into the planned orders but have no impact on the forecast.

To illustrate this concept, we'll return to the model supply chain we set up earlier in the chapter. Figure 7.3 shows what a Flowcasting plan might look like for a new product at store 108, in weekly time periods.

PRODUCT: 12345100 – New product

LOCATION: Store 108

Current On Hand Balance:	0 units
Minimum Store Ordering Quantity:	1 unit
Store Receiving Schedule:	Monday, Wednesday and Friday only
Replenishment Lead-Time from RDC1:	2 days

	Weeks											
	1	2	3	4	5	6	7	8	9	10	...	52
Total Forecast								1	2	2	...	2
Min Display Qty							8	8	8	8	...	8
In Transits											...	
Projected On Hand							8	8	8	8	...	8
Planned Arrivals							8	1	2	2	...	2
Planned Orders							8	1	2	2	...	2

Figure 7.3: Flowcasting plan for a new product at store 108.

Notice that the new product is planned to start selling in week 8 and has forecast quantities beginning that week. In addition, a shelf change (Min Display Qty) has been planned in week 7, indicating that the shelf display for this store will be a minimum of 8 units. The effect is that a planned arrival has been calculated in week 7 for 8 units. Since the lead time from RDC1 to this store is only 2 days, the planned order date for this arrival is in the same week.

Similarly, a Flowcasting plan for the new product in store 602 is shown in Figure 7.4.

PRODUCT: 12345100 – New product

LOCATION: Store 602

Current On Hand Balance:	0 units
Minimum Store Ordering Quantity:	2 units
Store Receiving Schedule:	Tuesday, Thursday and Saturday only
Replenishment Lead-Time from RDC1:	3 days

	Weeks											
	1	2	3	4	5	6	7	8	9	10	...	52
Total Forecast								10	11	13	...	12
Min Display Qty							36	36	36	36	...	36
In Transits											...	
Projected On Hand							36	36	37	36	...	36
Planned Arrivals							36	10	12	12	...	12
Planned Orders							36	10	12	12	...	12

Figure 7.4: Flowcasting plan for a new product at store 602.

Again, the forecast starts in week 8 and the shelves will be set up in week 7, but in this case, store 602 is expected to have a higher sales forecast for the new item. The RDC-level Flowcasting plan for

PRODUCT: 12345100 – New product

LOCATION: RDC1

Current On Hand Balance:	0 units
Minimum DC Ordering Quantity:	36 units
DC Receiving Schedule:	Monday to Friday
Replenishment Lead-Time from MDC1:	4 days

	Weeks											
	1	2	3	4	5	6	7	8	9	10	...	52
Store Planned Orders							44	11	14	14	...	14
Safety Stock						48	48	48	48	48	...	48
In Transits											...	
Projected On Hand						72	64	53	75	61	...	56
Planned Arrivals						72	36		36		...	36
Planned Orders					72	36		36			...	36

Figure 7.5: Flowcasting plan for a new product at RDC1.

the new product, using the combined planned order streams from stores 108 and 602, is depicted in Figure 7.5.

Because we are using our simplified example, the "top line" for MDC1 consists of the planned orders from RDC1, as illustrated in Figure 7.6 below.

PRODUCT: 12345100 – New product

LOCATION: MDC1

Current On Hand Balance:	0 units
Minimum DC Ordering Quantity:	72 units
DC Receiving Schedule:	Seven days a week
Replenishment Lead-Time from Factory:	7 days

	Weeks											
	1	2	3	4	5	6	7	8	9	10	...	52
RDC1 Planned Orders					72	36		36			...	36
Safety Stock					96	96	96	96	96	96	...	96
In Transits											...	
Projected On Hand					144	108	108	144	144	144	...	108
Planned Arrivals					216			72			...	
Planned Orders				216			72				...	

Figure 7.6: Flowcasting plan for a new product at MDC1.

As the forecast cascades through the supply chain, the planned orders for MDC1 become the demand plan for the factory, which would plan material requirements based on production run sizes, safety stock, and other parameters. At this point, the Flowcasting process has seamlessly linked the entire retail supply chain from factory to shelf.

Additionally, the Flowcasting process is constantly updating itself, and as actual sales are transacted for the new product, new forecasts will be generated. As time passes, the new item will be using its own historical data instead of the artificial history that was created during the introduction stage of its lifecycle.

The bottom line is that Flowcasting dramatically changes the new product introduction process for the better; instead of scrambling to add a new product to the assortment, retailers can now plan every aspect of a product introduction months in advance, if the information is available.

Cannibalization

If a new product is being added to an existing assortment of similar products, then this expansion to the assortment may actually result in lower sales of existing products; it will therefore be necessary to create a revised (and reduced) forecast for cannibalized items.

For example, introducing a new and improved shovel may mean that the sales of existing shovels will suffer as customers are lured instead to the new-and-improved model. Again, human judgment is the best tool for predicting behavior in such a circumstance. Planners would use their judgment, collect advice from a number of different sources (including the supplier and store personnel), and accordingly reduce the forecast of an existing item that will experience reduced sales when the new product enters the assortment.

Introducing New Product Lines

So far, our explanation has focused on using Flowcasting to plan for the introduction of a single item. In practice, retailers typically revamp entire lines of business on an annual basis and introduce many new products at the same time. Since the Flowcasting process provides extensive visibility for all nodes in the retail supply chain, it enables retailers to anticipate and preempt future constraints in production, transportation, receiving and shipping labor, and available warehouse space.

Suppose that a retailer intends to introduce a number of new products in a specific product category, and these products will be distributed from an RDC to all the stores. Further suppose that the forecast start date was the same for all the new items. As shown in Figures 7.3 and 7.4, the initial distribution to the stores can often be much larger than the week-in-week-out distribution. The question then arises, "Can the RDC handle the volume -- both inbound and outbound -- for the new items?"

Since the people in the RDC can see the expected volumes well in advance, they have the information necessary for determining if the RDC has the inventory and capacity, and if not, to take measures for reducing the RDC's capacity constraints (see Chapter 10 for more information on capacity planning). These measures could be as simple as changing the shelf dates for the new products for some stores, which would result in the required volume being shifting to earlier weeks. The point is that the unprecedented visibility provided by the Flowcasting process allows Flowcasting teams to make intelligent, cost effective, service-oriented decisions, and then execute them. For the first time, a common game plan can be created, agreed upon, and then put into play for the entire retail supply chain.

New Store Openings

A close relative to a product introduction, from a supply chain planning point of view, is a new store opening. While introducing a new product involves developing Flowcasting plans across multiple stores for an item, a store opening involves developing Flowcasting plans across multiple items in a single store. As previously described, for a product introduction, sales history is copied from a similar item in all participating stores in order to create a baseline forecast.

For a new store opening, sales history is copied from a similar store for all items that the new store will stock. Similar to the cannibalization effect within product assortments, cannibalization can also happen geographically. For example, if the new store is to be located near existing stores, then the existing stores may experience a downturn in sales as some of their customers begin shopping at the new store instead. Within a Flowcasting environment, this cannibalization effect can be planned for in advance by reducing the forecasts in the existing stores shortly after the new store is planned to be opened.

Product Discontinuations -- Out With the Old

Once a retailer has decided that a product is nearing the end of its lifecycle, the goal is usually to deplete as much inventory at the stores and RDCs as possible before discontinuing it. The less that discounting is needed to clear out obsolete inventory, the better. The key is to determine the run-out date, store by store, and consume as much of the available inventory from the RDC as possible.

PRODUCT: 9876543 – Product to be discontinued

LOCATION: Store 108

Current On Hand Balance:	10 units
Minimum Store Ordering Quantity:	1 unit
Store Receiving Schedule:	Monday, Wednesday and Friday only
Replenishment Lead-Time from RDC1:	2 days

	Weeks											
	1	2	3	4	5	6	7	8	9	10	...	52
Total Forecast	1	2	2	2	2	2					...	
Min Display Qty	4	4	4	4							...	
In Transits											...	
Projected On Hand	9	7	5	4	2						...	
Planned Arrivals				1							...	
Planned Orders				1							...	

Figure 7.7: Flowcasting plan for a product to be discontinued at store 108.

Figure 7.7 shows the Flowcasting plan for a product that is to be discontinued at store 108, in weekly time periods:

Notice that the forecast for this product ends in week 6. This is based on how long the last planned arrival to this store is expected to last from the distribution center that supplies it -- in this case, RDC1.

But why is an arrival planned from RDC1 in week 4, given that this product is being discontinued? Because we have full visibility into the stores and RDC1, we can simultaneously plan to deplete the inventory in all locations before discontinuing the product. In Figure 7.7, it was determined that store 108 had low enough inventory and a high enough rate of sale to "pitch in" and accept an additional shipment from RDC1.

A run-out calculation for a store is made on the basis of when the last shipment of this product from the RDC is expected to be depleted at the store (that is, the projected on hand goes to zero for this store). The run-out date for a product could, of course, be different for different stores. If sales transpire at rates different than that forecasted, the planned arrivals and run-out dates would be re-calculated, store by store and the information would be communicated throughout the retail supply chain in the form of dependent demand (i.e., planned orders). Based on all of the planned product flow in and out of store 108, the run-out date would be sometime in week 6.

PRODUCT: 9876543 – Product to be discontinued
LOCATION: Store 602

Current On Hand Balance:	48 units
Minimum Store Ordering Quantity:	6 units
Store Receiving Schedule:	Tuesday, Thursday and Saturday only
Replenishment Lead-Time from RDC1:	3 days

	Weeks											
	1	2	3	4	5	6	7	8	9	10	...	52
Total Forecast	10	12	12	12	12	12	11	13	2		...	
Min Display Qty	24	24	24	24	24	24					...	
In Transits											...	
Projected On Hand	38	26	26	26	26	26	15	2			...	
Planned Arrivals			12	12	12	12					...	
Planned Orders			12	12	12	12					...	

Figure 7.8: Flowcasting plan for a product to be discontinued at store 602.

Similarly, Figure 7.8 illustrates the Flowcasting plan for the product to be discontinued in store 602.

At this store, additional planned arrivals totaling 48 units are scheduled in weeks 3 to 6. This is because of store 602's high rate of sale and favorable inventory position when compared to store 108.

For store 602, the forecast will consume all supply early in week 9, a longer time horizon than at store 108. Again, the Flowcasting plans for a discontinued item would be different for each store, and would be continuously re-calculated based on actual sales and inventory levels.

For RDC1, the Flowcasting plan would reflect the aggregate plans of the stores that it services. The planned orders from the stores would be aggregated and used as the demand plan for the DC. In our example, the Flowcasting plan for the RDC1 is shown in Figure 7.9:

PRODUCT: 9876543 – Product to be discontinued

LOCATION: RDC1

Current On Hand Balance:	50 units
Minimum DC Ordering Quantity:	36 units
DC Receiving Schedule:	Monday to Friday
Replenishment Lead-Time from MDC1:	7 days

	Weeks											
	1	2	3	4	5	6	7	8	9	10	...	52
Store Planned Orders			12	13	12	12					...	
Safety Stock											...	
In Transits											...	
Projected On Hand	50	50	38	25	13	1	1	1	1	1	...	1
Planned Arrivals											...	
Planned Orders											...	

Figure 7.9: Flowcasting plan for a product to be discontinued at RDC1.

The top line for RDC1 is the sum of the planned orders from the stores that it services. In addition, given that this product will be discontinued when it sells out, the safety stock has already been set to zero. For each store, future planned arrivals are calculated based on inventory available at the RDC. If RDC1 was overstocked, then additional planned arrivals would be calculated at the stores until the inventory was depleted.

In this case, the RDC inventory was not run down to exactly zero. This can happen when the product is nearing the end of its lifecycle and the market has completely dried up. In these situations, the residual inventory at the RDC would not be consumed, and the retailer would mark down the product to attempt to sell it or, in some cases, write it off -- both potentially costly propositions to be mini-mized wherever possible.

Because replenishment at RDC1 was "shut off" when the deci-sion to discontinue was made, the supplier would see that there are no planned orders for this item and would plan distribution and pro-duction accordingly. If you think about the generic sales lifecycle described previously, this makes good sense. For some period of time in the product's lifecycle, the supplier will see a future projection of planned orders from RDC1. As time passes and the product approach-es the end of its lifecycle, the planned orders will eventually trail off and then show zero in future time periods (indicating that the retail-er is phasing the product out). The supplier would aggregate the planned order projection with projections from other retailers and customers to arrive at a total demand plan (as was described in Chapter 5).

Product Replacement -- Out With the Old, In With the New

The proliferation of offerings is a challenge that many retail organi-zations face. The law of diminishing marginal returns precludes retailers from just expanding their assortments indefinitely. For this reason, annual line reviews are often used to rationalize and refresh product categories. Decisions on which products will stay and which will go are made simultaneously. This section outlines how Flowcasting can be used to plan for this situation.

Consider a new product that will replace an existing one once it's introduced. Ideally, the new product will be hitting the shelves at about the same time as the existing product sells out. The key to achieving this optimal timing is to link the new product's forecast start date to the existing product's run-out date. As sales for the exist-ing item are recorded, the run-out date is recalculated, and the fore-cast start date for the new product can be adjusted. If there's a change, the entire retail supply chain will be recalibrated in near real time.

Figure 7.10 illustrates the Flowcasting plan for the product that's being replaced at store 108 in weekly time periods.

PRODUCT: 12121212 – Existing product

LOCATION: Store 108

Current On Hand Balance:	6 units
Minimum Store Ordering Quantity:	1 unit
Store Receiving Schedule:	Monday, Wednesday and Friday only
Replenishment Lead-Time from RDC1:	2 days

	Weeks											
	1	2	3	4	5	6	7	8	9	10	...	52
Total Forecast	1	1	2	1	1	1					...	
Min Display Qty	2	2	2	2							...	
In Transits											...	
Projected On Hand	5	4	2	2	1						...	
Planned Arrivals				1							...	
Planned Orders				1							...	

Figure 7.10: Flowcasting plan for existing product store 108.

The sales forecast for the product at this store ends in week 6 because that's when it's predicted to run out of stock. In addition, the minimum shelf display has been set to zero in week 5, because the last shipment from RDC1 will be arriving at store 108 in week 5. After this week, no more stock is planned to be available in RDC1, so store 108 won't receive any more replenishments.

Of course, the likelihood of running out at the stores and the RDCs at exactly the same time is low. However, by planning to attempt this optimal timing, you will minimize the amount of residual inventory of the product you are phasing out -- a problem that has plagued retailers for years. The timing of the new product's introduction has been set to coincide with the run-out date of the existing product, as shown in Figure 7.11.

As stores sell off the inventory of the existing product, the Flowcasting process will recalculate the run-out dates. Stores that are selling at a faster rate will have an earlier run-out date which, in turn, will move the start date for the new product to an earlier date. Stores that are selling the existing product at a slower rate will have their run-out date pushed out into the future which, in turn, will move the start date out for the new product.

PRODUCT: 13131313 – New product

LOCATION: Store 108

Current On Hand Balance:	0 units
Minimum Store Ordering Quantity:	1 unit
Store Receiving Schedule:	Monday, Wednesday and Friday only
Replenishment Lead-Time from RDC1:	2 days

	Weeks											
	1	2	3	4	5	6	7	8	9	10	...	52
Total Forecast						1	1	1	2	2	...	2
Min Display Qty						2	2	2	2	2	...	2
In Transits											...	
Projected On Hand						2	2	2	2	2	...	2
Planned Arrivals						3	1	1	2	2	...	
Planned Orders						3	1	1	2	2	...	

Figure 7.11: Flowcasting plan for new product store 108.

Since the product introduction and run-out calculations are being done store by store, the RDC that supplies the stores will have an accurate view of the expected timing of the demands. Each day, the demand pattern at RDC will be recalculated and refreshed, based on the latest information.

Product Lifecycle Management -- Recap

While the approaches to category management can vary, the overall goal is the same: to cost-effectively bring new products to the marketplace with minimal disruption and obsolete inventory. Flowcasting is an excellent means for achieving that goal given the visibility it provides across the entire supply chain. As shown in this chapter, retailers can leverage this visibility to make good decisions regarding product introduction and discontinuation dates, safety stock quantities and timing, and capacity requirements. Further, the Flowcasting process is self adjusting, so that a change in plan for one supply chain trading partner is immediately communicated to all parties within the extended retail supply chain. This provides unparalleled opportunities to plan in advance. Finally, Flowcasting closes the traditional gaps between merchandise plans, category plans, and plan-o-grams by allowing them to be factored explicitly into the store replenishment calculations.

Summary

In this chapter, we've looked at the product introduction and discontinuation process and how these core processes can be improved using a Flowcasting process. Here are the key points to remember:

1. All products have a sales lifecycle. Flowcasting provides the ability to translate lifecycle into actionable information for all trading partners.

2. The Flowcasting process provides the visibility required to effectively introduce new products to the marketplace. Store-level forecasts and inventory projections give planners the ability to see the impact of their decisions long before they will occur. This provides all trading partners, through their Flowcasting teams, with the opportunity to create, agree to, and execute a plan.

3. Product-level visibility can be converted into capacity requirements to ensure that initial store distributions of new products will not create a bottleneck anywhere within the extended retail supply chain. In the event they do, decisions can be made in advance to avoid constraints.

4. Store-level visibility and the ability to calculate store-by-store run-out dates of an existing product make it far easier to introduce a new product while discontinuing an old one.

5. Since the entire supply chain is linked by a series of cascading planned orders (dependent demand), all trading partners have advance notice of product introductions and discontinuations and the impact that these events will have on their operations.

The next chapter covers another key planning process for retailers and their trading partners: seasonal planning. You'll learn how the Flowcasting process greatly improves seasonal setups and takedowns and decision-making in advance of the season. The result is improved service levels and reduced costs throughout the extended retail supply chain.

C H A P T E R   8

Seasonal Planning
Managing Micro Seasons

Many retailers and their supply chain partners maintain an assortment of items that are seasonal. Baseball equipment sells much better during spring and summer months in the United States while hockey equipment would sell during the fall and winter months. Yet, as important as seasonality is to retailers, today's approaches for planning seasonal product flows often result in excess carry over inventory for items that didn't sell as well as hoped, and mid-season out-of-stocks for items that sell better than expected. For non-apparel lines, it's been estimated that between 15-25 percent of the inventory bought during the season ends up being carried over into the off-season.

Once again, the "every-node-for itself" forecasting approach is the major culprit; with each trading partner "guessing" at the seasonal pattern of sales, the supply chain can't cannot respond to true demand signals from at the retail shelf. The Flowcasting process is far superior to today's practices since seasonal flows are planned store by store, and forward-looking exceptions alert planners about potential problems in time for them to make decisions that minimize seasonal inventory carryover, thereby reducing costs.

In this chapter, we'll explore:

1. How Flowcasting can be used to plan seasonal products

2. Planning next year's season today

3. Using visibility to make better decisions

4. Planning special seasons (e.g., holidays) using Flowcasting

Seasonal Planning Using Flowcasting

1. Using Flowcasting to Plan Seasonal Products

Once again, we'll continue to use the basic retail supply chain shown in Figure 8.1 to illustrate core Flowcasting concepts.

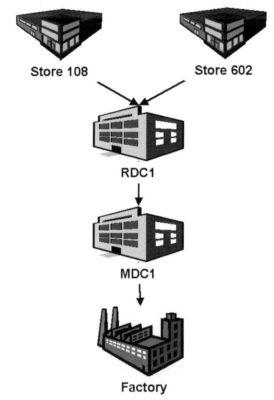

Figure 8.1: Sample retail supply chain.

Imagine that we are planning the upcoming spring season for a gardening product that will be carried in stores 108 and 602. Both stores are supplied by RDC1.

Managing the retail supply chain for these items is different than managing items that sell year round. Store shelves must be stocked and displayed in advance of the selling season, then taken down and replaced by other items when the season ends. An aisle that displays patio furniture in the summer may display snow shovels in the winter.

In planning seasonal merchandise flows, *timing* is everything. The ideal scenario would be to run out of the current season's merchandise just before setting up the merchandise to sell for the next season to minimize carryover without leaving sales on the table. While it may be unrealistic to expect seasonal inventory at every location will drop to zero as the season winds down, a Flowcasting process will give you the best chance of reaching this optimal balance.

Forecasting a seasonal item

As is the case for all products, the starting point for planning a seasonal item is the store-level consumer demand forecast. The typical sales pattern for a seasonal item is shown in Figure 8.2, a summer product, with sales peaking in June/July.

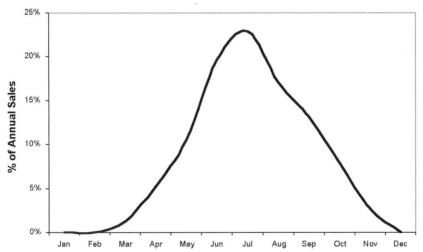

Figure 8.2: Generic sales profile for a summer seasonal item.

Because forecasts are created at store level, the Flowcasting process can provide unprecedented precision in managing seasonal products. Geographically, stores in different regions can have vastly different seasonal profiles for the same item. For example, stores in colder climates may experience demand for gardening supplies only in the spring and summer months, whereas other stores may sell them year round.

Seasonal curves can also vary dramatically, even among stores that are geographically close. In a Flowcasting simulation for beer sold in Quebec convenience stores, it was noticed that out of 8 stores in the Montreal market, 7 of them had a spring/summer selling season, but one store had a fall/winter selling season. After an investigation, it was determined that the 8th store was located close to a university. Because the population of students was low in the spring/summer months and high in the fall/winter months, that store experienced an "upside-down" seasonal pattern.

For many items, the timing of the start of a selling season is often dictated by the weather. Snow shovels sell when the snow starts falling, and that could be in October or December, depending on the locale. Although the weather cannot be forecasted with any degree of accuracy, with Flowcasting, a precise prediction of weather patterns isn't necessary for planning seasonal product movements; estimating when you would like merchandise to be on the shelves can ensure that product will be available to customers before the season actually begins.

Planning the Season Start

Planning seasonal items not only involves the use of historical point-of-sale information to forecast future sales, but it entails assessing risk with regards to the season start date. Many retailers stock their shelves in advance of upcoming seasons. The risk assessment is a management decision concerning how early you want product to be on the shelf before sales are expected to occur.

For example, suppose sales for a seasonal item at a store traditionally begin by March 1st. If you took no action, then the process would plan an arrival of inventory just before March 1st. To mitigate the risk of losing sales if the season breaks early, it might be decided to have the shelves merchandised by February 15th, using the time-phased minimum shelf display. The Flowcasting system would now plan for inventory to arrive in mid-February even though actual sales were not expected to happen until March. This hedge could vary category by category and store by store, depending on the sales/inventory risk assessment.

A Flowcasting plan for a seasonal item at store 108 is shown in Figure 8.3 below.

PRODUCT: 12121212 – Seasonal product

LOCATION: Store 108

Current On Hand Balance:	0 units
Minimum Store Ordering Quantity:	4 units
Store Receiving Schedule:	Monday, Wednesday and Friday only
Replenishment Lead-Time from RDC1:	2 days

| | Weeks | | | | | | | | | | | |
	1	2	3	4	5	6	7	8	9	10	...	52
Total Forecast						6	8	16	19	22	...	0
Min Display Qty					40	40	40	40	40	40	...	0
In Transits											...	
Projected On Hand					40	42	42	42	43	41	...	0
Planned Arrivals					40	8	8	16	20	20	...	
Planned Orders					40	8	8	16	20	20	...	

Figure 8.3: Flowcasting plan for a seasonal product at store 108.

As you can see from the Total Forecast line, this product is expected to begin selling in week 6. This store is planning to set up their display in week 5, as indicated by the Min Display Qty line. The Flowcasting logic then plans product to be ordered and delivered in week 5 to set up the display. As in the previous examples, this new information is automatically communicated as dependent demand to RDC1.

Store 602 has a different plan for this item, as shown in Figure 8.4 below.

PRODUCT: 12121212 – Seasonal product
LOCATION: Store 602

Current On Hand Balance:	0 units
Minimum Store Ordering Quantity:	12 units
Store Receiving Schedule:	Tuesday, Thursday and Saturday only
Replenishment Lead-Time from RDC1:	3 days

	Weeks											
	1	2	3	4	5	6	7	8	9	10	...	52
Total Forecast					24	29	36	41	44	47	...	0
Min Display Qty			80	80	80	80	80	80	80	80	...	0
In Transits											...	
Projected On Hand			80	80	80	87	87	82	86	87	...	0
Planned Arrivals			80		24	36	36	36	48	48	...	
Planned Orders			80		24	36	36	36	48	48	...	

Figure 8.4: Flowcasting plan for a seasonal product at store 602.

For store 602, the selling season is expected to begin in week 5 instead of week 6, and the display quantity will be set up in week 3 instead of week 5.

The Flowcasting system provides RDC1 with an accurate projection of store requirements, despite the fact that each store has a completely different seasonal setup strategy for this product. The RDC-level Flowcasting plan for the seasonal product is outlined in Figure 8.5.

PRODUCT: 12121212 – Seasonal product
LOCATION: RDC1

Current On Hand Balance:	0 units
Minimum DC Ordering Quantity:	48 units
DC Receiving Schedule:	Monday to Friday
Replenishment Lead-Time from MDC1:	7 days

	Weeks											
	1	2	3	4	5	6	7	8	9	10	...	52
Store Planned Orders			80		64	44	44	52	68	68	...	
Safety Stock		96	96	96	96	96	96	96	96	96	...	
In Transits											...	
Projected On Hand		96	112	112	96	100	104	100	128	108	...	
Planned Arrivals		96	96		48	48	48	48	96	48	...	
Planned Orders	96	96		48	48	48	48	96	48		...	

Figure 8.5: Flowcasting plan for a seasonal product at RDC1.

With a complete demand picture that accounts for each store's individual strategy, the RDC has planned for 96 units of safety stock to arrive in week 2, just prior to the first week's shipments to the stores. The planned orders for RDC1 constitute the demand plan for the seasonal item at MDC1, as shown in Figure 8.6.

PRODUCT: 12121212 – Seasonal product

LOCATION: MDC1

Current On Hand Balance:	250 units
Minimum DC Ordering Quantity:	72 units
DC Receiving Schedule:	Seven days a week
Replenishment Lead-Time from Factory:	7 days

	Weeks											
	1	2	3	4	5	6	7	8	9	10	...	52
RDC1 Planned Orders	96	96		48	48	48	48	96	48		...	
Safety Stock	144	144	144	144	144	144	144	144	144	144	...	0
In Transits											...	
Projected On Hand	154	202	202	154	178	202	154	202	154	154	...	0
Planned Arrivals		144			72	72		144			...	
Planned Orders	144			72	72		144				...	

Figure 8.6: Flowcasting plan for a seasonal product at MDC1.

Once MDC1 shares its planned orders with the factory, the entire supply chain will be automatically synchronized for the upcoming season.

Planning the Season End

Getting out of the season without a lot of excess inventory can be just as challenging as getting into the season without missing out on sales.

Let's see how the Flowcasting process works in planning for the season end. Figure 8.7 depicts the Flowcasting plan for the seasonal item at store 108, in weekly time periods.

In week 34, sales will start to decline, and by week 41, it's expected that the season will come to an end. Store 108 has decided to stop replenishing the shelf display in week 36. Most of the residual inventory will be consumed by the end of season -- the current plan is to have 2 units left after week 40. Similar logic would be applied to planning the season end for the product at store 602.

PRODUCT: 12121212 – Seasonal product

LOCATION: Store 108

Current On Hand Balance:	52 units
Minimum Store Ordering Quantity:	4 units
Store Receiving Schedule:	Monday, Wednesday and Friday only
Replenishment Lead-Time from RDC1:	2 days

	Weeks											
	32	33	34	35	36	37	38	39	40	41	...	31
Total Forecast	24	26	22	18	13	10	8	6	3		...	21
Min Display Qty	40	40	40	40							...	40
In Transits	12										...	
Projected On Hand	40	42	40	42	29	19	11	5	2	2	...	42
Planned Arrivals		28	20	20							...	
Planned Orders		28	20	20							...	

Figure 8.7: Flowcasting plan for a seasonal product at store 108 at season's end.

By using the Flowcasting process, retailers can make merchandising decisions several months in advance of the actual season. Store-level plans can be set up to precisely depict when inventory will flow into the stores and when it will begin to decline as the season winds down. In other words, the Flowcasting system provides the RDCs and other trading partners with demand profiles that are directly linked to the retail store shelf.

Contrast this tight linkage with the way each node in a supply chain forecasts its own demand profiles independently of the levels above them. There is simply no chance that the individual plans will be synchronized, especially at the beginning and end of the selling season. When true demand signals indicate that it's time to reduce ordering, it will be too late for the various trading partners to take corrective action. While it was mentioned that seasonal inventory carryover is costly at store level, in today's disconnected environment, it's also a problem at the RDC level and throughout the rest of the retail supply chain. Flowcasting eliminates the carryover problem at all levels of the supply chain, from the retail store to the manufacturing plant.

2. Planning Next Year's Season Today

An experienced merchant will tell you that the best time to make decisions about next year's season is immediately following a post mortem review of the current season.

For example, suppose that a poor initial merchandising decision was made for a category of products; the season started earlier than expected, and sales were lost. Since the Flowcasting process covers a 52-week time horizon, you could immediately input revised merchandising shelf dates and quantities into the Flowcasting plan for next season. When the beginning of the next season rolls around, the product flow throughout the supply chain has already been planned for months, and the ordering is automatic.

3. Using Visibility to Make Better Decisions

The long-term planning horizon built into Flowcasting provides the visibility necessary for making end of season decisions. Since the Flowcasting process produces a time-phased plan by product and location, it's possible to see what your future inventory levels will be -- by product, product category or any other combination that might be useful. And since the process is forward-looking, potential problems can be identified before they materialize. Excess inventory carryover is one problem that can be identified and potentially resolved before it occurs.

Suppose that you're a retailer who carries 3 different garden shovels, and the end of the gardening season is approaching. Because you are able to see your future inventory levels and consumer demand forecasts out to the end of the season, you can easily calculate your projected days of supply, each day, to the end of the selling season.

For example, if you think you'll have 20 units in inventory on a particular day and you're forecasting that you'll sell 10 units per week, then you would have 2 weeks of inventory coverage for the item. Figure 8.8 illustrates what a time-phased days of supply picture might look like for 3 shovels in store 108.

Store 108	Days of Supply by Week											
	1	2	3	4	5	6	7	8	9	10	...	52
Shovel 1	21	14	7	21	14	7	180	171	165	158	...	21
Shovel 2	21	14	21	14	21	14	7	0	0	0	...	0
Shovel 3	21	14	7	21	14	7	190	183	180	180	...	0

Figure 8.8: Projected inventory coverage in days of supply for three shovels at store 108.

In week 7 for shovel 1, the days of inventory coverage jumps to 180 days. This is a common occurrence for items at the end of the selling season, and it makes perfect sense. A minimum store order quantity may only last a few days when the product is in season, but the same order minimum may take months to sell down if it's bought at the end of the season.

Of course, for products that look like they'll end the season with minimal inventory carryover, you'd expect the process to run as normal -- that is, to plan arrivals of inventory to meet forecast sales. But in the situation shown in Figure 8.8, it's easy for the Flowcasting process to warn you that your plans will result in inventory carryover for shovels 1 and 3, with enough time to take action before it happens.

You might, for instance, create an end of season clearance promotion to sell out items that are projected to be in a carryover position. Or you may decide to avoid replenishing some items in week 5 or 6. Still another option may be to rebalance inventory among the stores to capture as many sales as possible while minimizing overall carryover inventory throughout the chain. The point is that the visibility provided by the Flowcasting process provides the information you need to make better decisions.

Without the time-phased view of demand, supply, and inventory information provided by Flowcasting, it's virtually impossible to make such decisions far enough in advance to have strategy choices.

4. Planning Special Seasons Using Flowcasting

So far, we've shown how the Flowcasting process enables accurate planning of seasonal items. But what if the season is very short and very specific, such as the Christmas holidays? Christmas happens every year at the same time and usually results in a surge in demand across a wide variety of items. Other examples are Father's Day, Mother's Day, Easter, and Halloween, to name a few.

Should planning items for these "special seasons" be any different than planning any other seasonal items? Think of it this way: Although the "season" is much smaller, the planning principles of the process remain the same. Store by store plans reflect the sales forecast and merchandising decisions about planned arrivals. The forecasts are translated into planned orders and are communicated to the RDCs which, in turn, communicate their planned orders to their supplier. This process continues until the entire retail supply chain is linked.

The point is that planning for seasonal items and specific holidays follows the same process. That makes it simpler and easier to understand; after all, people manage Flowcasting processes, and the more things can be standardized for people, the better.

Summary

In this chapter, we've looked at how to manage seasonal products using a Flowcasting process. Here are the key points to remember:

1. Seasonal planning requires decisions on a store-by-store basis, especially merchandising decisions regarding shelf changes for season start and end dates.
2. The Flowcasting process provides the visibility required to manage seasonal products. Dependent demand communicated to trading partners will reflect when a season starts and ends.
3. Seasonal products can have store specific selling patterns. A Flowcasting process provides the ability to translate these patterns into actionable information for all trading partners.
4. Future visibility regarding inventory projections provides people with the information they need to make good decisions regarding end-of-season inventory levels.
5. There is no difference in planning seasonal items and items whose season's are holiday driven.

The next chapter will focus on planning and managing slow selling items. In it, you'll see how Flowcasting greatly simplifies managing slow sellers and ensures that a consistent planning process is used for all products.

C H A P T E R   9

Managing Slow Sellers
Changing the Forecast Horizion

In the previous chapters, we've shown how a single forecast of consumer demand, generated at the retail store level, can be used to
profitably manage the flow of inventory throughout the extended
retail supply chain. We've also shown how Flowcasting eliminates, or
significantly reduces, a number of planning problems that have
plagued retailers for years: maintaining the right level of inventory
during retail promotions, introducing and discontinuing products,
and conducting effective seasonal planning.

Another area where Flowcasting can make dramatic improvements in retail supply chain management concerns the management
of "slow sellers" -- items that sell very few units over a relatively long
period of time. Traditionally, retailers have found it a burden to manage slow sellers, since they typically require the same resources (people time and computational power) as high-velocity items.
Nonetheless, in aggregate, slow sellers can make an important bottom line contribution. This chapter will demonstrate how
Flowcasting enables you to easily manage slow selling items at the
retail shelf level.

Flowcasting Slow Sellers

Flowcasting slow sellers at store level is made possible by deploying a technique that has been around for years and has been successfully applied in manufacturing and distribution: the computation of forecast consumption.

In this chapter, we'll review:

1. Forecast consumption
2. Developing Flowcasting plans for slow sellers
3. Benefits of a consistent planning process

Forecast Consumption

As outlined in previous chapters, Flowcasting produces forecasts of consumer demand at store level in specific time periods for a year into the future. While the forecast period for many products is weekly, the process allows forecasts to be developed for monthly or quarterly time periods (or longer), if necessary. A longer time period can be used for items that are very slow sellers, since they require less forecasting effort, are easier to understand, and are more accurate. For example, suppose that an item sold 2 units per month, on average. That's easy to understand versus stating that the same item sells "half of one unit per week."

Once you decide to forecast an item over a longer time frame, the question becomes, "What happens to the remaining forecast as you move through that time period?" In other words, if in the example above the forecast was for 2 units for the month, what happens to the forecast as the first day passes into history, then the next day, the next day after that, and so forth until the current month becomes history?

Forecast consumption is a technique for dealing with the unknown timing of actual demand within a forecast period.

For example, you may be able to say, with some degree of accuracy, that a given product will sell 3 units during a month. Suppose that the 3 units forecasted to sell during the month are spread evenly across each week, or 0.75 units per week. Now suppose that you sold 2 units during the first week as shown in Figure 9.1.

	Weeks			
	1	2	3	4
Sales	2			

Figure 9.1: Overselling the first week for an item selling 3 units per month.

The question then becomes, "What will the sales forecast be for the rest of the month?" Using forecast consumption, treat this as a timing problem by first assuming that the best estimate of sales for the entire month is still the original forecast of 3. The fact that 2 have sold in the first week means that the remaining unit should sell sometime in the next three weeks. The calculation takes the remaining forecast for the month (1) and divides it by the remaining periods in the month (3) to give a revised weekly forecast of 0.33.

Without forecast consumption, the first week will be dropped off into history -- that is, the time period has passed, and it was assumed that since the forecast for that week was 0.75, then 0.75 units were sold. Three weeks remain with an average forecast of 0.75 per week. This gives a remaining forecast of 2.25 for the rest of the month. This would have the effect of inflating the forecast to 4.25 for the month (the 2 that have already sold, and the remaining forecast of 2.25). It is generally not prudent to change the forecast on the basis of the higher than the expected average first week's sales. That's because the first week may be a poor indicator of the total month, and a longer forecast period can compensate for weekly variations.

There is another forecasting alternative for the preceding situation. Some supply chain management professionals would argue that since 2 sold in the first week, the best estimate of sales for the month would be 8. Yet, if you look at the statistical results for all products that sold more than expected in the first week of a month, most did not maintain the same weekly rate of sales for the month; otherwise, over time, their monthly average would be higher. There were some peaks and valleys, and it just happened that the first week was a peak.

It's an interesting exercise to ask those people who would argue that the most accurate forecast is 8 what the monthly forecast should be for the product below, depicted in Figure 9.2?

	Weeks			
	1	2	3	4
Sales	0			

Figure 9.2: Underselling the first week for an item selling 3 units per month.

If you apply the same logic used to get 8 in the example above, the answer would be zero, because you're assuming that what happened in the first week will happen in the remaining weeks of the month. Yet most people would be uncomfortable with predicting zero for the entire month, based on the first week's results.

Flowcasting is a natural fit for using forecast consumption to plan slow sellers since it replans every item, in every store as daily sales are recorded. The forecasts are constantly being reviewed and compared to actual sales and, if necessary, adjusted via the consumption logic outlined above. If the forecast changes, then this triggers a re-calculation of dependent demand throughout the entire retail supply chain.

At store level, forecast consumption works equally well for high- and very low volume items. Some products will be forecasted in weekly time periods. Others will be forecasted in monthly, quarterly, and even half-year time periods.

The mechanics of forecast consumption are the same regardless of the time period. We expect to sell some inventory over the time period, but cannot say exactly when in the time period the sales will actually take place. Even if one or several days (or weeks) have sales that are higher (or lower) than normal, there's no reason to change the sales forecast, because you don't have good information to make that prediction, given the nature of how the product sells (e.g., sometimes this period, sometimes the next).

Developing Flowcasting Plans for Slow Sellers

A good Flowcasting process makes use of forecast consumption to forecast and manage slow selling items at store level. First, specific items that need longer forecast periods must be identified. It is a straightforward matter to review the items and determine which ones should be forecast and what time periods (weekly, monthly, or quarterly) are desirable.

They're usually products that are not driven by promotions or advertising; people have a specific need for them and make a purchasing decisions when they need the item. In other words, they sell randomly. And trying to predict random sales is fruitless. Yet, today, considerable computational effort is spent trying to develop algorithms to predict precisely when a slow selling item will move off the shelves.

In addition to using a longer forecast period and forecast consumption, a good Flowcasting process uses an approach called "integer forecasting*" for slow selling items. If an item normally sells in volumes of ones or twos, then doesn't it make sense that the forecast should be in ones or twos as well? The process determines the average integer rate of sale and uses this number to randomly place this quantity on a specific day during the forecast time period.

Given enough slow selling items for a specific store, the random nature of the forecasts will naturally place the forecasts on different dates within the overall forecast period -- that is, all the integer forecasts for the potentially hundreds of slow selling items will not fall on the same day of the forecast period.

If the forecasts are not placed randomly, all the products would have some portion of the forecast in the first time period. This is a problem with most approaches for forecasting slow sellers. First, it is not indicative of how the product will sell. Customers don't go to the store to buy 0.2 units of a product; they go to buy the product. And, if the forecast is a small amount in the first time period, the replenishment plan could easily generate a planned arrival for this product and all other slow selling products. People using this information for operational and financial planning would be using erroneous information and potentially making poor decisions as a result.

* The authors wish to acknowledge that the idea of integer forecasting is that of Darryl V. Landvater. Mr. Landvater is one of the pioneers in time-phased planning systems and has worked closely with the authors for more than 15 years.

For example, let's consider a product at store 108 that sells on average 2 units a month, and has been doing so for some time. Further, suppose that the 2 units are sold in ones. That is, sometime during the month someone will buy one unit and, at some other time, someone else (presumably) will buy the other unit.

The Flowcasting process would forecast this item for store 108 in monthly time periods. Given that the selling pattern is 1 unit per sale, the process would randomly forecast 1 unit on a specific day during the month and then another unit on another day during the month.

Figure 9.3 depicts the Flowcasting plan for the slow selling item, forecasted in monthly periods. The monthly forecast is for 2 units.

PRODUCT: 12131415 – Slow selling product

LOCATION: Store 108

Current On Hand Balance:	2 units
Minimum Store Ordering Quantity:	1 unit
Store Receiving Schedule:	Monday, Wednesday and Friday only
Replenishment Lead-Time from RDC1:	2 days

	Days									
	M	T	W	Th	F	Sa	Su	M	T	W
Total Forecast						1				
Min Display Qty	2	2	2	2	2	2	2	2	2	2
In Transits										
Projected On Hand	2	2	2	2	3	2	2	2	2	2
Planned Arrivals					1					
Planned Orders			1							

Figure 9.3: Daily Flowcasting plan for a slow selling product for store 108 using integer forecasting.

Notice that a forecast of 1 unit has been randomly assigned to the first Saturday of the month and perhaps the second unit is on Tuesday of the last week (not shown).

In addition, notice that a planned arrival is scheduled to arrive on Friday in order to keep the shelf display (Min Display Qty) at 2 units. By now you know that this planned arrival will be passed to the RDC as dependent demand. The RDC will use and aggregate that number with store 802's dependent demand for this item, thereby arriving at the RDC's total forecast. The RDC would develop a time-phased plan to support the demand and pass its dependent demand on to the MDC, and so on, until the retail chain is linked from store shelf to factory floor.

To return to our example, suppose that Monday passes and no sales occurred for the item. No re-forecasting will be required, since the assumptions have been true so far (i.e., we expected zero on the Monday and zero occurred). Suppose that the first Thursday passes and no sale occurred on that day, even though our integer forecasting approach forecast one unit. The process will then keep the monthly forecast at 2 units and randomly assign the forecast of 2 single units somewhere across the remaining days in the month. Once this product is re-forecast and the 2 units were randomly assigned to the remaining days of the month, the Flowcasting process would calculate a new plan (such as the one is shown Figure 9.3) and the resulting dependent demand would cascade throughout the entire retail supply chain.

To show the ramifications of not using forecast consumption/integer forecasting, suppose that the forecasting process was in monthly time periods, but that the forecast was spread evenly across the month. That is, 1/30 of the 2 units, or approximately .07 units, are expected to sell each day. The Flowcasting plan in this case is exhibited in Figure 9.4.

PRODUCT: 12131415 – Slow selling product

LOCATION: Store 108

Current On Hand Balance:	2 units
Minimum Store Ordering Quantity:	1 unit
Store Receiving Schedule:	Monday, Wednesday and Friday only
Replenishment Lead-Time from RDC1:	2 days

	Days									
	M	T	W	Th	F	Sa	Su	M	T	W
Total Forecast	0.07	0.07	0.07	0.07	0.07	0.07	0.07	0.07	0.07	0.07
Min Display Qty	2	2	2	2	2	2	2	2	2	2
In Transits										
Projected On Hand	2.93	2.86	2.79	2.72	2.65	2.58	2.51	2.44	2.37	2.30
Planned Arrivals	1									
Planned Orders										

Figure 9.4: Daily Flowcasting plan for a slow selling product for store 108 with forecast spread evenly across each day of the month.

Notice the difference between this plan and the Flowcasting plan depicted in Figure 9.3. Which one is more realistic and likely to happen? In Figure 9.4, you expect to sell .07 units on Monday. Suppose that Monday passes and you don't sell any units -- the forecast will only be for the remaining 29 days x .07, or 1.93 units. Worse, suppose that one unit did sell on the first day. In that case, the remaining forecast for the month would still be 1.93 units. But now you've changed your monthly forecast to 1 (the actual sale on the first day) plus 1.93, which equals 2.93 units. This hardly makes sense and is quite dangerous from a planning perspective.

Now let's return to the Flowcasting plan shown in Figure 9.3 and apply the integer forecasting approach. Remember that the integer forecasting approach will determine that this item sells -- based on history -- 1 unit at a time and, in total, about 2 per month. Integer forecasting will forecast 2 units per month and randomly place two specific forecasts of 1 unit on two days during the month.

If Monday passes and no sales occur, then the remaining forecast will still be 2 units, which are planned (in units of 1) on the original forecast dates. If one sale did occur on Monday, the remaining forecast for the month (based on the forecast assumption) would be 1 unit (the original forecast of 2 units, less 1 unit of actual sales to date). This one unit would then be randomly placed on a specific day during the remaining 29 days of the month. By chance, if on the Monday 2 units sold, then the remaining forecast for the rest of the month would be zero. Forecast consumption avoids the problem of lack of forecast integrity -- that is, keeping the forecast the same for the time period as this time period becomes history. This ensures that the forecast is stable and doesn't react to "noise," thereby ensuring that downstream planning is stable as well.

Another problem that the integer forecast approach avoids is that of "bunching" of planned arrivals. To illustrate the problem, let's return to the example shown in Figure 9.4. Notice that the projected on hand balance requires an immediate planned arrival, since .07 units are expected to sell on the first day. The effect is that a number of planned arrivals would be "bunched" around similar dates, which is not realistic.

This "bunching" situation would apply to many items in a retail environment if the forecast is evenly spread across the monthly planning horizon. Suppose you had hundreds, perhaps thousands, of items that could potentially "bunch" around specific dates. This situation would not only be an invalid simulation of reality, but it would send the wrong signals to all members of the extended retail supply chain. The RDC would see demand forecasts in "lumpy" patterns around the bunched dates. In turn, they would calculate Flowcasting plans that would also reflect this bunching phenomena and the dependent demand passed among supply chain partners would be erroneous. Further, people working in operational planning could make capacity-related decisions based on a distorted view of projected demand (Operational Planning will be discussed in Chapter 10).

The use of integer forecasting and forecast consumption makes all of the preceding problems disappear. Since the forecasts are random, there is little chance that all the item forecasts will be bunched around the same date. Integer forecasting reflects the manner in which the product will sell (i.e., people buy products, not .07 of a product), while forecast consumption maintains the forecast integrity for the forecast time period. Both are fundamental approaches used in Flowcasting to manage slow selling items. The result is that a consistent planning approach can be used for all products across all trading partners.

Benefits of a Consistent Process

An important benefit of Flowcasting is that a single, consistent process is used to plan all items throughout the extended retail supply chain. While the techniques and approaches may differ somewhat for specific types of items, the basic planning approach remains the same. Forecasts of consumer demand at store level drive all other demand in the retail supply chain. While slow selling items naturally lend themselves to forecasting over longer time horizons, integer forecasting and forecast consumption ensure that the planning process is the same. A Flowcasting plan is developed at store level for all items. Dependent demand is then calculated and cascades down the entire supply chain.

Today, for most retailers, there is no single, consistent process for managing the most difficult challenges facing a retail supply chain: slow sellers, promotions, seasonal items, product introductions, and discontinuations. The result, as shown in previous chapters, is poor performance, lower customer service levels, and lost sales.

By contrast, a consistent process -- Flowcasting -- enables a retail supply chain to function with maximum efficiency and profitability. While it may be tempting to "skip over" slow selling items in the planning process, you would still be left with two separate processes for managing items, likely supported by two separate systems. In addition, you would only provide supply chain visibility for only a portion of the total volume. Trading partners would need to perform additional forecasting in order to develop plans. And there is little chance that the forecasts would be in synch with current marketing and merchandising plans.

The approaches and techniques outlined in this chapter eliminate the need for a separate process for slow selling items. While slow sellers do have their nuances, they follow the same basic planning approach used for other items.

Summary

In this chapter, we've shown how to manage slow selling items by using a Flowcasting process. Here are the key points to remember:

1. Slow selling items can be forecast over longer time horizons at store level. This simplifies forecasting and makes it easier for demand planners to predict the slow sellers' behavior.
2. Forecast consumption is a technique used to maintain the forecast integrity over the forecast time horizon.
3. For slow selling items, integer forecasting is a technique that ensures that sales plans reflect the sporadic selling pattern of these types of items.
4. Flowcasting uses a single process for both slow sellers and faster sellers, thereby reducing costs for education, training, and system support and maintenance.

The next chapter covers another important planning process for retailers and their trading partners -- operational planning. You'll learn how the Flowcasting process greatly improves operational planning and results in better asset utilization and reduced costs.

CHAPTER   10

Operational Planning
Planning Future Capacity

At this point, you've seen how Flowcasting uses a single forecast of consumer demand, generated at the retail store level, to manage the flow of inventory through each node of the supply chain. And you've seen how Flowcasting greatly reduces retail out-of-stocks for promoted items; how Flowcasting simplifies the introduction and discontinuation of products in the retail supply chain; how Flowcasting minimizes many of the problems that plague seasonal planning today; and how forecast consumption and integer forecasting can be used within the Flowcasting process to manage slow moving items. On a day-to-day basis, Flowcasting also provides the information needed to ensure that product is delivered on-time and cost-effectively; that is, Flowcasting makes it possible to conduct effective operational planning.

Operational planning, a key component of any supply chain, concerns the management of capacities. By capacities we mean *people, equipment, space, and capital.* Regardless of the company or industry, these capacities represent limited resources and often become major constraints in a company's ability to produce, distribute, market and sell products across retail supply chains. The best way to avoid a constraint (a shortage of capacity) is to anticipate the problem and find a solution. This chapter explores how Flowcasting can be used to zero in and solve problems before they become constraints.

Operational Planning Using Flowcasting

Those who work in retail supply chain management know how operational capacity issues can prevent the flow of goods from the factory to the store shelf. They're especially frustrating and damaging when they occur during promotional periods, or worse, during make-or-break periods such as the back-to-school and holiday seasons. The rule is simple: no product, no sale. And for product to be available, operations — primarily transportation and distribution — need to deliver — on-time and cost effectively.

Operational planning involves processes that are used to plan the capacity of people, equipment, space, and capital, necessary to distribute and transport product within the extended retail supply chain. Many retailers have well-defined distribution functions for receiving shipments from suppliers and preparing shipments to stores. In addition, retailers usually have transportation departments that schedule deliveries to the stores and, in some cases, are responsible for picking up shipments from suppliers.

The operational planning challenge for retail supply chains is volume — keeping track of large numbers of shipments and deliveries, and determining if, when, and where capacity is needed. To add to the challenge, capacity must be added cost effectively; unexpected capacity needs can be extremely expensive to fulfill, due to the lack of visibility on the part of the trading partners. Flowcasting provides the required visibility for all nodes and functions in the retail supply chain. It provides actionable information that can be used to make cost-effective decisions and lay the foundations for operational excellence.

In this chapter, we'll review:

1. Foundations for operational excellence
2. Capacity planning using Flowcasting
3. Transportation planning using Flowcasting
4. Improving product flow using new distribution methods

Foundations for Operational Excellence

For years, the people working in operations, particularly on the retail side, have been hampered by processes and systems that can't provide long-term visibility into what's planned. Rather, the systems are focused on the next order, the next shipment, or the next receipt. To compensate, people in operations planning often develop their own forecasts of future volumes, shipments, receipts, inventory projections, and capacities. They piece this information together through a combination of history, experience, and what's been planned in marketing. The result, of course, is a set of numbers that likely has little to do with demand at the retail shelf — which, in turn, means that operations will not likely be in sync with the real needs of the supply chain.

Flowcasting makes such guessing a thing of the past by providing:

1. *A single set of numbers* — the Flowcasting process plans the entire retail supply chain from store shelf to raw material supplier. As such, everyone working in operations (i.e., DC planners, transportation planners) is "singing from the same hymnbook", so to speak.
2. *Long-term visibility is provided* — therefore, all *"ad hoc"* operational forecasting is eliminated; the outputs of the Flowcasting process are converted into the "language" of operations planners: cube, weight, picks, hours, etc.

Single Set of Numbers

Figure 10.1 outlines pictorially how the Flowcasting process dramatically simplifies operational planning. Since the information is at the most granular level possible, projections can be calculated based on multiplying specific information by a specific unit of measure; this provides what's needed for specific tasks. For example, multiplying each product's planned arrivals by the cubic feet of each product and summing the results provides a projection of the cubic volume to be received. This volume can be compared to available capacity.

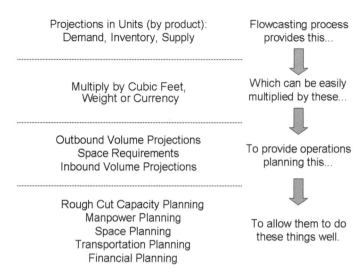

Projections in Units (by product): Demand, Inventory, Supply	Flowcasting process provides this...
Multiply by Cubic Feet, Weight or Currency	Which can be easily multiplied by these...
Outbound Volume Projections Space Requirements Inbound Volume Projections	To provide operations planning this...
Rough Cut Capacity Planning Manpower Planning Space Planning Transportation Planning Financial Planning	To allow them to do these things well.

Figure 10.1: Converting demand projections into the language of operations.

Note that, at the bottom level, the projections inform the financial process of expected dollar projections which is important for financial planning and activities like Sales & Operations Planning (S&OP). Flowcasting ensures that these financial projections are directly linked to current business plans and reflect what is actually transacting at the retail shelf. (Financial Planning is covered in depth in Chapter 11).

With Flowcasting, product plans, transportation, and capacity plans for stores, distribution centers, and plants are developed from the same set of numbers. As a result, the effects of decisions in one department are visible to others. For example, buyers won't create space constraints for distribution by unknowingly planning more product purchases than can be stored. Instead, the distribution staff and buyer can see the impact ahead of time and develop a plan that either handles the volume or changes the purchase.

The key point is that, in a Flowcasting world, all the time and effort that people in operations planning spend trying to predict their future is eliminated. Their effort is replaced with accurate, up-to-date projections of the future formatted in the language of operations. People spend their time preparing for and managing the future, rather than guessing what will happen and reacting to unexpected — and often unwelcome — events.

Visibility

Imagine how unproductive you would be if you knew only your daily schedule for the next hour or your weekly schedule for the next day. You'd be hard pressed to be prepared and conduct your business proactively. The same is true for supply chain planning. Visibility of required capacity is the key to good planning and to operational excellence.

The Flowcasting process provides planners with a long-missing tool: a consistent planning approach that provides supply chain-wide visibility for both the short and long term. Let's say that the situation represented in Figure 10.2 represents the cubic volume of prod-

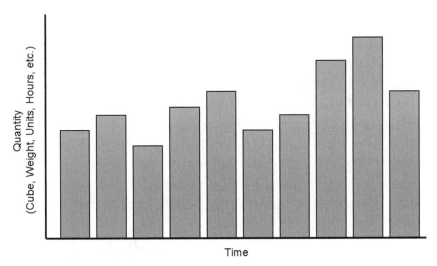

Figure 10.2: Visibility of required capacity provided by Flowcasting.

uct that a DC needs to receive during the next few weeks. The spikes in volume towards the end of the chart represent more volume than can be received in a week. Without the visibility provided by Flowcasting, this represents a major problem; since the volume was unplanned, additional cost will be incurred in terms of short-term overtime or outside storage space.

Most DCs respond to peaks in receiving by adding overtime *after* a backlog has occurred or by forcing trucks to wait for an appointment. The former is expensive while the latter jeopardizes product availability. The reason for these backlogs is limited visibility of the projected inbound flow of products. Flowcasting changes this situation since the visibility of the inbound flow is provided and can be converted to any operational language. So, in the example above, the chart could represent a number of different views of capacity including:

- Cube to be received
- Hours needed to unload
- Hours needed to put away product
- Weight to be shipped between a particular source and destination
- Inventory space required at any location
- Number of trucks to be received

2. Capacity Planning Using Flowcasting

The visibility provided by the Flowcasting process puts the power of operational planning where it belongs: with people. Since people can see what is likely to happen, they can identify potential capacity problems and develop preemptive solutions. In our collective experiences, people will always arrive at better solutions to resolve problems than trying to program a computer to handle them. The Flowcasting process forces people to collaborate. And since everyone is working from a single set of numbers, they understand that any proposed change ripples through the supply chain in a predictable manner. What a contrast to the traditional way of doing business in a supply chain, whereby one department or trading partner optimizes its operations at the expense of others!

Rough Cut Capacity Planning

The Flowcasting process produces planned shipments and resulting inventory projections from supplier to retail store for all locations in the retail supply chain. These could be from an RDC to a store, an

MDC to an RDC, a plant to an MDC, or any combination of the preceding. These shipment and inventory projections are used for rough cut capacity planning. As the name suggests, rough cut capacity planning is a rough check to determine if demand and capacity are in balance; that is, whether the capacity of manpower, transportation equipment, storage space, and receiving and shipping equipment is available to satisfy projected demand.

Receiving Capacity

Figure 10.3 shows projected receiving volumes at RDC1. It illustrates how Flowcasting provides planners with expected inbound volumes which, in turn, will require people and equipment (i.e., capacity) in order to receive the quantities of product that will arrive.

The aggregate planned receipts, which will impact RDC1, were developed by multiplying the product-by-product planned receipts by their respective cube and weight, then totaling them to provide an aggregate projection of future receiving capacity. While the plan shown in Figure 10.3 only depicts the next few weeks, the

Receiving Measure	Week 1	Week 2	Week 3	Week 4	Week 5	Week 6
Number of trucks	161	185	194	221	269	184
Weight (000's lbs)	6,440	7,380	7,708	8,824	10,700	7,280
Cube (cubic feet)	248,000	304,000	296,000	344,000	412,000	280,000

Figure 10.3: Receiving volume for RDC1.

Flowcasting process would provide a capacity plan for many weeks and months into the future. This allows planners to develop capacity plans for meeting future projections and eliminating (or dramatically minimizing) the surprises mentioned earlier. The result will be improved product flows and reduced costs.

Suppose that, for an initial rough cut at capacity planning, the operational people at a distribution center have reviewed the planned inbound cube and compared it to normal operating capacity, as outlined in Figure 10.4.

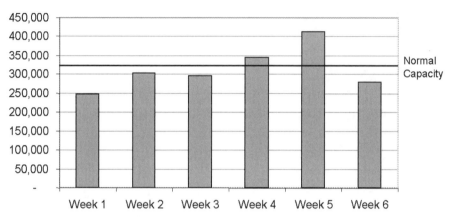

Receiving Capacity Plan

Figure 10.4: Receiving capacity compared to normal capacity for inbound cube.

This complete picture give distribution professionals visibility into what is required in terms of receiving capacity days or weeks into the future, and how that capacity requirement maps to their available capacity.

In the example shown in Figure 10.4, the DC would have to consider other options for receiving the inbound cube in weeks 4 and 5. For example, they could decide to work additional overtime to meet the inbound volume. Or they could work with the Flowcasting teams to potentially move up an inbound receipt to an earlier week when capacity is available (e.g., in week 3). Regardless of the choice, the Flowcasting process enables people to work together and see the supply chain-wide impacts of any decision they make.

As a rule, capacity plans such as the one represented in Figure 10.4 are shown in days for the first two weeks, then in weekly intervals. Once a plan has been developed that is within the capacity of the DC (manpower, equipment, and storage space), the focus shifts to execution. Since the capacity plan generated by Flowcasting provides visibility many days and weeks into the future, it's possible to make changes for receiving some products earlier than originally planned.

By making decisions in advance of the actual receipt, DC professionals can avoid capacity constraints and improve on-shelf availability while reducing operating costs.

Traditional planning processes are not integrated to this extent. Since they provide little, if any, visibility beyond the next order, they force operations teams into a continual fire-fighting mode. In a Flowcasting environment, the focus shifts to fire prevention. Good forward planning information allows people to make good decisions that will keep product flowing with minimal disruption.

Space Planning
In addition to receiving capacity, the Flowcasting process provides the information necessary to answer the following operations questions: How much space will you need next month? Next year? Will you need to rent space at any time, and if so, for how long? Without Flowcasting, it is difficult to answer these questions, since they are dependent on a number of variables such as sales forecasts, new product introductions, changes in product sizes and weights, or any other factors that may impact space requirements.

In the same way that the Flowcasting process provides planned receiving capacity by location, it can be used to predict space requirements by location. The projected on hand balance extended by the cube or number of cases or pallets, per product, yields the total space requirements. Figure 10.5, which shows the projected inventory space required for RDC1, illustrates this concept.

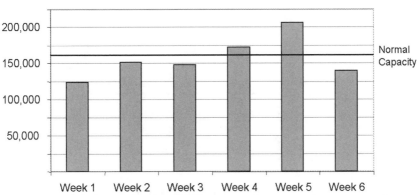

Figure 10.5: Space plan for RDC1 compared to normal space capacity.

The situation shown in Figure 10.5 requires that action be taken in weeks 4 and 5 to avoid a space constraint at RDC1 — plenty of time to choose an appropriate option. Imagine having this kind of information weeks, months and an entire year into the future! It would provide the timely information required to make decisions regarding planned product flows, including when to acquire additional space.

Manpower and Equipment Planning

Distribution and logistics managers also need to be able to predict the manpower and equipment needs by location. Flowcasting makes such prediction easy. The calculation reflects the hours needed to load and unload trucks, railcars, etc. The planned receipts and planned shipments in and out of RDC1 represent the shipments that have to be loaded and unloaded at RDC1. By extending these planned shipments by the labor hours, capacity requirements can be generated and displayed. Figure 10.6 depicts the total manpower requirements for receiving and shipping at RDC1.

Although Figure 10.6 shows the number of required person hours at RDC1, the process it represents can also be used for forklift trucks or any other piece of material handling equipment, including delivery trucks. The point is that since the Flowcasting process pro-

Figure 10.6: Capacity planning for total person hours at RDC1.

duces projections at the most granular level possible, the data can be easily converted into any projection that any department or group needs to do its job.

Additional Views of Capacity

In Chapter 8, we outlined how the Flowcasting process provides a superior approach to managing a seasonal business. Given that the process starts at the retail shelf and cascades dependent demand throughout the entire supply chain, accurate projections of seasonal volumes, including timing of product flows, is provided. As shown above, these projections can be converted to capacity requirements and planned for in advance.

Long-term capacity planning is especially helpful for companies that have seasonal demands. It can help to eliminate the need for people who must be hired on short notice to cover seasonal peaks or other significant changes in the level of work. With Flowcasting, people can see such situations developing ahead of time and plan for them accordingly.

Similarly, the Flowcasting process provides the information needed to determine the number of order picks required by the distribution team to satisfy store demand. Since the process is driven by store-level projections, totaling the demand by product and by time period provides an excellent estimate of the picks required in the DC over the planning horizon.

Since the Flowcasting process links the entire retail supply chain, capacity planning can take place at every node. How often have store managers complained that they weren't prepared for the volume of receiving in a particular week? By using a Flowcasting approach, they would see projected receipts for weeks and would have planned accordingly. They would also be easily able to predict inventory investments (covered in Chapter 11) and space requirements using the approaches described above. The information provided by Flowcasting finally gives all members of the extended retail supply chain the information required to excel at operations planning and execution, regardless of location — store, DC, or factory.

So how significant is visibility for capacity planning? Pioneering companies that are using Flowcasting to plan capacities are realizing productivity improvements of 20-25 percent in asset utilization. The improvements result from being able to make decisions based on future plans, not what is happening today or tomorrow.

3. Transportation Planning Using Flowcasting

The Flowcasting process provides the accurate information needed to improve transportation planning, especially load building, which entails creating effective loads between source location and destination location, by shipping method (truck, railcar, boat, etc.). For example, effective load building would plan full truckloads from a retail or manufacturing distribution center while meeting the constraints of the affected trading partners.

The power of Flowcasting is extended by also factoring in operational constraints above SKU level; unless this is done, inventory will be ordered independently for each SKU exactly when it's needed. In retail, which typically has a large SKU count, it would not be uncommon to have a planned shipment from a supplier to a distribution center every day of the week. Obviously, ordering and delivering every day from the same supplier is costly in terms of receiving and transportation.

The solution is to use the planned shipments from the Flowcasting process, along with some simple consolidation rules for pulling ahead planned shipments into more cost effective (i.e., fuller) loads. The example shown in Figure 10.7 illustrates the concept. It shows how the planned shipments, in cubic feet, might look across 10 SKUs for a single source/destination pair. In this example, we consider the planned shipments from a supplier (MDC1) to the retail distribution center (RDC1). Note that the concept is exactly the same regardless of the source and the destination — we could just as easily be showing how the process works for the planned shipments from the RDC1 to a particular store, or a group of stores.

As you can see from the "TOTAL" line in Figure 10.7, shipments are scheduled on the supplier/DC link every day for the next 3 weeks.

Source   MDC1
Destination RDC1

SKU	Week 1					Week 2					Week 3				
	M	T	W	Th	F	M	T	W	Th	F	M	T	W	Th	F
1234567	100			100			300							100	
1234568		450				500				350					600
1234569					500								300		
1234570			300					300					300		
1234571				3000				100							50
1234572	100					150					150				
1234573			280						100				260		
1234574		100										100			
1234575				2000										100	
1234576			250								200				
TOTAL	**200**	**550**	**830**	**5100**	**500**	**650**	**300**	**400**	**100**	**350**	**350**	**100**	**860**	**200**	**650**

Figure 10.7: Planned shipments from source to destination for 10 products in cubic feet for the next 3 weeks, by day.

Given that a trailer can hold about 2,400 cubic feet of material, the total cube that's scheduled to be shipped most days is far less than a truckload. To make things more challenging, the total cube each day represents *planned* shipments. Transportation can't start scheduling pick-ups until they become firm purchase orders, at which point enough time is allotted only to transport them to the destination, with little opportunity for consolidation. As a result, the scheduling function will be forced to deal with 15 pickups from the supplier over the next 3 weeks. Assuming that transportation won't run out of trucks, they may try to fill up trucks across multiple suppliers in the same region on the same days. The alternative is to hold product until optimal truckloads can be filled and risk delivering late. Typically, this is how it is done today, requiring extra work by the transportation planners and costly, time consuming multi-stop pick-ups. This extra work by the transportation group is unnecessary for the sake of an extra couple of days of inventory.

While our example is somewhat exaggerated, you can see how this type of situation could occur if a large number of products is flowing between a source/destination. Once again, Flowcasting allows us to avoid the problem. To understand how, let's start with two key principles:

1. The output of the Flowcasting process is a schedule of planned shipments that must be adhered to in order to satisfy demand. As such, product may ship earlier than the date assigned by the process, but never later.
2. Load building can be done prior to order creation. This is because there is fundamentally no difference between a planned shipment and a purchase order line. They both contain a product number, a ship date and a unit quantity (which can be transformed into cubic feet by item).

Given these two principles, we know that all of the planned shipments for the entire planning horizon are available to build loads, and that shipments can be pulled ahead, but never pushed off for the purposes of load building.

If you now assume that the constraint on a truckload is 2,400 cubic feet, then the load building problem becomes easier. (Note that the same logic applies if different transportation modes exist between the source/destination, such as shipping containers.) All that remains is to decide how far in advance we are willing to pull ahead planned shipments to try to build efficient loads. For simplicity, we'll use 3 days (i.e., we're willing to hold a *maximum* of 3 days of additional inventory to gain transportation and operational efficiencies). Figure 10.8 outlines the initial step in the load building process.

As shown, we must ship 200 cubic feet on Monday of Week 1. We're willing to look ahead to Thursday (i.e., 3 days) for planned shipments that may be candidates to pull ahead to Monday. We also know that we can only pull ahead to top up the next incremental 2,400 cubic feet of product.

From the cubed out plan, we know that we can pull ahead all of the shipments for Tuesday and Wednesday into Monday without exceeding trailer capacity. If we do this, the truck will be filled to 1,580 cubic feet (200 + 550 + 830). We only have room for another 820 cubic feet, so we can't pull *all* of the planned shipments for

Source   MDC1

Destination   RDC1

SKU	Week 1					Week 2					Week 3				
	M	T	W	Th	F	M	T	W	Th	F	M	T	W	Th	F
1234567	100			100			300							100	
1234568		450				500				350					600
1234569					500								300		
1234570			300					300					300		
1234571				3000				100							50
1234572	100					150					150				
1234573			280						100				260		
1234574		100										100			
1234575				2000										100	
1234576			250										200		
TOTAL	200	550	830	5100	500	650	300	400	100	350	350	100	860	200	650

Figure 10.8: Initial step of load building process, consolidating planned shipments from MDC1 to RDC1.

Thursday ahead. But we can pull ahead the planned shipment for SKU #1234567, which is only 100 cubic feet. At this point, the load plan would be represented by the diagram shown in Figure 10.9.

The next "must" shipment is 5,000 cubic feet on Thursday of Week 1. This means that we have 2 planned trucks filled to capacity (2 x 2400 = 4800) plus 200 cube of spillover into a third truck. Adhering to the principles we have previously established, we know that we can't push off shipments. That means we need to try to build

Source   MDC1

Destination   RDC1

SKU	Week 1					Week 2					Week 3				
	M	T	W	Th	F	M	T	W	Th	F	M	T	W	Th	F
1234567	200						300							100	
1234568	450					500				350					600
1234569					500								300		
1234570	300							300					300		
1234571				3000				100							50
1234572	100					150					150				
1234573	280								100				260		
1234574	100											100			
1234575				2000										100	
1234576	250												200		
TOTAL	1680			5000	500	650	300	400	100	350	350	100	860	200	650

Figure 10.9: Continuation of load building process, consolidating planned shipments from MDC1 to RDC1.

a third load of 2400 units on Thursday for a total of 7,200 cubic feet. By using the same logic as before, we can look ahead for the next 3 days to find planned shipment quantities to add to the third load, as depicted in Figure 10.10.

Source   MDC1
Destination   RDC1

SKU	Week 1					Week 2					Week 3				
	M	T	W	Th	F	M	T	W	Th	F	M	T	W	Th	F
1234567	200						300							100	
1234568	450					500				350					600
1234569					500								300		
1234570	300							300					300		
1234571				3000				100							50
1234572	100					150					150				
1234573	280								100				260		
1234574	100											100			
1234575				2000										100	
1234576	250										200				
TOTAL	1680			5000	500	650	300	400	100	350	350	100	860	200	650

Figure 10.10: Continuation of load building process, consolidating planned shipments.

By continuing this process for the remainder of the planning horizon, we have time-phased loads built out into the future as depicted in Figure 10.11.

Source   MDC1
Destination   RDC1

SKU	Week 1					Week 2					Week 3				
	M	T	W	Th	F	M	T	W	Th	F	M	T	W	Th	F
1234567	200			300								100			
1234568	450			500				350				600			
1234569				500								300			
1234570	300							300				300			
1234571				3000				100				50			
1234572	100			150				150							
1234573	280							100				260			
1234574	100											100			
1234575				2000								100			
1234576	250							200							
TOTAL	1680			6650				1200				1810			

Figure 10.11: Output of load building process, consolidating planned shipments from MDC1 to RDC1 for a 3-week horizon.

By using simple logic based on sound principles, the number of loads has been effectively reduced from 15 to 4, with little additional inventory cost. The additional inventory cost will be more than offset by the transportation savings, making the effort well worthwhile. Companies that are using this approach to build effective loads typically see transportation savings of approximately 10 percent. It is the visibility provided by the Flowcasting process that makes this kind of planning possible — visibility that does not exist using conventional approaches to managing retail supply chains.

Our example is for a horizon of 3 weeks, but the planning horizon for load building can be as short, or as long, as required. Typically, it varies by source/destination combination. For example, you probably wouldn't build loads very far out for the planned shipments from RDC1 to the stores. However, you might plan loads out farther for planned shipments from the MDC1 to RDC1, because order lead time is longer. As a general guideline, the longer the average cumulative lead times between the source/destination combinations the longer the horizon for planning loads.

After the loads have been consolidated, the original Flowcasting plans (in units, for replenishment purposes) would be updated with the new ship dates and shared with the supplier for production planning. Additionally, the cubed out version of the plan would be used for rough cut operational planning (capacity, equipment and manpower) for all downstream facilities in the supply chain.

Accounting for Shipping Schedules

Many retailers work on a fixed shipping schedule between RDCs and stores. In our example, store 108 may only receive shipments from RDC1 on Mondays, Wednesdays and Fridays. The Flowcasting process would reflect this constraint, so planned arrivals would only be scheduled for Mondays, Wednesdays and Fridays. Any load building, as outlined above, would also respect these dates. As a result, store 108 could confidently plan on deliveries on Mondays, Wednesdays and Fridays (e.g., they may schedule receiving only on these days of the week).

Transportation Budgeting

Given that the Flowcasting process produces planned shipments for all source/destination combinations in the extended retail supply chain, information from a Flowcasting system can be a significant help to transportation professionals who create plans and budgets. For example, the plans can be totaled and used to negotiate transportation rates. In some cases, the plans provide powerful proof for the need to purchase additional equipment, such as trucks, trailers, and any other equipment needed to provide the capacity required. The point is that the single set of numbers is driving analysis and the decision making process. This makes budgeting easier, since guesswork is eliminated.

4. Improving Product Flow: Using New Methods

Flowcasting will also improve the methods by which product can flow to the retail store. One example is direct shipments from suppliers, either directly to the store or cross docked through an RDC. Figure 10.12, depicts the basic concept.

With visibility of planned shipments, the manufacturer or

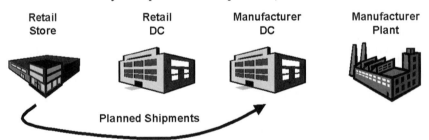

| Retail Store | Retail DC | Manufacturer DC | Manufacturer Plant |

Planned Shipments

Figure 10.12: Using Flowcasting information to plan and ship from supplier to store.

wholesaler can pick and pack the products by store. The store shipments are grouped and shipped either directly to the stores or to the retail RDC and cross docked for shipments to the stores. The Flowcasting process provides the necessary visibility, making the planned shipments to the stores available to the manufacturer weeks in advance.

Flowcasting also makes it possible to efficiently distribute products through a variety of alternative approaches. For example, it may make sense to skip the manufacturer's distribution center for certain shipments because the volume is great enough to justify shipments from the plant directly to the RDC or wholesaler. Many retailers and wholesalers do this today for products on a promotion. Yet, when the volume from a plant to a retail or wholesale DC is made up of many different products (some may be on promotion and others may not), the manufacturers typically do not have the ability to see the total movement of product between two points. That's because there may be many different purchase orders with different delivery dates constituting the load.

A key requirement for changing the distribution channel is visibility; the planned shipments must be available far enough in advance for transportation professionals to seize opportunities to more cost effectively move product via direct shipment. Visibility is critical, since direct shipment requires time to coordinate.

In addition to direct shipment, collaborative distribution also becomes possible when Flowcasting is used to manage a retail supply chain. In this model, manufacturers will be able to collaborate and combine their efforts to reduce the cost of distribution and increase product velocity (see Figure 10.13).

It will be possible for manufacturers to collaborate and partner

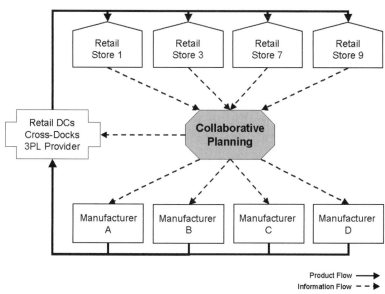

Figure 10.13: Collaborative distribution model.

with other manufacturers to deliver to a common customer at a specific store. Transportation volumes for a group of manufacturers could also be combined by store, affording additional economies. This will result in increased inventory velocity and reduced operating costs for trading partners

An intriguing possibility is the application of this concept to "etailing" and developing a more effective delivery model. Delivering to consumer's homes represents a major cost to etailers and, ultimately, the consumer. A variation on the model outlined above, along with the Flowcasting process, could help make etailing more cost effective, thereby lowering costs for consumers and making this channel more attractive.

Suppose that a number of etailers decided to combine forces and adopt the collaborative model depicted above. Say they decide to open a fulfillment center that stocks the combined offerings from all the etailers in the collaborative group. The distribution costs for all the etailers would be immediately reduced, since the group would share fixed facility costs such as utilities, rent, and depreciation. The etailers would use the Flowcasting process to provide demand projections for their manufacturing partners, thereby lowering inventory costs. And by using the methods outlined earlier in this chapter, the etailers would lower transportation costs to the fulfillment center as well.

The combined leverage on product volumes would also help in reducing outbound transportation costs. And, given the increased volumes, the etailers would also have greater leverage in negotiating freight rates and agreements with the carriers that fit their model. The benefits of a collaborative distribution model could make etailing more profitable in the future.

Summary

In this chapter, we've looked at how the Flowcasting process improves operational planning. Here are the key points to remember:

1. The Flowcasting process provides projections of demand, inventory, and supply at the most granular level (by store and by product). This information can be multiplied by product factors (such as cube and weight) to provide projections that are useful to operations planners.
2. The Flowcasting process provides both the short- and long-term information required to improve operational planning. Since the process is a simulation of what is going to happen in the future, this information can be used for capacity and transportation planning.
3. Operational planners cannot work in isolation from other departments and other companies (for example, suppliers). Rather, everyone must work together and arrive at solutions that provide top-notch service and reduce costs.
4. Since the Flowcasting process provides accurate projections, it can be used to develop transportation freight budgets, negotiate freight rates, and justify the purchase of equipment.
5. The Flowcasting process will enable the deployment of new distribution methods. The new methods will be used to avoid potential problems and reduce costs.

The next chapter covers another important planning process for retailers and their trading partners: financial planning. You'll learn how the Flowcasting process greatly improves financial planning which, in turn, results in better decision making and improved bottom line performance.

C   H   A   P   T   E   R   1   1

Flowcasting and Business Planning
Managing a Retail Business by One Set of Numbers

In the early days of data processing, financial systems were the first to be computerized in manufacturing companies. That's because financial systems worked well manually, and to automate a system that already works is a relatively straightforward process.

Many manufacturers, after putting payroll, accounts payable, accounts receivable and general ledger on the computer, found that while they might have eliminated some clerical help, the savings were usually more than offset by the cost of the computer and associated IT support. Attention then shifted to the development of management information systems that help people better run their companies. It took many years and millions of dollars to finally understand that the foundations of management information systems in manufacturing environments had to be based on systems that actually worked (just as payroll systems worked even before automation came along). Therein was the problem — back in the 1950s and early 1960s inventory management systems did not work well. At the time, production and inventory management systems were based on the reorder point technique for ordering materials to support production schedules. Reorder point systems were largely ineffective because they did not distinguish dependent from independent demand and were essentially ordering systems focusing attention on what they need and when they need it. In the late sixties, Material Requirements Planning (MRP) became the planning and scheduling tool of choice, because it distinguished dependent from independent demand and was essentially a planning system that focused attention on what was actually *needed*, rather than when product should be ordered.

Over the years, MRP morphed into manufacturing resource planning (MRPII). With a well-functioning MRPII system, people discovered that they could actually create a computer-generated model of their business. Ultimately, MRPII became the basis for what is commonly referred to today as ERP, or Enterprise Resource Planning.

Today, we are witnessing the same phenomenon taking place on the retail side of supply chains. Reorder point systems are proving to be ineffective for planning at the store level, let alone driving the activities of an entire supply chain. And just as reorder point systems were replaced by MRP systems, reorder point-based inventory management and replenishment systems in retail are being replaced by Flowcasting. Retailers and their trading partners are turning to Flowcasting for managing the extended retail supply chain. And they're using output from Flowcasting as inputs for a variety of critical business planning processes.

This chapter illustrates how Flowcasting facilitates superior business planning at three levels: store, RDC, and corporate. It also introduces the concept of Retail Sales & Operations Planning (RS&OP), the counterpart of a process that has been successfully used for years in manufacturing companies to mesh sales, production and inventory goals.

Flowcasting and Business Planning: Store Level

Flowcasting provides opportunities for business planning, whether you're on the management team in finance, merchandising, marketing, sales, store operations, purchasing, transportation, or warehousing.

To use Flowcasting as a business planning tool, we need to start at the "atomic level" — the product at the store shelf. The ability to start planning and modeling at this level sets the stage for multiple levels of aggregations. This can be done by day, week, month, or year, as well as by product, category, store, region, or the company in total. Figure 11.1 shows an example of a Financial Plan for store 108 for product 12345678 for the first seven days of the planning horizon. In this plan:

Total Forecast $ is the forecast in units multiplied by the selling price.

Min Display $ is the minimum display quantity in units multiplied by the projected landed cost.

In Transit $ is the in transit quantity in units multiplied by the store landed cost.

Projected On Hand $ is the projected on hand quantity in units multiplied by the projected landed cost.

Planned Arrivals $ is the planned shipment quantity at receipt date in units multiplied by the projected landed cost.

Gross Margin $ is the gross margin dollars on the sales forecast.

Product: 12345678
Store 108: Plan in $

	Current	1	2	3	4	5	6	7
				Days				
Forecast		9.00	9.00	9.00	24.00	21.00	21.00	24.00
Min Display	4.50	4.50	4.50	4.50	4.50	4.50	4.50	4.50
In Transit								
Projected On Hand	13.50	9.00	22.50	18.00	24.00	13.50	57.00	45.00
Planned Arrivals			18.00		18.00		54.00	
Gross Margin		4.50	4.50	4.50	12.00	10.50	10.50	12.00

Figure 11.1: Store-level financial plan for one product.

The Financial Plan shown in Figure 11.1 is simply the conversion of the Flowcasting plan for store 108 to dollars (or whatever currency would apply). This can be aggregated to serve a variety of purposes. For example, the projected sales, inventory, purchases, and gross margin can be seen on a daily, weekly, monthly, or yearly basis and compared to budgets. The advantage is that financial planners can immediately see any projected variances, rather than waiting until after the period is over (day, week, or month). Assume for example that store 108 has a sales budget of $385K for all products for the coming week. It also has a budget of $1.5 million in inventory, and it will realize $175K in gross margin.

Product: All Products

Store 108: Plan in $ (000's)

	Current	1	2	3	4	5	6	7
		Weeks						
Forecast		386	425	393	400	460	445	475
Min Display	756	756	756	756	756	756	762	762
In Transit		25						
Projected On Hand	1,254	1,203	1,260	1,335	1,185	1,475	1,220	1,150
Planned Arrivals		202	180	250	165	325	220	140
Gross Margin		178	159	185	202	164	175	179

Figure 11.2: Aggregate store-level financial plan.

The latest projections from Flowcasting (Figure 11.2) shows expected sales of $386K for the coming week, inventory of $1.2 million, and a projected margin of $178K. Therefore, store management already knows that current projections are in line with the budget for the coming week.

As can be seen from the preceding example, management gets a clear indication of whether the current plans will support their financial objectives. If the plans do support the goals, all that remains is to execute well. If, however, the Flowcasting projections differ from the budgets, store management — working with people at headquarters — must either change the marketing/merchandising plans, assortment, promotion schedule or the financial plans themselves.

Before the advent of Flowcasting, it was not possible to conduct this kind of dynamic financial planning — that is, financial planning driven by store-level forecasts that cascade through the entire retail supply chain. Financial plans were disconnected from the very systems used to buy, transport, receive, and ship products to RDCs and stores. As a result, stores had to use historical reference points — what happened last year multiplied by a factor thought to represent what might happen this year. By contrast, Flowcasting provides unparalleled opportunities for financial planning because it is based on the very system that a retailer uses to run its business. It provides a mirror image, in financial terms, of how much product a retailer will buy, distribute, and sell today, tomorrow, and well into the future.

Flowcasting and Business Planning: RDC Level

In Figures 11.1 and 11.2, we demonstrated how Flowcasting can be used as the store level to generate financial plans. Now we'll drive the planning to the RDC level and show how it integrates with supplier scheduling. In Figure 11.3 we show a financial plan for product 12345678 at RDC1, which supports, among others, store 108.

Product: 12345678
RDC1: Plan in $

		Days					
	Current	1	2	3	4	5	6
Planned Shipments: Store 108		12	0	12	0	216	0
Planned Shipments: All other stores		84	72	108	108	624	0
Total Forecast		96	72	120	108	840	0
Safety Stock	200	200	200	200	200	1000	1000
In Transit		288					
Projected On Hand	150	342	270	294	330	1074	1074
Supplier Schedule: Receipt Date				144	144	1584	
Supplier Schedule: Ship Date			144	144	1584		

Figure 11.3: RDC1 financial plan for a single product.

You might notice that Figure 11.3 reflects certain changes from the displays shown in previous examples used in this book. For example, we've separated the planned shipments to store 108 from the remainder of the chain to show the relationship between planned shipments to the store and demands on RDC1. The line for Planned Arrivals is now labeled *Supplier schedule (receipt date)* and the line for Planned Orders now reads *Supplier schedule (ship date)*. That's because the Supplier schedule line shows each supplier what's needed to meet the needs of RDC1. This line, in fact, represents what the retailer intends to buy from the supplier. It is time-phased one year out into the future. As conditions change, the information is refreshed daily and communicated to the supplier. For the supplier, this represents a forecast of what the retailer intends to buy in a time-phased fashion. *The focus is on which product, how much, and when it is needed.*

For the buying organization, these supplier schedules can be summarized by supplier and extended by the applicable currency, thereby generating a total buying plan for the next 52 weeks. The plan represents the total amount of business the retailer intends to commit to the supplier. As such, it is an excellent means for fostering collaborative efforts between retailers and suppliers. For the first time, trading partners can easily make a variety of important comparisons, such as:

- Total projected volume of business compared to past quarters and past year.
- Total projected purchase investment compared to past periods.
- What will be the resulting inventory, compared to plan?
- Comparing the actual performance of new product introductions to the original plans.

We predict that Flowcasting will lead to an adaptation and greater acceptance of supplier scheduling in retailing. Flowcast-mediated supplier scheduling offers enormous potential for simplifying the procurement process for retailers and their suppliers. It also has the potential to eliminate the need for retailers to release purchase orders and for suppliers to issue invoices.

Retailer XYZ Supplier Schedule for Company ABCD Inc			Week of xx/xx/xx							
Location: Los Angeles DC Firm Zone: 2 weeks										
									Schedule Number: ABCD 432	
Buyer: John Doe			Scheduled Requirements					UOM: Selling units		
Item Number	Description		Weeks							
			Past Due	2	3	4	Next 4	Next 4	Next 4	Next 12
23.426	26" color TV			60		60	240	180	180	660
		PO No.	B1203							
Unit Cost/Value	$1175			70500		70500	282000	211500	211500	775500
23.432	32" color TV		30	30	30	30	90	160	160	330
		PO No.	B1204							
Unit Cost/Value	$1475		44250	44250	44250	44250	132750	236000	236000	486750
23.442	42" color TV		30		30		30	60	60	300
		PO No.	B1205							
Unit Cost/Value	$1875		56250		56250		56250	112500	112500	562500
23.450	50" color TV			20		10	20	40	30	100
		PO No.	B1206							
Unit Cost/Value	$2175			43500		21750	43500	87000	65250	217500
Weekly Total Value $:			100500	158250	100500	136500	514500	647000	625250	2042250
Cumulative Total Value $:			100500	258750	359250	495750	1010250	1657250	2282500	4324750
Weekly Total Weight:			4950	8150	4950	7150	27050	33100	32100	104650
Cumulative Total Weight:			4950	13100	18050	25200	52500	85350	117450	222100
Weekly Total Standard Hours:			2	4	2	3.5	13.3	15.4	15	48.6
Weekly Receiving Capacity:			400							

Figure 11.4: Supplier schedule.

To illustrate the power of Flowcast-mediated supplier scheduling, we have reproduced a supplier schedule that one of our clients is sharing with suppliers at the time of this writing (see Figure 11.4[14]). This supplier schedule represents the sum of the planned orders for the next 28 weeks for the intended purchase of television sets from a particular television manufacturer. As you can see, the current plan calls for the purchase of $4,324,750 worth of television sets over the next 28 weeks. The TVs will be delivered to the retailer's DC in Los Angeles. Note that the supplier schedule has a number (ABCD 432) and a specific purchase order number (P.O.) for each television set represented on the schedule. The combination of the schedule number, the P.O. number, and the specific week of planned delivery is used

14 Company names, item numbers, and cost data have been modified to maintain client confidentiality. Line item data is unaltered.

as the unique identifier on all paperwork created by the retailer and supplier.

For example, a shipping manifest with the number ABCD 432-B1203-4 would represent the planned shipment of sixty 26" television sets in week 4. This numbering approach eliminates the need for the retailer to issue purchase orders. It also eliminates the need for the supplier to issue invoices for shipments made. In place of purchase orders and invoices, a purchase contract exists whereby the supplier ships against the supplier schedule, references the appropriate identification numbers, then issues monthly statements. The monthly statements show the value of all the shipments made during a given month against a specific supplier schedule number.

Prior to engaging in the Flowcast-mediated supplier schedule shown in Figure 11.4, the two companies issued *thousands* of purchase orders and invoices annually. Today, they issue less than 20 invoices and P.O.s each!

The ability to create supplier schedules also enables management to get a handle on cash flow requirements for supporting the retailers total purchase commitments with its suppliers. Remember that supplier purchases represent more than 70 percent of the cost of doing business for retailers. With supplier schedules, retailers can sum planned purchases, group them by supplier, offset them by the negotiated payment terms, and then generate a highly accurate projection of cash flow requirements to pay for supplier purchases. For example, assume that payment terms between a retailer and a supplier are 2 percent ten days or net 30. The total value of purchases to be delivered in week 4 amounts to $136,500. If week 4 is the week ending April 1st, then payment for 2 percent ten days would have to be made on or by April 11.

Projections of planned purchases, transportation, receiving into RDC's and shipping and receiving into stores opens up a multitude of financial and operational planning opportunities. The ability to convert these projections into applicable currencies and operating measures (hours, cases, pallets, weight, cube, numbers of trucks, etc.) provides all the functional areas of a retail company with the potential to greatly increase productivity and reduce costs.

Flowcasting and Business Planning: Corporate Level

So far we've seen how Flowcasting makes a great deal of sense for business planning at the store and RDC levels. The opportunity also exists to aggregate store plans, RDC plans into category plans, and overall corporate plans. This was not feasible until recently, and as a result, higher level category and corporate plans were often disconnected from day-to-day operations. Consequently, the Flowcasting approach opens the door to a very powerful management concept that has its roots in manufacturing companies and has yielded enormous operational and financial benefits to companies that have used it well. In manufacturing companies, this concept is referred to "Sales & Operations Planning" (S&OP).

Sales & Operations Planning									
All numbers in 000's									
Time periods = months									
Sales		-3	-2	-1		Curr	+1	+2	+3
Plan		240	250	260		270	250	240	240
Actual		235	252	261		268			
Difference		(5)	+2	+1					
Cumulative Difference	0	(5)	(3)	(2)					
Purchases		-3	-2	-1		Curr	+1	+2	+3
Plan		260	260	260		260	260	260	260
Actual		258	266	260		260			
Difference		(2)	+6	0					
Cumulative Difference	0	(2)	+4	+4					
Inventory		-3	-2	-1		Curr	+1	+2	+3
Plan		740	750	760		750	740	730	730
Actual	740	735	747	758		753			
Difference		(5)	(3)	(2)					

(Column between -1 and Curr labeled "Today")

Figure 11.5: Classic Sales & Operations Planning template in manufacturing.

S&OP is the process through which the sales and manufacturing arms of a company align their objectives. Figure 11.5 shows the classic S&OP template commonly used in manufacturing companies. Typically, S&OP plans are developed by groups of products that share similar production capacities. The key objective of the S&OP process is the marriage of three key operational activities that represent the "pulse" of a manufacturing company: Sales, Production, and Inventory. Just about everything a manufacturing company does will be affected by how well it marries sales objectives with production capabilities and resulting inventories. Over-production can result in excess inventories and unnecessary added costs. Under-production can result in lost sales, out-of-stocks, poor customer service, lost revenues, and discontented customers. Lower sales can result in lost revenues, higher inventories, and added costs. Higher than expected sales can result in out-of-stocks, poor customer service, and higher cost of production due to overtime and production disruptions. The key is the continual monitoring and refining of these three key objectives. Although a complete discussion of the S&OP management process is beyond the scope of this book, we will highlight some of the potential benefits that S&OP[15] can bring to retailers.

Introducing Retail S&OP

Management in retail companies face many of the same issues as their counterparts in manufacturing companies. Business plans (financials) are disconnected from category plans which, in turn, are disconnected from day-to-day planning and execution. The situation is even more challenging in retail since day-to-day planning and execution are not properly connected. Fortunately, the Flowcasting business process makes it possible to connect the pieces between business plans, category plans, and day-to-day operating plans. It is entirely possible today to start with store level product plans and aggregate up to category plans, then up to Sales & Operations plans. Retail S&OP plans, in this context, would be a new level of aggregation and would represent the aggregation from category plans to a higher level where management responsibility and accountability for operating performance is clearly defined. In other words, the S&OP level of aggregation should be wherever top management can specifically assign responsibility for revenue, profit, and asset objectives.

---

15 You can learn more about the S&OP management process by visiting the Web sites of The Oliver Wight Company (www.oliverwight.com) and APICS (www.apics.org).

Consequently, the sum of the S&OP plans would be aggregated to the company business plans. These new levels of aggregation are shown in Figure 11.6.

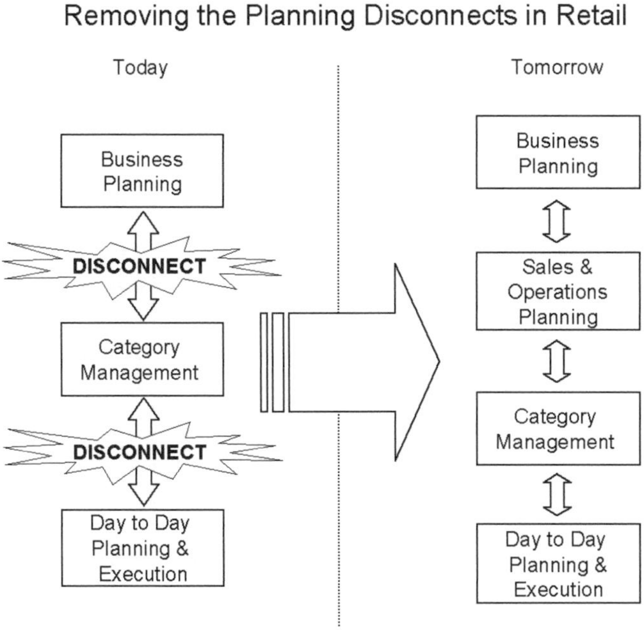

Removing the Planning Disconnects in Retail

Figure 11.6: Removing the planning disconnects in retail.

S&OP in retail will enable retail top management to connect business plans to category plans. Top management will then be able to integrate into a very cohesive set of plans the three key objectives that drive any retailer's business plan: *total sales plans, total inventory investment goals, and total required purchases by area of responsibility and accountability.*

Another way to look at these three key corporate objectives is to think in terms of attempting to balance *demand* from consumers (*Sales* at store level and its various levels of aggregation) with the proper level of *supply (Inventories and Purchases)*, aggregated to a corporate level. This approach is shown in Figure 11.7, which depicts a retail style version of the S&OP template used in manufacturing companies (refer to Figure 11.5). Since retailers are in the business of buying and selling product, the section on production is instead labeled "purchases."

Sales & Operations Planning

All numbers in 000's

Time periods = months

Sales		-3	-2	-1		Curr	+1	+2	+3
Plan		240	250	260		270	250	240	240
Actual		235	252	261		268			
Difference		(5)	+2	+1					
Cumulative Difference	0	(5)	(3)	(2)					
Purchases		-3	-2	-1		Curr	+1	+2	+3
Plan		260	260	260		260	260	260	260
Actual		258	266	260	Today	260			
Difference		(2)	+6	0					
Cumulative Difference	0	(2)	+4	+4					
Inventory		-3	-2	-1		Curr	+1	+2	+3
Plan		740	750	760		750	740	730	730
Actual	740	735	747	758		753			
Difference		(5)	(3)	(2)					

Figure 11.7: Classic Sales & Operations Planning template in retail.

To summarize, Retail S&OP is an aggregated mirror image of a retail business, segmented by specific area of responsibility. It provides visibility into the pulse of any retail business at a level of aggregation that management is comfortable to work with in answering the following questions:

- What are we going to sell in retail stores?
- Where will we sell it (which store)?
- What do we have in-stock?
- What do we have on order?
- And finally, what do we have to get?

Annual Budgeting

Even though budgeting may not be the most popular activity in management today, it is still essential for business planning. Part of the problem is that traditional tools for budgeting force people to guess and use rules of thumb, which are of limited use in predicting the future. Let's say a retailer predicts that a particular category — say frozen meats — will increase by 12 percent in the coming year. The company must accordingly account for increased capital investments in freezer equipment, additional space for the freezers, the impact on transportation, etc. Guesses and rules of thumb will not answer these questions sufficiently.

Flowcasting, by contrast, makes budgeting in retail companies far easier and accurate, given its ability to model an entire retail supply chain for one year into the future from store shelf to raw materials and all of the resources and capacities needed to meet demand. With a Flowcasting business process, the people must provide answers to questions like, "What capital investments must we make?" and arrive at reasonable numbers. All they need to do is change the sales forecast for the products affected by the projected sales increase — Flowcasting plans will be revised accordingly.

As you have seen thus far in this chapter, Flowcasting business processes enable people to plan at all levels of the business. Inherent in the process is the ability to aggregate from the atomic level of the business (store/SKU level) to the business plan level. All that is needed is the establishment of general budgeting guidelines for starting the annual budgeting process. In Figure 11.8, we have identified a likely sequence of events that would support the annual budgeting cycle.

At the base level (General Budgeting Guidelines, Step 0), top management would issue budgeting guidelines for the

Figure 11.8: Annual budgeting process.

General Annual Budgeting Guidelines		
Brick & Mortar	**Products**	**People**
# New stores	# New products	# New hires
# Store closings	# Product deletions	Organizational structure changes
# Store renovations	Etc...	Compensation guidelines
# New DC's		
New office space		

Financials			
% Sales Increase	**% Purchase Increase**	**% Inventory Increase**	**Working Capital**
Existing stores	Existing stores	Existing stores	Required cash flow
New stores	New stores	New stores	
Renovated stores	Renovated stores	Renovated stores	
New store formats	New store formats	New store formats	
# of promotions	# of promotions	# of promotions	
Etc...	Etc...	Etc...	

Figure 11.9: Sample general annual budgeting guidelines.

coming fiscal year. A sample of typical budgeting guidelines is shown in Figure 11.9.

At the next level (Day-to-Day Planning and Execution, Step 1), the budgeting guidelines would be incorporated into the Flowcasting model of the business. The budgeting process begins at Step 2 (Category Management). Here people look at outputs from Flowcasting, aggregate them into specific category plans and make comparisons. Changes are incorporated, and the plans are recalculated. Eventually, after several iterations, the budget planners create a model that incorporates all the major budgeting guidelines provided by top management. At that point, the sequence of aggregation, review, and negotiations from category plans to S&OP plans (Step 3) and from S&OP plans to Business Plans (Step 4) as depicted in Figure 11.8 can begin.

Eventually this approach to creating the annual budget will gain in popularity and greatly reduce the time and trouble people go through every year in putting them together.

Summary

This chapter has outlined how Flowcasting supports total business planning for the retailer. The key points to remember are:

1. The Flowcasting process provides the capability to do store-level business planning and calculates all other demand and supply projections throughout the extended retail supply chain. This makes it possible to conduct business planning at all levels by simply converting planned product flows into financial flows. The result benefits the entire supply by providing a single set of numbers for planning.
2. Flowcasting makes it possible to use supplier scheduling in retail environments since accurate projections of future purchases, inventory levels, and sales are provided a year into the future.
3. Flowcasting facilitates and improves category management processes. With Flowcasting, projections of sales and inventory can be aggregated by category, division, or whatever aggregate display is needed.
4. Retail Sales & Operations Planning (RS&OP) will emerge as an improved way to gain control of the Business. Retail S&OP, like its manufacturing counterpart, Sales & Operations Planning, will help ensure that everyone in retail is "on the same page."

In the following chapter, we focus on the planners who will execute the process and outline what is required to implement Flowcasting. The Chapter also covers the aptitudes and attitudes needed by those who will manage the flowcasting process.

C H A P T E R   1 2

Fourteen Steps
How to Successfully Implement Flowcasting

W hen you total up the volume of data that is generated within the extended retail supply chain, retailers win the "infoprize" hands down. Retail stores generate massive volumes of data on a daily basis, and depend on systems to do the number crunching. The challenge, however, is to make sure that computers and systems are adapted to the needs of people, rather than the other way around. In other words, computers and systems at the retail stores and DCs level must help Flowcasting teams answer routinely and daily the "universal retail supply chain" questions:

- What are we going to sell in retail stores?
- Where will we sell it (which store)?
- What do we have in-stock?
- What do we have on order?
- And finally, what do we have to get?

The bottom line is that people, not computers, are responsible — and rightly held accountable — for sales, in-stocks on the shelf, inventory investment, and operating costs. Therefore, people must be in total control. When a store or retail DC goes out of stock, no one can blame the computer; it's knowledgeable people who know the products, consumers, and suppliers that make the decisions. In a Flowcasting world, hardware and software are to Flowcasting teams what drills, hammers and saws are to the carpenter — a set of tools to get the job done. And it's people who will ultimately solve business problems. Show people how to get accurate foundational data, and give them the necessary education and training, and they will generate valid models that will enable others to do their job in a superior way.

Flowcasting is thus a mix of human judgment and sophisticated technology. And given that it represents a sea change in the way a company does business with its trading partners, a formal implementation process is necessary to ensure a success. Figure 12.1 outlines fourteen basic steps for implementing Flowcasting. The steps represent an adaptation of the Oliver Wight "Proven Path" methodology used to implement MRPII, DRP, and ERP. Over the years, the Proven Path methodology has been used with hundreds of companies worldwide in a broad range of sectors, and refined accordingly. Each step in the plan will be described below in the context of implementing Flowcasting.

A note of caution: since Flowcasting is a new type of planning, it will likely reveal previously hidden problems. Unfortunately, the problems don't go away just because you've identified them. But at least you can see what has to be done. This puts you in a much stronger position to preempt problems before they manifest themselves and impact your bottom line.

Step 1: Conduct Audit Assessment 1

Before a Flowcasting (or any other kind of) plan can be put together, you must know what is in place today — who does what, how it is done, and what kind of tools are used to complete the job. (Appendix E provides examples of typical questions for which answers are required in order to obtain a valid assessment of current conditions.)

The assessment phase determines the integrity of the foundational data currently in place, and what the costs and benefits would be should an implementation follow. The assessment may determine that the company is ready for implementation, or that it must shore

A Basic Flowcasting Implementation Plan

Audit Assessment I	Initial Education	Flowcasting Teams			
	Project Initiator Organization	Education/Consulting			
	Performance Goals		Demand Management		
		Business Process Redesign	Data Integrity		
			Software	Performance Measurements	
			Conference Room Pilot & Live Pilot	Roll-out	Audit Assessment II

Figure 12.1 The 14 basic steps of a Flowcasting implementation plan

up weaknesses before the implementation can proceed. For example, the assessment might reveal that inventory record accuracy is deficient due to poor operating practices and procedures. Contrary to some popular beliefs, inventory record accuracy is normally a people issue, not a system issue. Computers do not make inventory records inaccurate — people do.

There are a number of techniques you can use to document your initial Flowcasting audit assessment. One technique, Business Process Blueprinting, is particularly well-suited to the task. It uses a series of business process maps or "blueprints" for planning and satisfying consumer demand. Appendix F outlines this approach.

Step 2: Provide Initial Education

Once the initial audit assessment determines that the company is ready to begin implementing a Flowcasting business process, initial education sessions would be conducted with top management and a Flowcasting project team. For the retailer and wholesaler, a Flowcasting project team would be cross functional and would include people from sales, stores, distribution, customer service, purchasing, finance, and IT. For a manufacturer, the Flowcasting project team would consist of people from sales, distribution, customer service, manufacturing, finance, and IT.

Top management education. This would consist of a single half-day education session that focuses on the concepts and benefits of the Flowcasting process. This group would not participate in subsequent process redesign sessions, nor would it receive any training in the actual Flowcasting software tools.

Project team education. This is typically a single-day education session on the concepts and benefits of Flowcasting. The number of sessions depend on how many people are, or will be, on the project team. In addition, those who become members of Flowcasting teams (see Step 5) will also receive additional education and training at a later date.

Step 3: Assemble the Project Initiator Team

The project initiator team is responsible for the day-to-day management of the Flowcasting implementation process. Figure 12.2 illustrates the composition of the team (note that the nomenclature may differ from company to company). Let's consider each role.

The executive torchbearer represents the top management group and takes personal responsibility for the success of the imple-

Project Initiator Organization

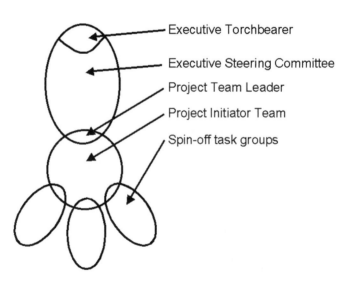

Figure 12.2 Project initiator organization.

mentation. The executive torchbearer is the person with the "fire in the belly" needed to make the implementation happen. The executive torchbearer puts his or her reputation on the line. In addition, one of the torchbearer's most important roles is to defend the implementation against diversions. Most companies have good ideas and more good initiatives than they have the resources to implement. Consequently, someone needs to keep the organization focused on bringing the Flowcasting implementation through to completion.

Executive steering committee members are concerned more with strategy and resources than with tactics — they focus on the overall management of the project and make major decisions, such as, "Do we have the needed resources?" If there's a management problem, the project initiator team needs to raise the flag and alert the steering committee. The steering committee, in turn, needs to make whatever decisions or get whatever resources are needed to correct the situation. For example, the project may be in trouble because the accuracy of the inventory records is lagging and creating difficulties. The steering committee would need to determine the course of action to address this issue. *Overall responsibility for the success of the implementation rests with the steering committee.*

The project team leader is also a member of the executive steering committee and serves as the primary interface between the two groups. He or she attends all the steering committee meetings and updates the steering committee on the progress of the implementation tasks.

Project initiator team members represent their respective functional areas. For example, if the initiator is a retailer, the team would have representatives (typically the department heads or someone assigned by them) from sales, stores, distribution, customer service, purchasing, finance, and IT. The members of the project initiator team work on, and manage, implementation tasks. A project initiator team member may, for instance, undertake responsibility for working with store operations to develop procedures to assure 95 percent inventory record accuracy. The project initiator team typically meets weekly.

Spin-off task groups are small groups assigned to various tasks. These tasks could include revising the process for how a buyer does his or her job as a member of a Flowcasting team, developing a better flow through the distribution center, working to create different models for forecasting, and so on. The spin-off task groups are important for several reasons. First, they provide a practical way to get work done in an organization that is probably overloaded. In addition, better decisions are made when the people closest to a situation are part of the problem-solving process.

Finally, spreading the work also spreads the ownership. One of the primary objectives of the implementation is to have people take "ownership" in both the changes and the new ways of running the business.

The spin-off task forces need to be coordinated so that the different groups aren't working at cross purposes or wasting time and energy by duplicating activities.

Step 4: Establish Performance Goals

While the initial audit assessment described in Step 1 identifies where you are today, performance goals represent *quantitative* measures of what you expect to achieve in the future. It's important to articulate and agree upon these goals in advance so people in the organization clearly know what is expected of them.

Performance goals should be stated concretely, as in, "We expect an improvement in customer service at store level (percent in-stock) to rise from the current range, 90 to 92 percent, to 98 to 99 percent, consistently. We expect a 30 percent reduction in inventory, and a 5 percent reduction in purchase and administrative costs."

If the performance goals are not set properly, you run the risk of everyone developing a different set of expectations about what "acceptable" performance means. You might hear questions like, "We lowered inventory by 10 percent — that's certainly good, isn't it?" Or "We increased productivity in purchasing by 4 percent — that's better than the national average, isn't it?" The best performance goals are "stretch" goals that challenge and motivate people.

Finally, performance goals must be meaningful in terms of the potential financial benefit. After all, if a company commits the resources necessary to implement Flowcasting and only sets goals of 2 or 3 percent improvement, this communicates a low self-assessment in terms of what the management and the workforce are capable of doing. In fact, a talented and aggressive management team should be able to realize substantial improvements by driving the business with Flowcasting.

Calculating Cost/Benefit

Once the company establishes performance goals, it should quantify in financial terms the overall costs and benefits of a full implementation. The size of the benefits will depend on a variety of factors. For example, when it comes to logistics excellence, many strive for it but few, if any, ever achieve it. Some retailers and their suppliers are excellent performers while others have more opportunities to excel. The size of the benefits will depend on where you are today in terms of fill rates, percent out-of-stock at store level, days of inventory on hand, purchased and other operating costs, etc.

This being said, having the ability to eliminate sales forecasting uncertainty at all levels of the retail supply chain, except at the final point of sale, offers a huge potential to reduce operating costs. Based on our analysis, 82 percent of the price consumers pay, on average, is made up of the cost of producing, marketing, distributing, and selling products (see Appendix G for details). By now, you've seen how Flowcasting can help in the very areas of producing, marketing, distributing, and selling products.

As an assist in calculating the cost/benefit goals of a Flowcasting implementation, we suggest basing the potential total benefits on 1 percent to 6 percent of your total sales. If your total annual sales are $1 billion, then the range of potential savings for your company would be from $10 million to $60 million. Where you should be in that range will depend on two factors. The first concerns where you are today versus your competition. The second concerns how aggressive you want to be in rolling-out the Flowcasting process to as many suppliers as possible.

Step 5: Select Flowcasting Teams

This step starts with the project initiator deciding who will participate in the initial pilot program. Once selected, the retailer and/or the supplier must begin assembling a Flowcasting team. Once the Flowcasting process is in place, this team will have the responsibility for orchestrating how both companies will do business in the future. In addition, they will serve as models for other retailers and suppliers as the Flowcasting implementation rolls out.

Figure 12.3 shows how retailers and suppliers would work in a complementary fashion on a Flowcasting team.

The New Flowcasting World of Communications

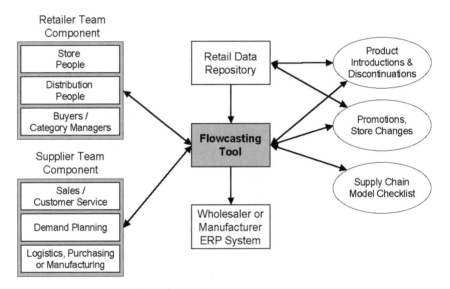

Figure 12.3 Flowcasting team components.

The retailer's core team is made up of representatives from the functional areas traditionally responsible for buying, distributing and selling products. Other people can be added to the core team as necessary. The same applies to supplier's representatives (manufacturer or wholesalers).

If this approach to total supply chain management seems foreign, be assured that forming Flowcasting teams doesn't require a major reorganization. After all, customer focused teams already exist in many manufacturing companies involved in VMI or CPFR endeavors. What's new is the intra-company focus revolving around *one consistent model for doing business.* Flowcasting teams manage to one set of numbers from factories to retail store shelves.

The establishment of Flowcasting teams must be taken very seriously if the Flowcasting approach is to yield results. Top management must provide visible support in order to bring about real changes in the authority/responsibility structure, and to ensure that team members have the opportunity to develop and implement their ideas for changing the way the company does business.

The early establishment of Flowcasting teams is the best approach we know of for breaking down intra-company departmental barriers and, at the same time, providing a company with the basic internal tools it needs to realize the full potential of this new business process. With the Flowcasting team in place, a company is ready to break down the toughest hurdle of all: inter-company boundaries.

Firms that develop effective cross-company Flowcasting teams will be on the cutting edge — completely changing the way they do business with their trading partners — and reap the associated rewards.

Step 6: Carry Out Education and Consulting

By this time, the initial retailer or supplier has been selected, meetings have been held, agreement has been reached, and the composition of the first retailer/manufacturer Flowcasting team has been established. An initial education program has already been completed (Step 2), and top management and other potential players have bought into the process and have acquired a general level of understanding of the Flowcasting concept. The next step is to educate the key people who will have the responsibility for implementing the Flowcasting business process (both retailer and supplier).

Part of the education process entails debunking common misunderstandings.

Some people, for example, may see Flowcasting as a computer system —"put two programmers on it for three months, and you're there." Others may see it as a way to improve forecasting and replenishment. Other people again see it for what it really is: a new way of doing business that unites the entire retail supply chain behind a single set of numbers. It's critical to get everyone on the "same page" so that a consistent message about Flowcasting and its benefits will propagate through the organization. If there isn't a consistent message, you'll spend more time answering questions than actually implementing the process. Education, therefore, plays a critical role in focusing people on the tasks at hand.

The education/consulting phase is where the key decision makers and those who will serve on Flowcasting teams learn what the Flowcasting process is all about and how it will work. Key decision makers will typically attend a half-day educational session. Future Flowcasting team members and other key operating personnel will attend a more detailed one-day educational session that will help them define the benefits of Flowcasting so they can assist management in their functional areas.

After these sessions have taken place, the key decision makers meet and review the range of benefits identified in Step 1. By this time, they will have obtained the necessary knowledge to narrow the range of benefits. They will also have a better feel for the resources that will be required. Once a consensus is reached, it should be communicated to everyone in the organization. This consensus helps give a clear and consistent message to the rest of the organization. Key decision makers can work out differences among themselves, rather than have their people bump into one another in the hall, compare notes, and create confusion.

The initial education phase is followed by a more expansive education and consulting phase, geared for everyone else in the company. Sadly, most companies do minimal initial education, let alone follow up education and consultation. What little education is done often turns out to be classroom-oriented and designed to impart education through the "grade-school method." As a result, it is usually ineffective as a means for introducing sea change within an organization. A better model is based on the "business meeting" in which a leader taps the collective knowledge of participants. This approach recognizes the experience and intelligence of the people in the organization, and as a result, builds high levels of ownership and enthusiasm. This, in turn, leads to a company best positioned to take advantage of the powers of Flowcasting.

Step 7: Redesign the Business Process

During this phase, members of Flowcasting teams hold a series of meetings to discuss and eventually agree on, new ways of doing business. The business process blueprinting approach is used again here, this time to document how the company will do business in a Flowcasting environment.

As we've stressed, Flowcasting represents a significant change in the way retailers and suppliers do business with each other. As a rule, people prefer the status quo — there's a natural tendency for people to resist change and stay within their "comfort zones." The key is to remove the fear of the unknown and answer the questions that most people raise when asked to embrace a new system or process: "What's in it for me? ... for my department? ... for my company?"

The questions usually come in that order; most of what we do is driven by assumptions and hidden agendas rather than intentional thought. And within large organizations, people don't typically assume that *anything* is ever done for a good reason! So when giving your Flowcasting team new tools, it's important to help the members develop an open mind-set so that they can learn to use the tools without preconceived assumptions.

Step 8: Consolidate Demand Management

In the context of Flowcasting, demand management comes down to the ability to create, and agree on, a unique store-level sales forecast. This represents a leap of faith for most people in retailing, as most forecasting activity is carried out the retail DC level. At that level, it's typical to use a moving average, or some derivative, in their purchasing systems to suggest orders to the buyers.

Step 9: Ensure Data Integrity

In his book *MRPII: Making It Happen*, Tom Wallace explains that there are two types of data: "forgiving" and "unforgiving." Let's look at both types and how they affect the foundational data necessary for a Flowcasting process to function properly.

"Unforgiving" Data. Unforgiving data causes serious problems if it's not accurate. In a Flowcasting environment, unforgiving data includes inventory record accuracy at the stores and distribution centers. That's because if the inventory records are incorrect, the planning will be wrong. If you think you have one hundred cases of light bulbs in the DC and, in fact, you only have fifty, then the planned orders will be incorrect. This, in turn, will spawn incorrect distribution replenishment plans, incorrect supplier schedules, and so on. Similarly, if you think you have five cases in a store and you really have just one, then you will most likely experience an out-of-stock situation in that store as well as incorrect store replenishment plans, incorrect demand on the retail DC servicing that store, and incorrect schedules to the supplier of the product. The effect cascades from one level of the retail supply chain to the next. In the past, we were oblivious to the cascading errors since the various levels of the retail supply chain were not connected. We felt the pain of out-of-stock situations and had to expedite orders and incur additional costs to compensate without knowing the root cause of the problem. With Flowcasting, such problems become highly visible and can be eliminated before they create difficulties.

It's also important to represent the distribution network accurately. If a particular store is supplied by a particular distribution center, but for operating reasons, another distribution center will supply the store as of a certain date; this information must be communicated so that changes to the distribution network can be made inside the Flowcasting system. Otherwise, the demands from that store will not show up as demand at the right distribution center.

For an effective Flowcasting process, the necessary data accuracy levels for effective operation are as follows: Inventory records, 95 percent; distribution alignment, 100 percent (i.e., proper representation of which retail DCs service which stores). Note that the 95 percent inventory record accuracy is not calculated in the applicable currency (the way accountants measure a physical inventory). Using the accounting measure, an error of +50 cases on clear light bulbs, and an error of -50 cases on frosted light bulbs, results in a very small error, or no error, in financial terms. And while such an error has little or no impact on the company's financial books, it can have a significant impact on the company's ability to satisfy consumers, because the store's replenishment schedules for both products will be wrong.

The target of 95 percent inventory record accuracy used for a Flowcasting planning process means that 95 percent of the SKUs are within counting tolerance. As an example, if one hundred items were cycle-counted, and ten were found to have differences between the on hand balance in the system and the actual count that was greater than the counting tolerance, the resulting accuracy would be 90 percent. The tolerance is generally based on how the items are counted: zero percent for case packaged items, 2 percent or so for weight counted items, like apples or bananas.

Experience has shown that levels of inventory accuracy for most retailers and wholesalers at the distribution centers already exceed 95 percent. The same is true for wholesalers and manufacturers in their distribution centers. The implementation challenge lies in achieving this kind of accuracy at the store level. Accuracy of scanned data becomes an issue in this context because of the use of the multiplier key. While scanning ten cans of cat food that bear the same price only once (by hitting the multiplier key) instead of capturing each flavor will get consumers through the checkout line quicker, it will compromise the accuracy of the on hand balance and increase the cost of doing business through lost sales and the cost of expedited shipments. To mitigate this, many retailers have adopted "scan every item" policies. Some have even gone so far as to disable their multiplier keys altogether.

A distribution network alignment accuracy of 100 percent says it all. With a Flowcasting business process, the idea is to model the way products will flow from factories to retail store shelves. If the connections are wrong or missing, the stores will experience stock-outs and the concomitant loss of sales.

You may wonder, "Do we really have the ability to achieve such high levels of accuracy?" The answer is a resounding yes! There is a tested and proven process for achieving inventory record accuracy, as outlined in Appendix B.

"Forgiving" Data. With forgiving data, "reasonable" accuracy is acceptable — and generally fairly easy to achieve. Forgiving data includes order quantities, safety stock levels, and lead times. If the order quantity is two days of supply, is three days of supply incorrect? No — two days of supply may be better than three, but neither is "wrong." The objective is to get to the point where you are ordering every day, or every other day, to avoid an out-of-stock situation and not determining a "right" order quantity. Put another way, what good would it be to receive the right order quantity one or two days after you have run out of stock?

Safety stock is a function of the uncertainty in either demand or supply. If demand is fairly unpredictable, then more safety stock will be needed. Again, the objective is to do a better job of predicting demand and managing distribution so safety stocks can be safely reduced. As planners become versed in how the logic of DRP (the underpinnings of Flowcasting) actually works, especially at store level, they will quickly discover that DRP's rescheduling power goes a long way to compensate for forecasting errors. In other words, when you significantly undersell or oversell the forecast, the logic will move planned orders in or out. (For example, moving a planned arrival from day 4 to day 2 or from day 2 to day 4). As a result, over time, you will be able to safely reduce safety stocks.

With respect to lead times, the objective is to provide those responsible for supplying products (retail, wholesale, manufacturing DCs and factories) with time-phased visibility of your replenishment requirements, refreshed daily, as you oversell or undersell the forecast. In the case of wholesalers and manufacturers, these time-phased replenishment requirements can be converted to supplier schedules (see Chapter 5). Consequently, lead times become a meaningless concept. Suppliers will be seeing schedules several weeks into the future and will convert planned demands into actual shipments in time to meet the delivery requirements. In a Flowcasting environment, those responsible for replenishment must only maintain reasonable lead times for all the different products under their purview.

Step 10: Choose the Right Flowcasting Software

Although software tools are essential for Flowcasting, the best software package is no guarantee of top-notch performance. What correlates with excellent performance is good management. To offer a golf analogy, it's not the clubs, but rather how you hit the ball. Similarly, a great set of tools does not make a carpenter.

Today, there is good, tested software that supports the Flowcasting business process. Every company, of course, has individual needs, but these needs typically require only minor changes to the software. Typical customization jobs might be the reformatting of a picking list or the addition of a particular calculation to determine the quantity that should be initially distributed to stores participating in a promotion.

Software Selection

While good software does not guarantee success, the wrong software guarantees failure. Selecting commercially available software to support your Flowcasting business process is a necessary and important step. So how do you ensure that you select the right software for your company? Answer: You buy Flowcasting software the same way you buy a car.

1. Make a list of the options you need and which ones would be nice to have.
2. Narrow down the list of dealerships you're going to visit.
3. Take some test drives.

Your business process tells you what functionality you need to look for. By writing scripts or test cases based on your process, you can mock up a step-by-step "day in the life" scenario of how the process will be executed. Of course, you can rank the functionality, or the test cases, since some features will be more important than others. For example, promotion planning might be very important if you do a lot of promotions.

Once this is done, you can work with your IT colleagues and industry groups to determine which technology providers are candidates. Then, as with buying a car, take some test drives. Invite the list of technology providers to demonstrate that they can execute your test cases with your data. By scoring each script, you have a basis for determining how well the software will support your business. Your team must be involved in running the test cases since you want an accurate, unbiased evaluation of how well your people can use the software to execute the Flowcasting process. In addition, it gives you a chance to assess the software vendor in terms of ability to work with you and responsiveness to your needs. Finally, you need to make sure that the chemistry between your IT people and the vendor is good for the short- and long-term.

Do bear in mind the following word of caution when you select Flowcasting software. Flowcasting is built around one simple and very critical premise: an unique sales forecast by product, by store drives the entire retail supply chain. This means that massive volumes of data must be processed rapidly, daily, and economically. Therefore, as part of the evaluation, you need to do a volume test to make sure the software can support the vast number of location/item combinations, not just today, but as your business continues to grow/change. Given this situation, you might insist that the software vendor demonstrate that it can meet the following specification:

"The planning software package should be capable of supporting the Flowcasting business process as depicted by the business process blueprint and should be able to model high quality time-phased store level sales forecast, time-phase inventory projections, and time-phased replenishment plans for all retail stores and distribution centers (plus wholesale and/or manufacturer's DCs if required) inside the same system. In addition to the above, it must be capable of generating action messages, by exception, for a minimum of 100 million product/location combinations over a 52-week planning horizon inside a 2-hour window on a computer or a cluster of servers costing $250,000 (USD) or less."

The last thing you want is to make a poor software decision and have the software become the focus of attention at the expense of the people responsible for the success of your implementation. Remember, Flowcasting is a people system made possible by the computer. If Flowcasting becomes a technical support issue, your implementation can become derailed and you will lose the immediate benefits that Flowcasting affords your company and its trading partners.

Step 11: Conduct a Conference Room Pilot and Live Pilot

Before rolling out the actual system (see next step), it is essential to conduct a Pilot approach consisting of three components. The first is the "software" pilot that is used to make sure the software is working as expected. The second is the "conference room" pilot. This is an extension of the education/consulting phase, where members of the Flowcasting team for the first group of products work with the system using actual data, create a model, and simulate how the company would use the system. The third is the "live" pilot and entails using the system to plan and actually ship orders for a limited number of planners who are responsible for specific products within their extended supply chain. By limiting the number of planners involved, there is a low risk to the business if the Flowcasting process needs adjustment. You can fix whatever problems appear, then continue doing business. After about a month of the pilot, you'll have identified most of the problems. Once you've solved them, add another planner or planners, and begin having them execute the new business process for their extended supply chain. Fix the problems that emerge, settle in, and continue until all products in all stores and DCs have been included. In this way, you will be ready to roll out the Flowcasting system companywide.

Step 12: Roll-Out the Flowcasting System

Once the results of the live pilot are in and there is consensus among all members of the Flowcasting team, it's time for the roll-out. The actual roll-out period must be planned carefully. The amount of time it takes will depend on the number of planners and products, stores, and DCs involved. It will also depend on the method of doing business between the retailer and the first pilot supplier. Normally, the roll-out approach would follow the normal product flow pattern and would be carried out, one group of planning teams at a time. The experience of the live pilot should serve as a guide as to how many planners and products should be rolled out at any one time for an extended supply chain.

Once the roll-out period has begun, it's important to complete it as quickly as possible. Remember that, as you're rolling out the new approach, the old way of doing business is still in effect. As a consequence, during the roll-out period, two approaches of doing business are still in use, and running two systems in parallel should be kept to a minimum amount of time. It is important to note that this roll-out should be conducted one planning team/supplier at a time for purposes of accountability.

Step 13: Establish Performance Measurements

How do you know that the pilot is working? How do you know whether to continue with it, as is, or make adjustments? Some of these questions can be approached subjectively. "Do people believe the replenishment schedules from suppliers' DCs to retailer or wholesaler DCs?" "Do people believe the replenishment schedules from DCs to retail stores?"

Another way to look at the output of the process is to ask, *"As a team, are we modeling the way product should flow from factories to store shelves?"* "Does the process make sense?"

Other questions can be answered only by establishing performance measurements. Be aware, though, that some of the performance objectives or goals are unlikely to be realized with just a pilot. Overall customer service, for example, will not probably improve as a result of a pilot implementation. Knowing this, you might start tracking customer service on specific product lines. Some companies compare customer service for products that are on the pilot with products that are not. You can take the same approach to productivity, although productivity is more difficult to measure on a product-by-product basis.

It's also quite common for inventory levels to actually increase on items that have been recently switched to the Flowcasting planning method. There is a logical reason for this. Flowcasting reviews and replans every stocking location every day. Items that are in dire need of replenishment will all be detected and reordered immediately after going live in a Flowcasting environment. For items that are overstocked, however, you simply have to wait a few weeks for the inventory to deplete. This results in net positive purchases in the short term after a Flowcasting implementation, followed by a gradual drop to a steady state.

The key issue at this point is to start measuring against the goals set at the very beginning of your Flowcasting implementation (refer to Step 4 covered earlier).

Step 14: Conduct Audit Assessment II

"Where are we?" "Did we achieve the goals we set for ourselves in the beginning?" "What's next?" "What other elements should we be working on?"

The initial audit identified the opportunities for improvement, and triggered a series of implementation activities. If those activities worked well, then the new way of doing business is improving fill rates, reducing store out-of-stocks, increasing inventory turns, and reducing operating costs significantly. The second audit might reveal that, while your organization has done certain things well, such as data accuracy, you are not optimally managing the Flowcasting process. Perhaps the forecasting process at store level is sub par. This would be problematic, since the store-level forecast drives the activity of all trading partners in the supply chain. Such deficiencies would become apparent in your forecast measurement metrics; once on the radar screen, you can set about fixing the problems and improving the Flowcasting process.

Resource Allocation

A major issue in implementation is how much you can realistically do within a given time frame. It's better to say you're going to do less and make it happen than to make major promises and then not deliver. If the task is manageable and people achieve success, everyone will be motivated to take on additional challenges. If people can never be winners, they'll be unmotivated, and the organizations involved in the implementation will achieve less. An excellent test of the maturity of a management team is its ability to set realistic goals and objectives for its people. You may need everything yesterday, but if it can't be done, your management team needs to step up to their responsibilities and produce realistic plans.

Our methodology is based on a proven approach that has successfully stood the test of time in retail, wholesale, and manufacturing companies. If you follow it, you'll maximize your chances of gaining unprecedented visibility into your supply chain from store shelf to the factory floor. To be sure, implementing Flowcasting is a major undertaking. But the benefits far outweigh costs of transforming your retail supply chain from a series of disconnected islands to a seamlessly integrated entity driven by a single forecast.

A P P E N D I C E S

Appendix A
A New Mindset for Supply Chain Management

To design, implement and manage a Flowcasting process requires that supply chain professionals think in new ways. The principles outlined below will help them do so.

One Supply Chain -- For too long, companies have thought of themselves as discrete islands within their extended supply chains. "Extended" rarely meant reaching outside an entity's four walls. Each trading partner focused too much on its own operations, neglecting the impact that its decisions had on other supply chain nodes. Flowcasters understand that the retail supply chain is one eco-system, and that decisions made by one trading partner affect the entire system. The Flowcasting process connects all the nodes in the ecosystem in a natural, seamless and continuously forward looking manner. The result is a single set of numbers that drives all supply chain activity.

Commit Time -- Since the Flowcasting process plans a continuum and this future visibility is shared amongst all trading partners, the traditional concept of lead time collapses. Before Flowcasting, lead times were comprised of buffer times at all levels of the retail supply chain. These buffers existed for only one reason: to guard against surprises.

With Flowcasting, this approach is replaced with an up-to-date projection of future product needs for the entire supply chain. As a result, lead times between supplier and customer collapse to the bare minimum, or what is referred to as "commit time." For example, commit time between a supplier DC and a retailer DC should consist only of "pick, pack, and ship and receive" time between the two facilities. If retailers spend the effort to educate suppliers and provide valid supplier schedules, commit times can be more than 70 percent less than traditional lead times.

Collaboration -- Traditionally, supply chain partners have not spoken the same language. Retailers talk about point-of-sale data, while distributors and manufacturers speak the language of purchase orders. The Flowcasting process provides the tools required to speak the same language: consumer demand. Now all trading partners can collaborate on a consumer demand forecast, focused on where they can add the most value.

For example, manufacturers might help retailers develop consumer forecasts for new items, and they might work together to develop promotional forecasts. The Flowcasting process translates the store-level forecasts into actionable information for all trading partners in the retail supply chain.

This breakthrough fosters in a new era in collaboration. Schedules are shared throughout the retail supply chain, and trading partners work on the principle of "silence implies consent." Since long-term visibility of product requirements is a given, unless your supplier indicates it will not be able to supply in the future, the assumption is that it can. In the event it cannot, a plan can be mutually developed, then shared and executed.

Channel Management -- Many retail supply chains consist of tens of thousands of products, hundreds or thousands of stores, and hundreds or thousands of suppliers. Over time, a number of different replenishment methods have evolved for distributing products from supply sources to retail stores. For example, replenishment approaches like flow through, cross dock, direct store delivery (DSD), and vendor managed inventory (VMI) have been used to reduce costs in the retail supply chain.

The Flowcasting process simplifies the application of these practices. One of the fundamentals of the process is that a store-by-store projection of planned needs by product is developed. These projections are not dependent on how the product will be supplied. Rather demand is mapped to its supply point and serves as the demand forecast for the supply location.

To illustrate, consider the following diagram, depicted in Figure A1.

This example could depict how the Flowcasting process supports a direct store delivery (DSD) or vendor managed inventory approach for replenishing the stores.

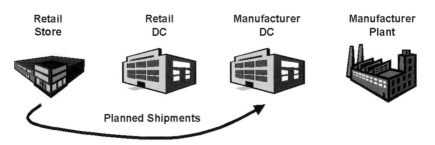

Figure A1: Mapping store-level demand.

The direct store delivery is where the manufacturer ships products to the store directly from its distribution centers. In this case, the store-level planned arrivals are mapped to the manufacturer DC, not the retail DC. This makes sense since the product will actually ship from the manufacturer DC. In addition, the retail DC will not see these demands, but operational planning will see an accurate picture of future capacity requirements. To date, this has not been possible. At the agreed-upon lead time, the store planned arrivals become firm orders for the supplier to ship to the stores.

Similar information is needed for a store-level vendor managed inventory program. In this case, the manufacturer usually has a representative who travels to the retail stores, counts the stock and replenishes any inventory needed. The Flowcasting process greatly simplifies this. Store-level projections provide the representative with precise product requirements, store by store, thereby eliminating any guesswork about the demand requirements. In addition, since the information is by store and delivery date, cost effective delivery routes can be planned since the store-level projections can be totaled and converted to cube or weight projections to assist the manufacturer plan their deliveries.

The concept applies to e-tailers as well. In this case, no retail stores exist since product is being demanded by customers' in their homes. Plans could be developed by ZIP code, state, or any geographic region that makes sense. The demand projection could be mapped to a fulfillment DC. The fulfillment DC would create Flowcasting plans and then provide the demand projections for its suppliers. For a retailer with both physical stores and online sales, some of the online demand can be mapped to the local stores for customer pickup or local delivery.

The point is, for the first time ever, professional planners in the retail supply chain have store-level visibility and they can "map demand at will" throughout the extended supply chain, as channel needs dictate.

Exception-Based Planning -- As mentioned earlier in this book, when it comes to information and data, retailers win the "infoprize." Developing store-level plans for all the store/product combinations can easily total in the tens of millions. To manage a problem of this magnitude, Flowcasters must spend their time on exceptions. In other words, firefighting is replaced by fire prevention. To date, many organizations have planned items based on how well they sell -- sometimes called ABC analysis. "A" items sell the most, "B" items sell less, while "C" items are the slowest selling. Conventional wisdom was for planners to spend the most time managing "A" items, less on "B's" and even less on "Cs."

In a Flowcasting world, that thinking is turned on its head. Flowcasters spend time on identifying and resolving exceptions before they occur, regardless of whether the item is classified as A, B, or C. In fact, what many people have found is that in terms of time management, the exact opposite is true. That is, "C" items produce the most exceptions, "Bs" the next, while "A" items have the least. Time is better spent resolving an exception on a "C" item than reviewing an "A" item that is flowing well.

Since the Flowcasting process produces time-phased projections at the most granular level and throughout the retail supply chain, specific exceptions can be identified and resolved before they occur. For example:

- At store level, an exception can be generated indicating that an inbound shipment will arrive soon, and that it will exceed the available shelf space for the product. This gives you the opportunity to make more shelf space available, change the ordering rules, or allocate some back room space for the item.

- A grocery retailer can flag that an item's current on hand balance will last beyond its "sell before" date. A markdown strategy can be employed to quickly sell the product and avoid spoilage.
- At the distribution center, inbound receipts can be converted to cubic feet, compared to available receiving capacity, and an exception can be generated to identify which days or weeks receiving capacity will be exceeded. The operational planners can then work with the Flowcasters to determine a plan for avoiding the problem.
- Instead of trying to build complicated constraint based planning, visibility is used to identify and resolve problems by people, not a computer. For example, capacity plans can be developed by space, equipment, labor hours, etc. and compared to available capacity. Problems are easily identified and resolved by people working together, both internally and externally.

The point is that since the Flowcasting process provides future visibility for all levels in the retail supply chain, exception-based planning makes people super-productive and provides them with the tools they need to develop superior service levels and reduce supply chain costs.

Appendix B
Inventory Record Accuracy

For Flowcasting to be successful, an inventory accuracy of at least 95 percent is required for all nodes in the extended retail supply chain. This means that 95 percent of the items have a physical on hand balance that is within an acceptable tolerance of the quantity recorded in the computer system. For example, if an acceptable counting tolerance for a group of items is one case, then 95 percent of the items counted should have an actual count that is within one case of the inventory number in the system.

A Flowcasting process demands this level of accuracy, even at store level. That's because the store level plans are the basis of all dependent demand plans throughout the extended retail supply chain. If the on hand inventory balance at store level is wrong, not only will that store's Flowcasting plan be wrong, but all other plans are wrong as well.

Contrary to what many people believe, a 95 percent accurate inventory level is attainable. Numerous companies have obtained this level of accuracy by using the following steps:

1. **Educate people**. Everyone must understand why it's important to have accurate information, and how other companies have been successful in achieving the established goals. If people do not understand the importance of inventory accuracy, there is little chance they will ever achieve it.

2. **Assign responsibility.** To date, most people who work in stores and distribution centers are not accountable for inventory accuracy. That must change and their jobs should emphasize the importance of keeping accurate inventory records.

3. **Provide the tools.** You need a simple and easy-to-use transaction recording system. A transaction recording system allows people to audit each and every inventory transaction, from receipt to shipment/sale. The only people who should be allowed to make inventory transactions are those who are responsible for it.

4. **Audit the accuracy.** For inventory records, the most common method is cycle counting, where a representative sample of items are counted on a periodic basis and compared to the on hand balance.

5. **Correct the causes of error.** The primary purpose of the audits is to find and fix the causes of the inaccurate data. Just as you cannot "inspect" quality into a product, you cannot "audit" accuracy into the information. It is not possible to cycle-count your way to 95 percent inventory record accuracy -- the root causes of the errors must be uncovered, and corrected.

Appendix C
Implementation Strategies

Chapter 12 outlined the Proven Path for implementing a Flowcasting process within your extended retail supply chain. This appendix expands on the ideas put forth in that chapter and outlines various implementation strategies for specific supply chain management goals. Remember that Flowcasting is first and foremost a people system made possible by technology. As such, the move to a Flowcasting business process requires change in how people work and how they are rewarded -- and, depending on who initiates the process, the Flowcasting-related tasks that people perform can change, supply chain by supply chain. For example, maybe the Flowcasting process is retailer-initiated and the planning is centralized. Or, maybe the planning is de-centralized. Each option is described below.

Retailer led, centrally planned -- In this case, the retailer is leading the move to Flowcasting, and central planners plan all product movements from suppliers to their retail stores. A planner may be responsible for a specific category of products from specific suppliers and be responsible for planning their flow into retail stores. The best approach is to implement Flowcasting planner by planner -- this way, all the products from the planner will be on Flowcasting at the same time, and there is no confusion about how to plan. If possible, try to implement the Flowcasting process for all the supplier's items as well.

If a single planner is responsible for all of the items from a supplier, the implementation will be easier. If not, try to add an additional planner to cover the remaining products for that supplier. You are trying to first move the central planner into the Flowcasting world and, if possible, ensure that their suppliers are also there as well. It may not be possible to satisfy all supply chain members, so the first priority should be to bend the implementation schedule to suit those people whose jobs will be changing the most.

Retailer led, de-centrally planned -- In this case, the retailer is leading the move to Flowcasting, but the planning takes place in two places: by store personnel for each store and by central planners who plan the DCs. Store personnel are responsible for planning all products in the store.

In this case, the store planners are changing the most since they do the store-level planning and are responsible for all items in a store. The implementation would be store by store, for all items in each store. This ensures that the store personnel are using the new process for all items, rather than trying to use it for some while using the current process for the others.

In a retailer led, de-centrally planned Flowcasting implementation, it is wise to continue to roll out the remaining stores until all stores are using Flowcasting to plan and order product. Once this is complete, the central planners can begin using Flowcasting, since their current demand forecasts would be replaced by the time-phased dependent demand from the stores. If this sequence isn't used, you would need to create a time-phased forecast at the retail DC level. This forecast would be thrown away once the stores were using Flowcasting and providing their dependent demand forecast.

Manufacturer led -- Under this scenario, the manufacturer is leading the move to Flowcasting, and the planning takes place at the manufacturer headquarters. In this situation, the retailer provides foundational data that will help the manufacturer develop Flowcasting plans from factory to shelf.

The Flowcasting implementation would be by planner and for a group of stores supported by one specific retail DC. This is necessary because the planner would likely manage a subset of the items supplied to the retailer. Again, it is desirable to ensure that the planners manage all the items supplied to the retailer with Flowcasting.

Appendix D
Flowcasting System Buyer's Guide

As mentioned earlier in this book, systems exist today that enable the Flowcasting process to be executed. Our advice is consistent with that outlined in Chapter 12: build and document your business process before selecting software. That way, you can develop a series of test cases or scenarios that software vendors must use to demonstrate their ability to support your business needs.

Business processes will vary slightly by company. However, this appendix is intended to provide you with a buyer's guide: that is, the features and capabilities that a system should have to support the standard Flowcasting business process. The principle a Flowcasting system should be built on is:

Valid simulation of reality -- A Flowcasting system must be able to simulate all flows in the extended retail supply chain from factory to shelf, for a year-long planning horizon.

We have listed the capabilities that a solid Flowcasting system should have by major function. These include:

- **Forecasting**
  - The ability to develop time-phased forecasts for a planning horizon of at least one year for all products at store level
  - The ability to recognize trends
  - The ability to recognize seasonality
  - The ability to smooth/filter out effects of past promotions
  - The ability to smooth/filter out effects of past stock-outs
  - The ability to smooth/filter out effects of moving holidays
  - The capability to forecast specific items at store level using different forecast horizons (e.g., weekly, monthly, quarterly), and to use forecast consumption to consume the forecast over the forecast horizon
  - The ability to develop integer forecasts for slow moving items
  - The capability to do mass copying of history for new items
  - The capability to do mass copying of history for new stores

- The ability to generate exception messages for managing large numbers of forecasts
- The ability to aggregate forecasts by groups of products or locations
- The capability to make mass changes to forecasts
- The ability to reconcile forecasts at the product / location level with higher level plans

- **Replenishment**
- The ability to develop time-phased Distribution Requirements Plans (DRP) for all nodes in the supply chain (including stores) for a planning horizon of at least one year
- The ability to set minimum and maximum display quantities at store level
- The ability to calculate projected shipment quantities by product/location
- The ability to calculate projected shipment dates based on lead-time offsets for all nodes in the supply chain
- The ability to calculate dependent demand for all levels below store level
- The capability to do re-planning on all items or selected items
- The ability to develop exception messages to alert users of various exceptions
- The ability to firm planned orders so that they will not be re-planned
- The ability to peg, or drill down, into demand projections to understand the components of demand
- The ability to view Available To Promise to show what can be allocated
- The ability to time-phase sourcing relationships
- The ability to handle assemblies for component products
- The ability to handle products that are sold in more than one configuration but are replenished in only one way

- **Aggregate planning (financial, space, capacity, and transportation)**
- The ability to create financial plans based on product/location projections including:
  - Projected sales forecasts
  - Projected purchases
  - Projected inventories
  - Projected gross margin
- The ability to create space plans based on product/location projections including:
  - Projected cubic volume
- The ability to provide capacity planning information including:
  - Projected picking hours
  - Projected receiving hours
  - Projected inbound cube
  - Projected outbound cube and shipments
- The ability to provide transportation planning information including:
  - Projected weight between any two nodes
  - Projected volume (cube) between any two nodes

- **Inventory transactions**
- The ability to maintain inventory position by product/location, including sales, receipts, in transits, adjustments, etc.
- The ability to produce a complete inventory transaction history to aid in finding the root causes of inventory errors and reduce a major cause of shrink

- **General use**
- The ability to develop and present exception messages
- The ability to prioritize exception messages
- The ability to perform mass maintenance
- The ability to quickly move through all nodes in the supply chain and view relevant information at every stage

- **Processing volumes**
  - The ability to develop Flowcasting plans for all products in the extended retail supply chain for a planning horizon of at least 52 weeks within an acceptable processing time

- **Hardware**
  - The ability to develop Flowcasting plans for all products in the extended retail supply chain for a planning horizon of at least 52 weeks using commercially available and cost-effective hardware

Appendix E
Sample Audit/Assessment Questions

Retailer and/or Wholesaler Questions
- What is the organizational structure of the company?
- What are the total sales?
- What is the total number of products sold?
- What is the number of stores and/or distribution centers?
- What is the total inventory investment? In dollars? In days of sale?
- What are the total selling costs as a percent of sales?
- What is the percentage of annual product returns as a percentage of sales?
- What is the shrink factor as a percentage of sales?

Wholesaler Questions
- Can you describe your contacts with retailer and general steps, or processes, the company is engaged in with the retailer? (VMI, CPFR, Two-tier, Co-Managed?)
- How many individuals are on the retailer team? How much of their time is spent on the retailer?
- What measurements and performance metrics are tracked with the retailer?
- Do you have returns from retailer? If so, how much annually as a percentage of sales?
- What are some of the issues and challenges you have with retailer and the local and corporate levels? Do some of these issues cost you money and profitability? What changes would you like to see made in the relationship?
- What is the total cost of distribution? Warehousing costs? Transportation including redeployment costs?
- What is the average customer service level at store level? Percentage of out-of-stock at store level? Average order fill rate at DC level? Average SKU fill rate at DC level?
- Can you provide an overview of the IT systems?

Manufacturer Questions

- What is the total raw material cost as a percentage of sales and days of sale?
- What is the total average costs of goods sold? Material? Labor? Factory overhead?
- What are the total sales to retailer (1st Flowcasting partner) as a percentage of total sales?
- What is the total number of products sold to this retailer?
- What is the number of retailer DCs serviced? Number of retailer stores serviced?
- What is the average customer service level? Average order fill rate? Average SKU fill rate?
- What is the number of individuals on the retailer team? How much of their time is spent on the retailer?
- What measurements and performance metrics are tracked with retailer?
- Do you have returns from retailer? If so, how much annually as a percentage of sales?
- What are some of the issues and challenges you have with retailer and the local and corporate levels? Do some of these issues cost you money and profitability? What changes would you like to see made in the relationship?
- Describe your contacts with retailer and general steps or processes the company is engaged in with retailer. (VMI, CPFR, Two-tier, Co-Managed?)

General

- How do you forecast your total sales internally within the company and in relation to the retailer?
- How do you forecast how much inventory you will need in your DCs?
- How do you forecast how much you will have to produce and how do you handle requirements over production and finished goods?
- If you import products, how do you forecast how many you

should buy? What are the applicable lead-times to purchase? How much inventory do you keep of imported products? In dollars? In days of sales?

- What challenges do you have in obtaining an accurate forecast? Do you and/or the retailer track and report forecast error, or forecast to actual order differences?
- What business problems are current issues within distribution, forecasting, manufacturing, etc? What are current plans to resolve?

Technical (Retailer and Manufacturer)
- What type of databases do you use?
- What type of application servers do you use?
- What is the hardware environment?

Appendix F
Business Process Blueprinting

The foundation for a successful Flowcasting implementation is a sound business process that describes, on paper, how the Flowcasting business process will work. It must also describe how the Flowcasting process links with other processes internally within the organization and externally with the processes of other trading partners.

Building a Business Process

The process of building a house is a well-defined, step-by-step process, with the blueprint as the guide for executing construction (see Figure F1). The blueprint tells you what people and materials are needed (inputs), the sequence of the construction project (process) in order to produce a house (output).

A business is nothing more than a series of processes, executed in sequence, that deliver a beneficial output to its customers. The outputs of business processes can sometimes be less concrete than a house -- a demand forecast, an advertising campaign, or a budget, for example -- but they are still created using inputs and a series of transformation steps. And just like construction projects, new business processes should be thoroughly worked out on paper before you do anything else (like install software or modify existing systems). As with building a house, failure to spend enough time on the design stage will make the implementation more lengthy and costly.

Inputs	Process	Output

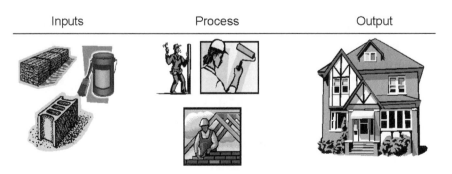

Figure F1: The process of building a house.

So how do you go about designing a business process on paper? It's actually quite similar to creating blueprints for a house:

1. Start out by describing the high-level activities in your business.
2. Once a high-level design is agreed upon, drill down to add details that are consistent with the design.
3. Continue drilling down to the specific activities and tasks that people in the organization will perform, to ensure that day-in, day-out activities are congruent with the high level design. At any stage, there may be several iterations before agreement.

When you're done, you'll have a paper representation (or blueprint) of what your business will be under the new system. You can then use this blueprint to:

- Make changes to existing policies and procedures
- Select new software and/or make changes to existing systems
- Develop education and training materials
- Design jobs and compensation schemes that support the process
- Develop measurements and key performance indicators (KPIs)

Business Process Blueprinting

To do a good job of business process blueprinting, we recommend that the process be conducted by a small team of people who have diverse backgrounds and roles within the organization. This won't make the job any easier, but expediency is not the goal -- you want to implement systems that have been well thought out from different perspectives.

We recommend a "clean slate" approach that allows people to explore how things should work. As far as documenting the current state, we suggest only doing so at a relatively high level, to point out redundancies that can be addressed by the new system and to help management understand the changes they will need to implement in the future.

Business Process Blueprinting Guidelines

Before we get into the mechanics of business process blueprinting, we need to establish some guidelines that will help to focus the activity and keep it on track:

- Always start with the ultimate consumer of your business activity and work all the way back.
- Think primarily in terms of what is being done and why. Put less emphasis on how the activity is performed and who performs it. Keep the company-specific jargon and acronyms to an absolute minimum. Anybody should be able to pick up the blueprint and understand it.
- Express sub-processes as boxes and inputs/outputs as arrows. Make sure process boxes are labeled using a verb as the first word. Input/output arrows should be nouns.
- Any process or sub-process may have multiple inputs, but should only have one output. Every time you follow a recipe for a chocolate cake, you should end up with a chocolate cake as output.

Starting with these initial guidelines (others will be introduced later), let's walk through a sample business process blueprinting exercise for fulfilling consumer demand in a typical retail business.

Developing a Level 1 Blueprint

The process box depicted in Figure F2 represents the most important -- but most often overlooked -- step in the blueprinting exercise. It seems obvious, but if the consumer doesn't execute the process, then there is no retail business!

The input received by the consumer is product displayed on the store shelf. The action they perform on the input is to "Acquire Product." The output of the process is the point of sale information that is recorded when the purchase is made.

Figure F2: The consumer process in the retail supply chain

Now we can start tracing back from the consumer. Where did the output "Product on Store Shelf" come from? What process created it?

Think about the activities that occur just prior to when consumers take the product off the shelf. The retail store would need to receive the product and place it on the shelf, as shown Figure F3.

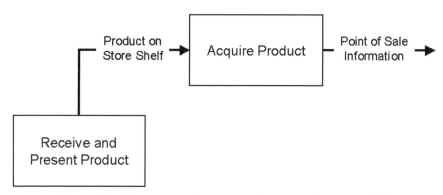

Figure F3: The process that gets product onto the store shelf.

The output of the process "Receive and Present Product" is the input of the process "Acquire Product." By continuing backwards in this manner, we may end up with the Level 1 process map shown in Figure F4.

A few elements have been added to make the blueprint easier to read:

- Process boxes have been numbered. This will make it easier to follow drill-downs.
- Solid and dotted lines have been used to differentiate between the flow of information and the flow of product.
- On the left hand side, a functional overlay has been added to categorize the sub-processes -- you can see that some of the sub-processes (2, 3, and 4) span across functions

Level 1: Fulfill Consumer Demand

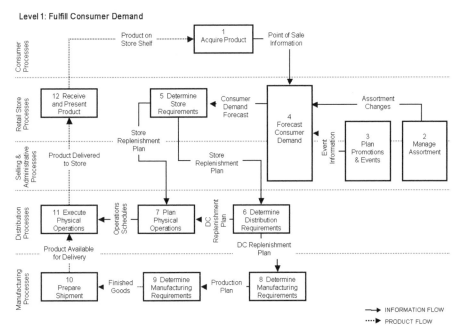

Figure F4: Level 1 business process blueprint for the Fulfill
Consumer Demand process.

Also, notice that the process flow is easy to follow and intuitive.
If you find it difficult to keep the flow lines from crossing, you may
have too much detail on the page, or your process may have redun-
dancy. If this is the case, it may be necessary to combine a few activities into one box and push the details down a level.

Once the Level 1 process blueprint has been agreed upon by
everyone involved in creating it, you would then -- and only then --
drill down to Level 2. You may choose to do a Level 2 drill-down on
every box or only on a select few processes that you're considering
changing.

Drilling Down

Once you have a closed-loop Level 1 blueprint, you can drill down to
Level 2. Each box on the Level 1 blueprint would be exploded into its
own blueprint. Take, for example, the "Forecast Consumer Demand"

sub-process from the Level 1 blueprint. In Figure F5, you can see that there are three sub-processes that provide input (sub-processes 1, 2, and 3) and one sub-process that receives its output (sub-process 5):

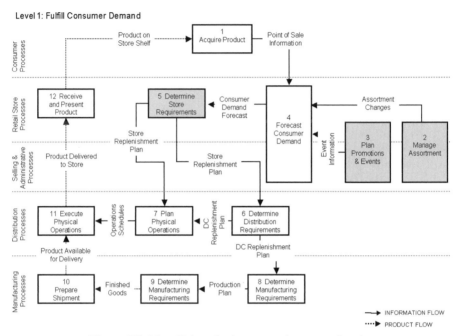

Figure F5: Identifying the inputs and outputs for the
Forecast Consumer Demand sub-process.

The first step is to create a new blueprint with the inputs on the left and the outputs on the right (Figure F6).

Now, use boxes and arrows again to document the steps that need to occur to transform the 3 inputs (Point of Sale Information, Assortment Changes, and Event Information) into the final output (Consumer Demand Forecast). This ensures that lower-level drill-downs will always link up with the higher-level processes that spawn them.

In our example, we end up with a glimpse into what is happening inside the Forecast Consumer Demand sub-process. The flow should be smooth and sequential from left to right as in Figure F7.

Note that there are 5 more granular sub-processes within the Forecast Consumer Demand sub-process. Also, the numbering con-

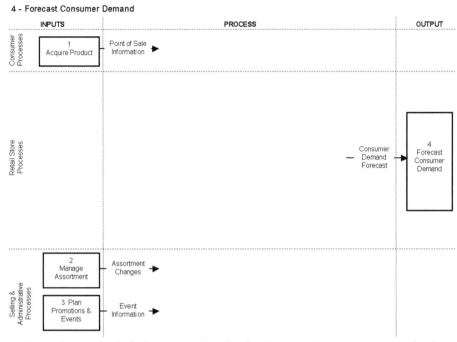

Figure F6: Sub-process drill-down template for the Forecast Consumer Demand sub-process.

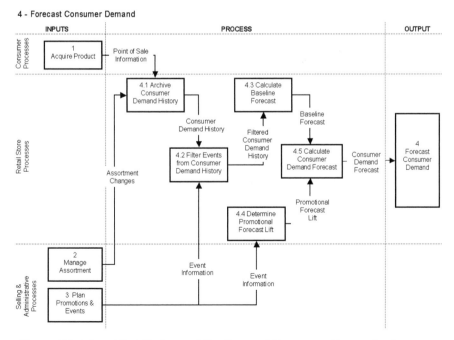

Figure F7: A Level 2 drill-down of the Forecast Consumer Demand sub-process.

vention is inherited from the higher level to ensure consistency throughout the blueprinting exercise.

You can continue to drill down in this fashion as much as you like, so long as the additional detail is useful. As before, don't proceed down to the next level until everyone is in agreement about the current level.

Once you're down to level 3 or 4, it may not be necessary to continue using boxes and arrows. You may instead want to just use a sequential list to document the details. Figure F8 shows how the drill-down for the Archive Consumer Demand History sub-process might appear:

Step	Activity
4.1.1	Extract date-stamped POS history from data warehouse
4.1.2	Determine which items entered the assortment less than a year ago
4.1.3	Retrieve superseded items and scaling factors for items with less than a year's worth of POS history
4.1.4	Copy scaled history from superseded items to new items
4.1.5	Delete history for superseded items

Figure F8: Archive Consumer Demand History sub process.

Supporting Documentation

One of the advantages to having business process blueprints is that you can make future process changes and determine the impacts early in the project. For example, if you want to delete an activity for efficiency's sake, you'll be able to see what other processes must also be changed. This can be very useful for change management purposes down the road.

For this reason, it's a good idea to have some background information about each sub-process, including:

- What the purpose of the sub-process is
- Which other sub-processes provide the input
- What input is supplied by these sub-processes
- Why the input is needed by the sub-process

For example, the background information accompanying our level 2 process blueprint could be depicted by the table shown in figure F9.

4 - Forecast Consumer Demand		
Process Purpose:	To predict, by item, the time-phased demands of consumers that will need to be satisfied by each retail store	
Process Inputs		
Supplier Process	**Input Supplied**	**Why Supplied**
1 Acquire Product	Point of Sale Information	To provide the historical demand data that will be used to generate a mathematical forecast model of future consumer demand activity.
2 Manage Assortment	Assortment Changes	To provide information about product introductions and discontinuations.
3 Plan Promotions and Events	Event Information	To provide information about past events so that we know which historical demand needs to be filtered from the baseline forecast calculation. To provide information about future events so that we can figure out how much additional demand needs to be added to the baseline forecast.

Figure F9: Level 2 process blueprint addition.

Summary

The implementation of a new business process is much like building a house. The time spent working out the details on paper before construction activities begin is well worth it.

Business process blueprinting is most effective when it's done as a collaborative team effort. This can sometimes make the process more difficult, but it's the best way to ensure you've captured everything. To keep things on track, start broadly and get agreement on the high level design before going into details.

Remember these key process blueprinting guidelines:

- Always start with the consumer, and work backward.
- A process blueprint is about what is done and why, not how it's done and who does it.
- When describing a process, use a verb as the first word.
- A process can have many inputs, but only one output.

When your blueprint is complete, the flow of the process should be easy to follow and intuitive. If you have a large number of boxes or flow lines that cross, look for ways to combine some activities, and relegate the details to the next level down.

Always get agreement on the level you're working on before drilling down.

And always provide supporting documentation that defines the purpose and inputs of each sub-process, so that others can retrace your steps at a later time.

Appendix G
Financial Benefits of Flowcasting

The Global Consumer Goods (CG) Industry is a $10.36 trillion industry. This makes it one of the largest, if not the largest, industrial sector in the world economy. Today, the potential exists to completely change the way retail supply chains are managed in the Global CG Industry. To support our claim in the introduction that Flowcasting can generate benefits in the range of 1 percent to 6 percent of sales, we have randomly sampled a representative number of manufacturers and retailers operating in the Consumer Goods Industry and have analyzed their financials statements.

Listed below are the 20 manufacturers and 5 retailers that we have sampled.

Manufacturers

Kellogg	Goodyear	Sara Lee
Corning	Tyson	Wyeth
Sony	Colgate Palmolive	Unilever
Johnson & Johnson	Coca-Cola	Danone
Black & Decker	ConAgra	Kodak
Bayer	Gillette	Procter & Gamble
Kimberly-Clark	Altria	

Retailers

Wal-Mart	Target	Costco
Kroger	Home Depot	

Our objective here is to provide a breakdown of the components of a dollar purchase we would make. In other words when we, as consumers, walk into a retail store and buy something for a dollar (USD) what are its cost components?

To find out, we analyzed the cost structure of the manufacturers and retailers listed above by looking at their last available annual reports. Reproduced in Figures G1 and G2 are the summary financials of these companies. These figures require some interpretation.

Looking at Figure G1, you will note that as a whole, the 20 manufacturers spent $332 billion (USD) producing their products. This represents, on average, **44.83** cents of the a dollar we would have spent had we purchased one of their products. They spent an additional $139 billion in selling, distribution, and general and administration activities. This represents an additional **18.82** cents of the one dollar we would have spent. The balance (R&D, Miscellaneous and Interest, Income Taxes, and Net Profit) adds up to $84 billion. The sub total of these costs is $554.6 billion. Thus far, in our analysis, the cumulative manufacturer's costs represent **74.97** cents of the a dollar we would have spent.

Components of a $1.00 (USD) Purchase			
(in Millions)			
	Dollars ($)	Percent (%)	Cumulative %
Manufacturers			
Cost of production	331,709	44.83	44.83
Selling, General & Admin	139,273	18.82	63.65
Research & Development	13,071	1.77	65.42
Miscellaneous & Interest	13,585	1.84	67.26
Income Taxes	16,519	2.23	69.49
Net Profit	40,522	5.48	74.97
Sub-total	554,679		
Retailers			
Operating Costs and S,G & Admin	135,784	18.35	93.32
Income Taxes	21,385	2.88	96.20
Net Profit	28,119	3.80	100.00
Total Cost to Consumer	739,967		

Figure G1: Components of a $1.00 (USD) Purchase.

This $554.6 billion represents the manufacturer's total sales to all their customers. Now, let us analyze the financial picture of the 5 retailers. Listed in Figure G2 is a summary of their last available financial statements.

	Sales (in Millions)	Cost of Goods Sold	Selling General & Admin	Research & Develop	Misc & Interest	Income Taxes	Net Profit
Dollars ($)	512,462	384,134	94,032		4,294	10,554	19,448
Percent (%)		74.97	18.35		0.84	2.05	3.80

Figure G2: Retailer Cost Breakdown.

Based on the numbers in Figure G2 these retailers had actually sold $**512** billion worth of goods to consumers. Their cost of goods sold (**COGS**) totaled $**384** billion. Their costs of Selling, General, and Administrative (**SG&A**) expenses were $**94** billion. The balance (R & D, Miscellaneous & Interest, Income Taxes, and Net Profit) adds up to $34 billion.

Assume, for purposes of this analysis that the 20 manufacturers sold their total production to the 5 retailers in our sample. Therefore, what is 100 percent of sales to the 20 manufacturer would represent a cost of acquisition of 74.97 percent to the 5 retailers on average.

Now let's apply a simple rule of three: If 74.97 percent equals $554.6 billion, then 100 percent equals $739.9 billion! This amount represents the total cost to the consumer as shown at the bottom of Figure G1.

To summarize our analysis to date: when we spend 1 dollar (USD) in a retail store (owned by any of the 5 retailers in our sample) and buy (on average) a product manufactured by one of the 20 manufacturers in our sample, the following picture emerges:

- **44.83 cents** paid by consumers is represented by the cost of production (the breakdown is: material 22.42 cents, labor 6.72 cents and factory overhead 15.69 cents)
- **37.17 cents** is represented in the way these 20 manufacturers and 5 retailers market, sell and distribute products (the breakdown is manufacturer SG&A **18.82** cents, and retailer OP/SG&A **18.35** cents).

The above costs add up to 82 cents of the 1 dollar we would have paid as consumers and they are the very costs that can be reduced by implementing the Flowcasting business process. In other words, Flowcasting can help trading partners' impact, on average, 82 percent of the cost of a product purchased for a dollar.

Where Are the Benefits?

The potential range of benefits that follow is based on our combined experience of having implemented DRP (the foundation of Flowcasting) with 40+ different companies operating in manufacturing, wholesale and retail over the last twenty plus years. It is also based on the fact that Flowcasting software tools are now available to drive retail supply chains from the beginning of the supply chain: the store. Manufacturers, wholesalers and retailers who utilize Flowcasting to do business with one another will gradually transform their supply chains from make and ship to stock supply chains to make and ship to order supply chains.

The **44.83** cents of the cost of production can be reduced as follows, based on actual results to date. Material 1% to 3%, Labor 3 percent to 10 percent and Overhead 5 percent to 15 percent. And the cost of Marketing, Selling, Distribution and Administrative (the **37.17** cents) can be reduced in the range of 5% to 10%. These are the percentages we applied to the financial numbers in Figures G1 and G2 to arrive at the potential range of cost reductions.

We calculated ranges because implementing the Flowcasting business process is a journey and is usually done one supplier or one retailer at a time, depending on who initiates the process. Therefore, the speed with which the process is implemented and the volume of business done by the participating trading partners will dictate the size of benefits achieved. Second, some companies are more efficient than others, and therefore, you have to allow for that.

Our Conclusion

Trading partners can reduce the 1 dollar selling price to the consumer in the range of 1 to 6 cents. To calculate the potential benefits for your company, apply these percentages to the total annual sales volume of your company.

As mentioned at the beginning, the Global Consumers Goods marketplace is a $10.36 trillion Industry. Reducing the costs of manufacturing, marketing, selling and distributing products to consumers by 6 cents on the dollar (the high-end of the range) would generate savings of over $600 billion (USD) to be shared by trading partners and the consumer.

We believe these benefit estimates to be conservative for the following reasons. We have purposely excluded in our calculations benefits derived from reductions in store out-of-stocks and the corresponding increases in sales and profits. We have also left out benefits in product shrink reductions as well as increases in Cash Flow due to inventory reductions.

Depending on the company and the degree of opportunities that exist in the aforementioned areas, it is not inconceivable that a few more percentage points could be added to both the low- and high-end of the benefits range we calculated.

Appendix H
The CPG Sales Force of the Future

Doubling Sales Force Productivity

Not only does Flowcasting drive tangible benefits in the form of fill rate and inventory turns, but for a supplier it can also lead to terrific increases in "white collar productivity."

In 2002, we surveyed twelve of our manufacturing clients with regard to how their sales reps spent their time (see Figure H1). We wanted to update a prior survey that had been published in the early 1990s. To our surprise we found no change -- the amount of time spent on various daily activities remained essentially the same!

What is so striking about the survey results is that on average, sales reps spend only *17 percent* of their time selling products. If this seems implausible, consider that other studies, such as one conducted by Proudfoot Consulting, have concluded that selling time can be as low as 10 percent! It is our opinion that manufacturing and wholesale companies can easily reduce the amount of time spent on administration, order processing, and expediting activities by 50 percent.

This type of reduction can be accomplished once companies adopt the practice of modeling the flow of products from their factories to customers store shelves as described in this book. With Flowcasting, most of the activities of order processing, expediting, etc become unnecessary. That's because after reviewing the supplier schedules provided by their retailer customers, sales reps already know how much inventory their customers have. They also know how long these inventories are going to last and when future replenishments should take place. If this approach is integrated with their company's own planning systems, they do not have to worry about booking orders to replenish their customer. Most important, they can spend their time on actions that are rewarding for them, their company, and their customers. These actions might include the planning of promotions, examining sales trends, talking about new products on the horizon, discussing achievements in service levels, and reductions in costs and inventories.

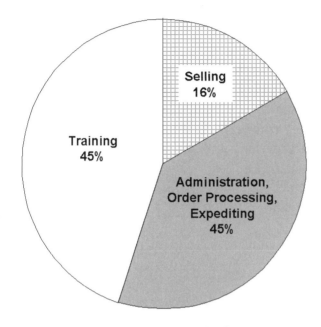

Figure H1: Typical day in the life of a CPG manufacturer's sales rep.

New Measures and Rewards for a New World

In a typical consumer product goods (CPG) manufacturing environ-ment, sales reps are recognized and rewarded for their ability to record sales for their company. The incentive is to push product out the door into the hands of retailers and distributors. What happens to the product after that is largely "not their problem." This can often lead to behavior that's very narrowly focused on the short term -- such as hitting monthly or quarterly sales targets -- which can create a snowball effect in later months. After "pushing" products to cus-tomers to hit the target for the current quarter, they'll need to buy less inventory in the next quarter, putting the target at risk again.

More progressive companies have sought to tie sales force com-pensation to forecast accuracy, rather than factory sales. The notion is sensible – the efficiency of the supply chain can be directly corre-lated to how well you can predict what your customers will need. But the focus of the activity is only on the next echelon in the supply chain.

As partners in the extended retail supply chain adopt the Flowcasting approach, the focus of everyone's activities -- from the retail store to the factory -- will be the end consumer. Therefore, the activities of the CPG sales force will change dramatically. They will still have close ties to their key accounts, but there will be no need to discuss "how much will you order from me next month?" This is an administrative effort that's handled by the Flowcasting process.

Instead, they will participate as members of a Flowcasting team, working with marketing counterparts from their retailer customers to develop innovative programs and promotions that will increase consumer demand at the store shelf.

Unlike the current "shell game" approach, everybody wins when consumers buy more product.

I N D E X

A U T H O R   B I O G R A P H I E S

ANDRÉ MARTIN

André is Co-founder of Factory2Shelf; a consulting organization focused on integrating the Retail Supply Chain from point of manufacture to final point of sale. With more than 35 years of experience in distribution and manufacturing, André created and pioneered the development and very first implementation of Distribution Resource Planning (DRP) at Abbott Labs in 1975. Since then, Andre has 43 successful DRP implementations to his credit.

He served as president of Oliver Wight Logistics Group for over 12 years. Also, he was the director of manufacturing and materials management at Abbott Canada. At Abbott, he was the driving force behind the successful implementation of the first integrated DRP/MRP II (Manufacturing Resource Planning) system in industry. In addition, he tied Abbott's financial and operating systems together.

Applying his expertise to wholesaler/distributors, André successfully helped pioneer the implementation of DRP in 1983 at two companies - American Hardware Supply (now called Servistar) and Mass Merchandisers Inc (now part of McKesson). In 1987 Andre worked with Sears on the first ever Retail DRP implementation.

As an educator and consultant for over 25 years, André is a worldwide authority on the subject of developing, refining, and successfully implementing customer E-connectivity programs. He is the author of two books: *Infopartnering, the Ultimate ECR Strategy*, and *DRP: the Gateway to True Quick Response and Continuous Replenishment*, as well as the Oliver Wight DRP Video Library. André wrote the DRP chapter for the revised edition of the American Production & Inventory Control Society (APICS) Handbook. He is a member of the Council of Logistics Management and APICS. He has conducted seminars throughout North America and Latin America, as well as France, Great Britain, Australia and New Zealand.

He has worked internationally with companies such as Coca-Cola, Colgate-Palmolive, Philips, RJR/Nabisco, Michelin, Digital, Procter and Gamble and Sears.

MIKE DOHERTY

Mike Doherty is co-founder of Demand Clarity Inc, and specializes in helping client's design and implement supply chain planning processes and systems. He has considerable experience designing and implementing Flowcasting processes for both retailers and manufacturers.

Prior to Demand Clarity, Mike was a partner with NuThink Inc, a supply chain consultancy. Previously, he was Team Leader for Canadian Tire Corporation. In this role, he led a team that designed and implemented a consumer-driven, integrated forecasting and replenishment process that linked the retail supply chain from point-of-sale to manufacturer. Previously, he was Manager of Inventory Control and Total Quality for Westburne Supply Ontario. He has also been a Logistics Manager for Loblaw Companies Ltd. where he led a team that successfully introduced advanced decision support technologies for logistics network optimization.

Prior to his industry experience, Mr. Doherty was a management consultant for Ernst & Young specializing in Manufacturing and Logistics.

Mr. Doherty holds a B. Math degree from the University of Waterloo.

JEFF HARROP

Jeff Harrop is a founding partner of Demand Clarity Inc. As a supply chain consultant with Demand Clarity (and NuThink Inc. prior to forming Demand Clarity), Jeff has helped several companies design and implement time-phased planning processes and supporting systems.

Prior to joining the consulting ranks in 1999, Jeff was part of a large project team that designed a completely integrated time-phased planning process - from the consumer right back to the supplier - for Canadian Tire Corporation. As one of the largest and most successful implementations of its kind in retail (50 planners and over 65,000 stock keeping units), Jeff was invited back to Canadian Tire in 2001 to help implement a similar process in their SKU-intensive Express Auto Parts division (120,000+ SKUs).

Previously, Jeff held various analytical and planning positions at TransCanada Pipelines and IBM Canada while working toward his honors degree in Economics from the University of Waterloo.